The Catholic Invasion
of China

Critical Issues in World and International History

Series Editor: Morris Rossabi

The Catholic Invasion of China

Remaking Chinese Christianity

D. E. Mungello

ROWMAN & LITTLEFIELD
Lanham • Boulder • New York • London

Published by Rowman & Littlefield
A wholly owned subsidary of The Rowman & Littlefield Publishing Group, Inc.
4501 Forbes Boulevard, Suite 200, Lanham, Maryland 20706
www.rowman.com

Unit A, Whitacre Mews, 26–34 Stannary Street, London SE11 4AB

Cover image: The 120 Catholic martyrs who died in China in 1648–1930, canonized
by Pope John Paul II in 2000. Painting commissioned by Cardinal Paul Shan
Kuo-hsi (Shan Guoxi) in 1996 and painted during an eighteen-month period by
Li Chien-yi, a Buddhist. The painting measures 3.9 × 2.6 meters and is preserved in
the Vatican Museum. Reproduced with the permission of the Chinese Regional Bishops'
Conference of Taiwan.

British Library Cataloguing in Publication Information Available

Library of Congress Cataloging-in-Publication Data
Mungello, D. E. (David Emil), 1943–
The Catholic invasion of China : remaking Chinese Christianity / D. E. Mungello.
    pages cm — (Critical issues in world and international history)
Includes bibliographical references and index.
ISBN 978-1-4422-5048-2 (cloth : alk. paper) — ISBN 978-1-4422-5050-5 (electronic)
1. Catholic Church—China—History—19th century. 2. Catholic Church—China—
History—20th century. 3. China—Church history—19th century. 4. China—Church
history—20th century. 5. Religion and culture—China—History—19th century.
6. Religion and culture—China—History—20th century. I. Title.
BX1665.M86 2015
282'.51—dc23   2015001698
ISBN 978-0-8108-9506-5 (pbc : alk. paper)

Contents

Illustrations

MAPS

FIGURES

Maps

Map 1   China in the late Qing dynasty, with marked sites treated in the book.

ix

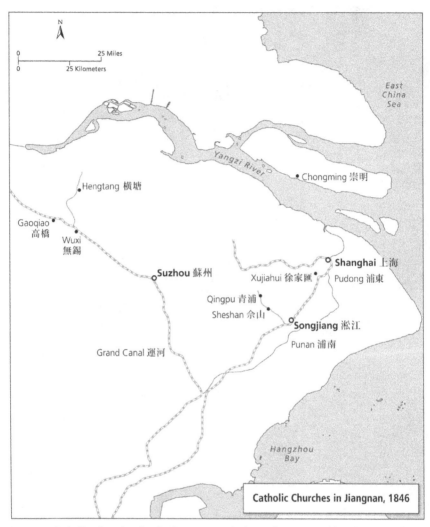

Map 2 Catholic churches in the lower Yangzi River (Jiangnan) region in 1846, show-
ing the sites associated with the composition of the *Open Letter* (*Zhaoran gonglun*).
© D. E. Mungello.

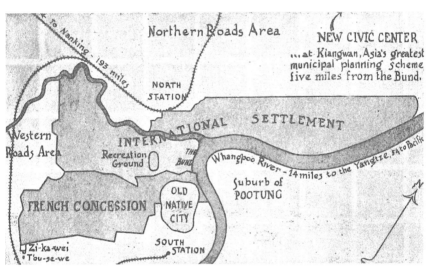

Map 3 Shanghai in 1936, with its three-part division into the old Chinese City, French Concession, and International Settlement. The Jesuit complex Zikawei (Xujiahui) is located in the lower-left corner of the map, approximately four miles from the center of Shanghai. From American Jesuits of Gonzaga College, *Portraits of China* (Shanghai: Tou-sè-wè Orphanage Printing Press, 1936), 42–43.

Maps

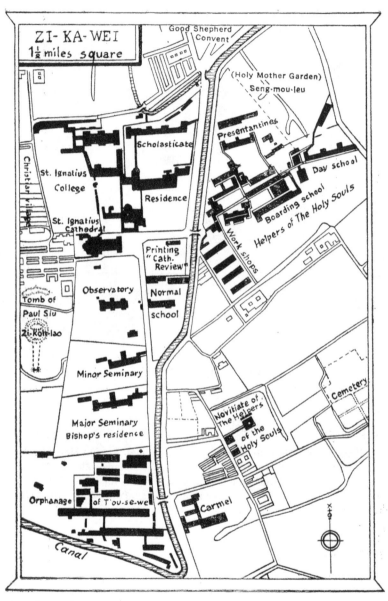

Map 4 The Jesuit complex Zikawei (Xujiahui) in Shanghai in 1936. From American Jesuits of Gonzaga College, *Portraits of China* (Shanghai: Tou-sè-wè Orphanage Printing Press, 1936), 66–67.

Chronology

1856–1860	Arrow War (Second Opium War)
1858	Treaty of Tianjin
1860	Anglo-French destruction of imperial garden Yuanming Yuan
	Treaty of Beijing
1876	Fr. Ma Xiangbo leaves Jesuit order in protest over French Jesuit arrogance toward Chinese
1884–1885	Sino-French War
1891	First six Canossian sisters arrive in Shaanxi province and establish an orphanage
1894–1895	First Sino-Japanese War
1898	Hundred Days' Reform led by Kang Youwei
	Reversal of reforms by reactionaries
1899–1900	Society of Righteous Fists (Boxers) Rebellion
1900	Fr. Alberico Crescitelli killed by a mob in Shaanxi province
1901	Fr. Vincent Lebbe arrives in Beijing
	G. L. Dickinson publishes *Letters from a Chinese Official, Being an Eastern View of Western Civilization*
1903	Fr. Ma Xiangbo and French Jesuits found Zhendan Daxue (Aurora University) in Shanghai
1906	William Jennings Bryan publishes *Letters to a Chinese Official, Being a Western View of Eastern Civilization*
1911	Xinhai Revolution led by Sun Yat-sen leads to dissolution of the Chinese monarchy
1912	Fr. Ma Xiangbo and Ying Lianzhi initiate the founding of Fu Ren Catholic University in Beijing
1912	Republic of China founded and dominated by military leader Yuan Shikai
1915	Gu Hongming publishes his attack on Western civilization, *The Spirit of the Chinese People*
1916–1928	Warlords dominate China
1919	Versailles Treaty signed in Paris
	May Fourth Movement begins in Beijing
	New Culture Movement initiated by Hu Shi and Chen Duxiu
1921–1927	First United Front between Nationalist Party (Guomindang) and Communists
1926	Six Chinese bishops consecrated by Pius XI in Rome
1926–1928	Northern Expedition led by Chiang Kai-shek
1937–1945	Second Sino-Japanese War
1939	Vatican reverses its 1742 prohibition on Catholics observing Chinese ancestral rites
1946–1949	Chinese Civil War

1949	People's Republic of China founded; Nationalists flee to Taiwan
1950–1951	Korean War
1951	Expulsion of Christian missionaries
	Founding of the Three-Self Patriotic Movement
	Martyrdom of Fr. Zhang Boda, SJ
1954	United States and Republic of China (Taiwan) sign mutual-security treaty
1955	Communist government intensifies anti-Catholic campaign
	Communist government imprisons Bishop Gong Pinmei of Shanghai
1956–1957	Hundred Flowers Movement
1957	Anti-Rightist Campaign
	Founding of Chinese Catholic Patriotic Association
1958	Religious Affairs Bureau consecrates first Catholic bishops without Holy See authorization
1958–1960	Great Leap Forward, forced collectivization of agriculture, and widespread famine
1966–1976	Cultural Revolution
1971	Failed coup attempt of Lin Biao
1976	Gang of Four attempts coup
1979	Diplomatic relations between mainland China and United States restored after thirty-year break
1981	Trial and condemnation of Jiang Qing (Madame Mao Zedong)
1985	Bishop Gong released from prison on parole
1989	Tiananmen (June 4) Incident
1997	British colony of Hong Kong restored to China
1999	Portuguese colony of Macau restored to China
2000	Vatican announces canonization of 120 Catholics martyred in China between 1648 and 1930

Acknowledgments

This work evolved gradually from my interest in the history of Christianity in China and in what happened after the Jesuits and their much-praised accommodation practices faded from the scene with the Society of Jesus's temporary dissolution between 1773 and 1814. The focus of my research intensified in 2000 with Pope John Paul II's controversial canonization of 120 Catholic martyrs in China. I am indebted to Fr. Dr. Roman Malek, SVD, of the Institut Monumenta Serica for supplying me with materials on the 120 martyrs in China and on Auguste Chapdelaine, MEP. I am likewise indebted to Fr. Otfried Chan and Sr. Emma Lao of the Chinese Bishops' Regional Conference for their assistance in obtaining the cover image of the 120 martyrs. Parts of chapter 5 on Fr. Auguste Chapdelaine I first presented at a workshop on Chinese religions at Harvard University in 2001, and I am grateful to my former mentor Professor Tu Wei-ming and the workshop participants for their comments. I am also grateful for assistance from Drs. Marina Battaglini, Ad Dudink, and Wang Meixiu, as well as from Professor Tsing Yuan and the late Professor Fr. John W. Witek, SJ, for their assistance in writing parts of chapters 2 and 4. I am particularly indebted to Dr. Dudink, who has responded to my queries on numerous matters, always with painstaking thoroughness.

I am indebted to the late Dr. Arne Sovik (1918–2014), formerly of the Lutheran World Federation, who first drew my attention in 1979 to the *Renmin ribao* article on Matteo Ricci and who more recently shared information on his friendship with David Macdonald Paton (1913–1992). Professor Jonathan Chaves has given me assistance in translating Chinese on numerous occasions. I am grateful to Fr. Gianni Criveller, Pontifical Institute for the Foreign Missions (PIME), for sharing his publications on the missionary Alberico Crescitelli, PIME (1863–1900), and for his crucial assistance in personally searching in Hong Kong for a copy of the biography of Zhang Boda,

SJ. Professor Eugenio Menegon provided me with helpful insights into the sexual charges against Fr. Francisco Fernandez de Capillas, OP.

Professor R. G. Tiedemann shared his extensive knowledge of the post-1800 history of Christianity in China by responding in detail to my numerous requests for information. I am indebted to Professor Paul Mariani, SJ, for his helpful responses to my queries and for sharing materials with me on the Communist anti-Catholic movement of the 1950s in Shanghai. Dr. Luisa M. Paternicò served as an indispensable intermediary with the archivist of the Canossian sisters in Rome in helping me to secure documents from their archive. Dr. Huang Xiaojuan shared some of her dissertation research on Chinese Christians in Jiangnan in the 1840s.

Professor Federico Masini provided assistance in helping me to secure Fr. Leone Nani's photograph of the Guluba orphans from the PIME photo archives in Milan. Dr. Wu Xiaoxin searched the Ricci Institute files and provided me with three photographs from the late Fr. Edward J. Malatesta, SJ. My colleague Professor Kenneth R. Jones served as a helpful consultant on several Latin terms. Professors Fr. Louis Gendron, SJ, Suzanne Barnett, Anthony E. Clark, and Nicolas Standaert kindly responded to my queries. Finally, I would like to express my gratitude to my editor at Rowman & Littlefield, Susan McEachern, who was particularly patient and steadfast in supporting the sometimes tortured evolution of this work.

This book is dedicated to my yet unborn grandson.

Chapter 1

Catholicism and Western Imperialism in China

The judgment of history is as inevitable as it is revealing. Although the nineteenth- and twentieth-century Catholic effort to convert the Chinese constituted an "invasion," it consisted of both negative and positive forces. On one side, the forces were chauvinistic, exploitive, and condescending, but on the other side they were kind, charitable, and inspirational. Today, as the number of Catholics in China grows well into the millions, the evidence becomes more and more compelling that the positive long-term effects of an indigenous form of Catholicism ultimately outweigh the negative short-term effects of this invasion.

The nineteenth- and twentieth-century history of Catholicism in China has undergone a great reevaluation during the last half century. In the 1960s historians viewed it negatively and as an appendage of Western imperialism. The physical incursion of thousands of religious into China ended with the expulsion of the missionaries in 1951, and a sense of defeat pervaded late-twentieth-century views of the Christian mission in China. These attitudes obscured how the anti-Catholic campaign of Communist persecution and imprisonment were generating spiritual growth in China rather than decline, a development completely misread by most foreign journalists and academics. Viewed from a short-term historical perspective, the Catholic invasion of nineteenth- and twentieth-century China was a very negative experience—a debacle—but viewed from a long-term perspective, the invasion contributed to the transformation of a mission church into an indigenous religion. In the process, the Catholic invasion enriched Chinese culture, while the Chinese church enriched Catholicism and made it more universal.

To understand this revised view of the history of Christianity in China, we need to examine certain aspects of Western imperialism that have not received much attention. Historians usually treat Western imperialism as a military, political, and commercial phenomenon. This book examines the history of Catholicism in China from 1834 to 2000 by focusing on imperialism in terms of Western feelings of superiority (chapter 1), spiritual domination (chapter 2), European resistance to the emergence of an indigenous Catholic Church (chapter 3), the love and hysteria associated with the Catholic orphanages (chapter 4), and the sexual domination of female parishioners by Catholic priests (chapter 5). The conclusion (chapter 6) challenges foreign China scholars' widespread misreading of the Christian mission of the nineteenth and twentieth centuries as a failure rather than as a movement with both positive and negative consequences in the development of Christianity in China.

WESTERN IMPERIALISM AS LOOTING

In 1973 Sotheby's established a branch auction house in Hong Kong and for twenty-seven years, with no objection from the mainland Chinese government, sold relics looted from the Yuanming Yuan (YMY) by Anglo-French forces in 1860.[1] The Yuanming Yuan (Garden of Perfect Clarity), sometimes called the Old Summer Palace, was a 775-acre (347-hectare) imperial residence and garden located on the northwestern outskirts of Beijing. The Kangxi emperor had started the garden in 1687, and his Manchu successors expanded it into one of the grandest garden-palaces the world had ever known.[2] After Anglo-French forces looted and burned it during the Second Opium War (1856–1860), the Yuanming Yuan was left a ruin and a symbol of national humiliation inflicted upon the Chinese by Western imperialists.

Western apologists continued to justify the destruction of the YMY on military and political grounds. Typical of these was Samuel Couling, a scholarly English missionary active in Hong Kong and Shanghai in the early twentieth century. Couling said that British leader Lord Elgin's decision to burn the YMY was a response to barbarous treatment of war prisoners by the Chinese and to the Chinese court's resistance to negotiating a treaty. Couling wrote that the destruction of the YMY "was less an act of vengeance than just punishment, falling on the Emperor himself and entailing no loss on the common people. It was said to have been most effective."[3] Couling makes no mention of the large-scale plunder of art objects by soldiers prior to the destruction. The colonialist plunder of subservient nations was a prominent characteristic of nineteenth-century Western imperialism and commonly referred to as "looting."[4] Colonizers regarded the question of ownership of looted objects as complex, as reflected in their appearance in forums as diverse as Western auctions, museums, and international expositions, each of which had a different function. The objects were seen as "curiosities," not in the seventeenth-century European sense of being remarkable, but rather in the diminished nineteenth-century view of China as merely exotic.[5]

In the following years, internal weaknesses limited assertions of Chinese nationalistic pride. But suddenly, in April 2000, the fine arts auction houses of Christie's and Sotheby's were shaken by the Chinese government's demands that they withdraw four relics from sale on the grounds that they were national treasures stolen by French and British troops in 1860.[6]

In the mid-eighteenth century, in the northeast corner of the Yuanming Yuan, the Qianlong emperor had commissioned a section of hybrid Sino-Western buildings constructed by Jesuit designers working with Chinese craftsmen. This section was called Multi-storied Western Buildings (Xiyang Lou) to distinguish it from the sections with one-story Chinese buildings. The owners of traditional Chinese gardens had long taken delight in guiding and diverting streams and lakes. Because of the Qianlong emperor's fascination with European mechanical fountains, French Jesuit Michael Benoist designed an elaborate fountain on the western facade of the Hall of Peaceful Sea (Hai-yangtang Ximian), which blended European design with Chinese technology. Water, under the pressure of gravity from an elevated storage tank hidden in one of the western buildings, cascaded down the stairways, alternately spouting water through the bronze heads of each of the twelve animals associated with the Chinese zodiac (rat, ox, tiger, hare, dragon, serpent, horse, sheep, monkey, fowl, dog, and boar), with each animal head spouting for a two-hour interval (the length of the Chinese hour) during the day and then spouting all together at noon.[7]

The deterioration in the maintenance of this zodiac fountain foreshadowed China's decline. By 1793 the pumps installed by the Jesuits had fallen into disrepair, and because the Jesuits had withdrawn from China due to Rome's 1773 dissolution of their religious order, no one knew how to repair them.[8] The long lengths of copper piping used in creating the waterworks at the zodiac fountain were dismantled for deployment elsewhere. To run the fountain for the Qianlong emperor's eightieth birthday in 1796, eunuchs laboriously generated the water pressure manually, using buckets to fill the reservoir.

The 1860 military campaign consisted of ten thousand British and eight thousand French troops organized to obtain an official apology for the Qing regime's rejection of British and French diplomats in June 1859 and to secure ratification of the Treaty of Tianjin (1858).[9] When the Xianfeng emperor fled north to Rehe, he assigned his twenty-seven-year-old brother, Prince Gong (Yixin) (1833–1898), to handle the peace negotiations.[10] The flight of the most important officials to Rehe and the seven to twelve days required for any communication with the court there made his task more difficult. Prince Gong was willing to ratify the Treaty of Tianjin, but Lord Elgin, the head of the British mission, insisted that the Chinese release Western war prisoners prior to any signing.

The initial plans had not called for a march on Beijing, but the stalled treaty negotiations led to a change. The British and French troops displayed minor behavioral differences in their plundering of the YMY.[11] In September the French troops, not as well supplied as the British, had been permitted to plunder for food and horses. The threat of a lashing with a nine-tailed whip called the "cat," however, restrained the British soldiers from doing likewise. The Chinese coolies accompanying these foreigners also plundered. Not only did the French forces, who arrived first at the YMY, plunder more freely than the British, but their descriptions of the YMY also indicate a greater appreciation for the beauty of the site.[12] These differences in reaction continued at the French and British capitals.

The French military commander Charles Coutin-Montauban ordered an escort of three lieutenants to carry certain selected works of plunder to Napoleon III. Empress Eugénie received the loot during a reception in the Tuilleries Garden in April 1861.[13] In contrast, the YMY art objects sent to Great Britain aroused little interest from Queen Victoria and were unceremoniously distributed among the various British museums. Later, Napoleon III's critics, most notably Victor Hugo, would condemn the burning of the YMY as a disgraceful act done in the name of civilization.

The sale of the bronze animal heads stolen from the zodiac fountain by the Anglo-French forces became the prime source of contention at the Sotheby's and Christie's auctions in May 2000. The ox and monkey heads in Christie's Hong Kong auction each sold for slightly over US$1 million, almost double the Christie's catalog estimate of their value at $500,000–$580,000.[14] Two days later, a bronze tiger's head sold at Sotheby's Hong Kong auction for over $2 million, far exceeding the catalog-estimated value of $580,000.[15]

Although these Chinese relics were being sold by Western auction houses, the outcome was very different from the previous two centuries. The three animal heads from the zodiac fountain were purchased by the China Poly Group, a state-run company that had been part of the People's Liberation Army until 1999, when a new law aimed at ending military involvement in business forced the two to sever ties.[16] Among its goals, the China Poly Group Corporation aimed to return to China treasures smuggled or taken out of the country. By 2000, the Chinese government had the wealth needed to compete in the international art market and to purchase these heads, which, after 140 years, were returned to Beijing and placed in the small museum maintained by the China Poly Group. The two-hundred-year cycle of Chinese weakness, humiliation, and powerlessness in the face of Western imperialism was over.

Despite minor differences in the conduct of the British and French during and afterward, this military expedition's main features were common to both forces and to the handling of the confiscated treasures. Of the major imperialist powers active in China, Christian nations, whether Protestant, Catholic, or Orthodox, shared common goals. The main imperialist nations with a presence in China were Great Britain, France, the United States, Russia, Germany, Italy, Belgium, and Japan. Japan was a non-Christian outlier whose full acceptance as an imperialist power the others resisted, in part, on cultural and racial grounds, at least until that nation's impressive performance in the 1904–1905 Russo-Japanese War. Several joint military, diplomatic, and commercial efforts by Western nations in China, including most notably the joint expeditionary force that marched to Beijing to lift the siege of the foreign legations in 1900, demonstrated the common core of imperialism. Differences notwithstanding, most of the nations that dominated the world during the nineteenth and first half of the twentieth centuries shared a common Judeo-Greco-Christian culture. The imperialism of the leading Catholic nation of this time, France, resembled that of the greatest Protestant nation, Great Britain. Germany's Catholics and Protestants shared these common features, as did American Protestants, who represented a predominantly New World extension of Old World Europe.

WESTERN IMPERIALISM AS "MIGHT-WORSHIP" AND "MOB-WORSHIP"

As the outside world penetrated China in the nineteenth century and disparaged traditional Confucian culture, many Chinese intellectuals rose to defend it. Gradually the defenders gained greater sophistication. Whereas initially Chinese traditionalists had avoided the study of Western culture, by the late nineteenth century, increasing numbers of Chinese lived and studied in the West. Some admired what they saw; others were critical, particularly with the onset of World War I (1914–1918). Using their knowledge of the West, the apologists of traditional Chinese culture critiqued the West and defended China by contrasting it with the failings of Western culture. One of the most articulate and knowledgeable defenders of traditional Chinese culture was Gu Hongming (1857–1928). Gu belonged to a significant segment of Chinese intellectuals who, from the early nineteenth century into the late twentieth, were deeply estranged from Western culture and resisted borrowing from it.

Gu's family was Overseas Chinese. His ancestors came from Tongan in Fujian province, near Amoy, but migrated to Malaya and lived there for several generations, working for the British.[17] Gu's father managed a British-owned rubber plantation. Gu was born in Penang in 1857, but after his father's death, when Gu was approximately ten, a Scottish friend of the family took him to Scotland. He received his master's degree from the University of

Edinburgh in 1877 and a diploma in civil engineering in Leipzig, Germany. After living for several months in Paris, he returned to Penang around 1880. As an Overseas Chinese, Gu came late to the study of classical Chinese culture. A high official of the China Merchants Steam Navigation Company encouraged him to adopt a Chinese queue (pigtail), wear Chinese clothes, and study classical Chinese. He lived for a time in Hong Kong.

In 1885 Gu began a twenty-year period of service on the personal staff of famous reformer and Self-Strengthener Zhang Zhidong (1837–1909). A leading advocate of the belief that Western learning could be grafted onto traditional culture, Zhang used the *ti-yong* (substance-function) formula ("old wine in new bottles") from the Neo-Confucian philosopher Zhu Xi (1130–1200) to justify it.[18] Gu served as a translator and interpreter rather than a close advisor. Zhang disregarded most of his suggestions as impractical, although Gu's bias against democracy and interpretations of the West did influence him. Gu was highly critical of the Christian missionaries, and his fluency in English enabled him to engage in public disputes with Western missionaries and businessmen in the treaty port English-language press in the 1890s.

In 1900 Gu's reactionary attitudes led him to defend Dowager Empress Cixi, Prince Duan, and the Boxers (Society of Righteous Fists). The Boxers were a peasant-based martial arts group that attacked foreigners and missionaries. Prince Duan was born Zaiyi, the second son of Yizong, who was the fifth son of the Daoguang emperor (r. 1821–1850). In 1860 Zaiyi became the adopted heir of Yizhi (Second Prince Rui) and inherited a fortune and rank of *beile* (prince of the third degree).[19] He was elevated in 1894 to the title of Prince Duan. When the Hundred Days' Reform occurred in 1898, he and his wife and brothers rallied around Dowager Empress Cixi to protect their privileges. After conservative resistance aborted the reform movement and the Guangxu emperor was placed under house arrest, Cixi treated Prince Duan as a favorite. The prince was active in a plot to assassinate the Guangxu emperor and replace him with Duan's son. When foreign diplomats and provincial officials blocked this effort, limiting his son to the status of heir apparent, Duan's hatred of foreigners caused him to support the xenophobic Boxers. In June 1900 he was appointed to the Zongli Yamen, which dealt with foreign affairs, and soon became its leader.[20] His influence on Cixi possibly played a decisive role in her support for the Boxers.

In 1905 Gu was appointed a foreign affairs ministry secretary in the Qing government, and in 1909 he received an honorary *jinshi* degree. The fact that the examination system had been abolished four years before underscored the reactionary nature of the honor. During the Revolution of 1911, Gu supported the Manchus, and when the emperor abdicated, he retired. Out of loyalty to the Manchus, he continued to wear his queue after most Chinese had clipped theirs. He wore it in defiance of the "masculine Christianity" of Europeans, for whom the queue symbolized the feminine and weak nature of Chinese men.[21] He supported the short-lived restoration of the last Manchu ruler, Puyi, to the throne in July 1, 1917, led by military leader Zhang Xun (1854–1923) and backed by several Qing loyalists, including Kang Youwei.[22]

In 1915, during the second year of World War I, Gu published his major critique of Western power, titled *The Spirit of the Chinese People*.[23] He believed that German "might-worship" (i.e., militarism) and British "mob-worship" (i.e., democracy) had caused this most destructive war in world history.[24] At the beginning of his essay, Gu expressed his concern that modernization threatened the traditional Chinese character, which he argued was gentler and less brutish than the European character.[25] He compared the difference to that between domesticated and wild animals. On the title page, Gu quoted eminent German author Johann Wolfgang von Goethe (1749–1832), who asserted that the two forces of peace in the world are *Recht und Schicklichkeit* (right and tact).[26] Gu claimed that these constitute the essence of Confucianism ("the Religion of good citizenship"). Judaism taught Europe to do right (i.e., instilled morality), but it did not teach tact. Gu believed that if Europe learned this quality from China, it would help to end the destructiveness of World War I. Although a thoughtful critique of Western culture, the treatise might also be read as a rationalization of China's powerlessness.

The Spirit of the Chinese People reflects a type of thinking widely practiced in the late nineteenth and early twentieth centuries, when traditional civilizations throughout the world confronted the question of whether modernization was synonymous with westernization. This led them to attempt to define their essential characteristics, often referred to as their national "spirit" or "soul." Today we would tend to view such characterizations as cultural stereotypes. Gu claimed that Chinese friendliness resulted from the cultivation of sympathy.[27] In comparison with the Japanese, the Chinese were more heartfelt in their politeness. He referred to the mental powers of the Chinese in terms of their superior memory and contrasted this with the inability of educated Europeans to learn Chinese.[28] The Chinese lack of precision, material progress, and abstract science stemmed from the cultural emphasis on the heart.

Gu attributed China's remarkable longevity, its "national immortality," to its civilization.[29] He argued that the key lay in the lack of conflict between the head and the heart, or the intellect and the soul. Unlike in Europe, the previous twenty-five hundred years in China had seen no conflict between the interests of science and art, on one hand, and religion and philosophy, on the other. Gu believed that the people of modern Europe had a religion that satisfied the head but not the heart. Europeans claimed that China had no religion, but Gu said Chinese culture did not need religion in the Western sense. Daoism and Buddhism were, in his view, more of a basis for tranquil regeneration than edification and dealt more with the aesthetic sensibility than with the moral or religious senses. Of course, Gu interpreted Daoism and Buddhism from a highly Confucian perspective.

Gu believed that Christianity was failing as a moral force and that Confucianism could serve as an effective substitute. He claimed that in China, schools functioned in the role of churches. While the modern schools in Europe and America taught students how to make a living and earn money, Chinese schools taught morality.[30] Clearly, he was thinking of education in the Confucian mode, although increasing numbers of Chinese believed that its individually focused pedagogy was elitist and inadequate to serve the modern needs of expanding literacy among the populace. Gu was an unapologetic and authentic voice of traditional Confucianism. He noted that Confucius, unlike other religious founders, did not evoke a following among the masses. He frequently compared Confucius to Goethe, the great figure of German elite culture. Traditional Chinese education awakened a feeling for the art of poetry, the essence of traditional Chinese culture. However, the masses could not appreciate great literature like Homer's epic poems, the *Iliad* and the *Odyssey*.

Gu took issue with his intellectual antithesis on the political left, Cambridge don Goldsworthy Lowes Dickinson (1862–1932). Clearly Gu's repetition of Dickinson's phrasing in the title *The Spirit of the Chinese People: With an Essay on "The War and the Way Out"* indicated that he intended the essay as a rebuttal to Dickinson's book *The War and the Way Out*, published in 1914 at the beginning of World War I.[31] Contrary to Gu, with his elite Confucianism, Dickinson expressed the socialist dream for Europe. Gu voiced a distrust of the common people, yet blamed the commercialism prominent in Great Britain and the United States even more than German militarism for causing the global conflict.[32] This link between self-interest and cowardice in commercialism created a religion of mob-worship in Great Britain that, in turn, generated the religion of might-worship in Germany.

Not surprisingly, Gu strongly opposed the New Culture Movement launched by a younger generation of Chinese intellectuals in 1919. He shared with Yan Fu, the famous translator of Western works, a dislike of the vernacular literature movement. He was particularly bitter in denouncing the westernized students returning from study in Europe and the United States who, he believed, were destroying traditional Chinese culture. He retained his reactionary vigor to the end. In 1921, in the city of Chongqing, English author W. Somerset Maugham interviewed Gu. Maugham's portrait emphasized Gu's eccentricity with the label of "philosopher," more inscrutable than appealing. He described Gu as a tall, thin man, shabbily dressed, with discolored and broken teeth, whose withered body contrasted with his fiery eyes.[33]

Those eyes conveyed an intense focus aimed at defending a civilization that, in Gu's eyes, refused to submit to Western power and might.

THE WESTERN RATIONALE FOR THE CHRISTIAN INVASION OF CHINA

G. Lowes Dickinson (1862–1932) was infatuated with China in a manner reminiscent of the eighteenth-century Sinophiles. Estranged from the capitalism and militarism of Western culture, Dickinson developed an image of China that bore only the vaguest relationship to reality. Although clearly alienated from the Western culture of his time and full of praise for his vision of Chinese culture, he was actually divorced from the reality of both the West and China while he promoted his vision of a utopian socialism. Known as "Goldie" to his friends, he spent most of his life at King's College, Cambridge, in England. As a Cambridge don, he was hard to categorize. The author of his entry in the *Dictionary of National Biography* called him a "humanist, historian and philosophical writer," though Dickinson referred to himself as a "teacher and man of letters."[34] He was more interested in shaping opinion than in scholarship, and the six books he wrote between 1901 and 1911 reflect the main concerns of his life. He was an internationalist and pacifist, part of the original Bloomsbury group, and member #209 of the famous informal Cambridge discussion group called the Apostles. He also organized an informal discussion group, known as Dickinson's Society, consisting of six undergraduates and six dons who met in his rooms.[35] In addition, he was an extremely repressed homosexual whose masochism involved a series of hopelessly unrequited romantic obsessions with heterosexual men and a pattern of masturbation to fantasies of domination by men whose shoes he licked.[36]

Dickinson based his first book dealing with China on an imaginative fabrication that criticized Western industrialization through the voice of a mythical Chinese visitor. *Letters from John Chinaman* was first published in London in 1901 and later reprinted in the United States under the title *Letters from a Chinese Official, Being an Eastern View of Western Civilization.* The book's surprisingly strong impact was due as much to the public receptiveness to Dickinson's message as to any popular interest in China. The idea of using a Chinese voice came from painter and art critic Roger Fry, a lifelong friend and one of Dickinson's five great unrequited loves.[37] Through the voice of John Chinaman, Dickinson attacked the West as the negative antithesis of his idealized China:

Your principle is the opposite to ours. You believe, not only that your religion is the only true one, but that it is your duty to impose it on all other nations, if need be, at the point of the sword. And this motive of aggression is reinforced by another still more potent. . . . It is a matter of life and death to you to find markets in which you may dispose of your manufactures, and from which you may derive your food and raw material. Such a market China is, or might be; and the opening of this market is in fact the motive, thinly disguised, of all your dealings with us in recent years.[38]

Dickinson's little book of less than a hundred pages found a broad readership that included William Jennings Bryan (1860–1925), the great orator of nineteenth-century American populism and Western Christianity. Dickinson and Bryan were almost exact contemporaries, but their viewpoints reflected the Old World/New World (European/American) contrasts quite prominent around 1900. Unlike Dickinson, Bryan wrote from an experience of having visited China between 1903 and 1906. He took issue with Dickinson's Chinaman. Shortly before Bryan's book was published, he learned that the author of the *Letters* was not a Chinaman, but rather "an Englishman" writing from "material furnished him by a Chinaman."[39] However, what Bryan defended was not exactly the same thing that Dickinson attacked. While both referred to a conflict between Eastern and Western civilization, Dickinson's critique aimed more at Europe, whereas Bryan was more clearly defending the United States and, more specifically, his view of a democratic, egalitarian, and Christianized America. He wrote, "By any standard—physical, material, intellectual, aesthetic, moral or spiritual—the average American is far superior to the average Chinaman."[40] The British humor magazine *Punch* had vividly characterized this widespread image of Western physical and moral superiority in a cartoon published in 1857 (figure 1.1).

Bryan visited China in the early twentieth century when it was nearing a low point in a two-hundred-year historical cycle (1800–2000). In his view, China compared poorly to an America then approaching a high point in its ascendant future. Biblical parameters defined Bryan's sense of civilization. He deemed a non-Judeo-Christian civilization inherently inferior. Bryan's confidence in America was as breathtaking as his ignorance of Chinese history. He wrote that the American "system of self-government has not only developed in a century and a third more great men than China has known in all the centuries of her existence, but it has produced a still larger number of competent and conscientious, if less conspicuous, officials and has educated the masses of the people in public affairs to a degree scarcely conceivable by the Eastern mind."[41]

Bryan ended his own book with a prophecy of a Christianized China. In his "time passes, history advances" view, he saw civilization developing around ever-larger bodies of water—first the Mediterranean, then the Atlantic. In the future, he predicted, civilization would develop around the Pacific. Here he

Figure 1.1 "A Lesson to John Chinaman. Mr. Punch: 'Give it to him well, Pam, while you are about it.'" This cartoon illustrates the low regard of nineteenth-century Europeans for the Chinese. The perceived inferior morality of John Chinaman, conveyed by the label "destroyer of women and children" (likely a reference to Chinese female infanticide), evokes a whipping from the Englishman Pam, who is depicted as superior in size, strength, and morality. Courtesy of John Leech Cartoons, *Punch* (weekly magazine), May 9, 1857.

adopted the voice of a biblical prophet as he concluded his book with this statement: "An unknown Presence moves up and down the shores calling men to follow him, and they are doing it. Another company of twelve is forming. And what took place in Palestine nineteen centuries ago is taking place again in our own day and under our own eyes."[42]

Significantly, Dickinson devoted less than four pages in his autobiography to his 1912–1913 journey in China. Although impressed by the civilized character of the Chinese in "manners, feelings, and art" to a degree that surpassed the West, he was aware of their decline. He wrote of the Chinese that "their civilization is decadent—I don't know when nor why it began to decline and nobody seems to know. Europe, I fear, will swallow it up, not revive it."[43] Thus, despite his initial positive view, he did not depart with a powerful impression of Chinese culture. Rather, his attitude seems to have remained what was when he wrote *Letters from John Chinaman*. Dickinson used China as an idealized model to criticize what Europe of his day had become. To that extent, Dickinson echoed the distortions and exploitation of the eighteenth-century philosophes in presenting China as an idealized rational model that Europe should emulate.[44] Unlike in the eighteenth-century philosophes, however, who represented a dominant point of view, Dickinson seems to have been part of a elite minority, alienated from the dominant culture by his effete tone and aberrant sexuality. Bryan, by contrast, represented a muscular American culture confident of the growing strength of its economy, the universality of its Christian beliefs, the political desirability of its democracy of the common people, and the propriety of its strict heterosexuality.

THE CATHOLIC INVASION OF CHINA

In 1842 the Jesuits entered China for the second time. Their entry and consequent penetration followed the rights given to missionaries in the unequal treaties of 1842, 1858, and 1860 and in the conventions of 1876 and 1895 forced upon China by the Western powers. Their first entry had begun in 1580 and ended with the papal suppression of the Society of Jesus in 1773. As in the first entry, the Jesuits became the intellectual leaders of the Catholic mission. But the second entry differed from the first in the political support of France, one of the leading imperialist powers of that time. The French government's support rested on diplomatic rather than religious grounds. The government was officially anticlerical, yet willing to work with the Catholic Church to advance French political and economic interests in China. This collaboration, called the French Religious Protectorate, involved French diplomatic leadership, including the issuance of passports and provision of protection to Catholic missionaries of multiple nationalities in China.

Historians have devoted a great deal of study to the Protestant missionaries in China during the nineteenth and twentieth centuries, due in part to the Protestant Christianity of the leading imperialist nations: Great Britain, the United States, and, to an extent, Germany. The different Chinese names for the two—*Jidujiao* (Christ Teaching) for Protestantism and *Tianzhujiao* (Lord of Heaven Teaching) for Catholicism—reinforced this division of Protestant from Catholic Christianity. The mutual hostility between Protestants and Catholics in the years between the Council of Trent (1545–1563) and Vatican II (1962–1965) magnified the theological differences between them. Considerable attention has been given to the old Jesuits in China, who have been praised as models of accommodation and used as a bridge in restoring relations between China and the West after the Cultural Revolution.[45] Post-1800 Catholicism has received far less attention, even though Catholics outnumbered Protestants in China until the second half of the twentieth century. The *Zhongguo zongjiao bangao 2013* (Annual Report on Religions in China 2013), also known as the *Blue Book of Religions*, reflects the ongoing division between Protestantism and Catholicism in China. This report defines the six officially recognized religions of China: Buddhism, Daoism, Islam, Christianity (*Jidujiao*), Catholicism (*Tianzhujiao*), and Confucianism.[46]

Protestant Christian missionaries arrived in China 227 years after the Catholic missionaries first entered the city of Guangzhou (Canton) in 1580. The first to do so was Robert Morrison (Malixun) of the London Missionary Society, who arrived in Canton in 1807.[47] The German Karl Gutzlaff (Guo Shili or Guo Shila), sent by the Netherlands Foreign Missionary Society, arrived on the China coast in the 1830s. The American Elijah Bridgeman, sent by the American Board of Commissioners for Foreign Missions, arrived in 1830. Bridgeman was joined in 1833 by another American, Samuel Wells Williams, who became involved with Bridgeman and Morrison in publishing the serial *Chinese Repository*.[48] Protestant missionaries expanded greatly in number after the Treaty of Nanjing (1842) gave them limited access to the Chinese interior through the establishment of five treaty ports (Guangzhou, Fuzhou, Ningbo, Shanghai, and Tianjin). The Treaty of Beijing (1860) opened the entire country to Christian missionaries and allowed for the establishment of Protestant mission stations. By 1877, these had increased in number to ninety-two stations (forty-three British, forty-one American, and eight continental European) where missionaries resided.[49] There were 13,515 Protestant communicants (8,308 male and 5,207 female) and seventy-three ordained pastors. In comparison, in 1870, 254 foreign and more than 138 native priests ministered to 404,530 Catholics.[50]

Between 1800 and 1950, sixty-three Protestant missionary societies (thirty-three American, eighteen British, three British colonial, and nine continental European) were active in China.[51] This compared to 214 Catholic religious communities (fifty-seven for men, eighty for foreign women, and seventy-seven for Chinese women).[52] According to estimates, by 1949, when the Communists took control of China, approximately 3.5 million Catholics outnumbered about half a million Protestants. By 2012, official figures indicated a reversal, with over 25 million Protestants outnumbering 12 million Catholics (divided evenly between the official and underground churches).[53] The faster growth of Protestantism has been due, in part, to its more flexible institutional organization and its ability to survive Communist persecution and develop indigenous and local churches without foreign control imposed by an ecclesiastical hierarchy in Rome. The consequences of the Catholic invasion of China from 1834 to 2000 also explain Catholicism's slower growth.

The Catholic invasion of China involved attitudes of superiority that transcended the realm of spirituality. This superiority involved cultural, economic, intellectual, moral, political, physical, and racial spheres. Most nineteenth-century Catholic missionaries believed the culture of the West (Europe and North America) was superior to Chinese culture. They shared the view of the atheist Karl Marx, who in 1857 described China as "the rotting semi-civilization of the oldest state in the world."[54] They believed that Chinese female infanticide reflected a lower state of morality, that the Chinese political structure was antiquated, and that the Chinese were physically weaker than and even lacked the courage of Westerners. In sum, they deemed the Chinese an inferior race.

Not all Catholic missionaries thought this way, but these assumptions were widespread and dominated the Catholic attitude toward the Chinese in the years between the mid-nineteenth and mid-twentieth centuries. These beliefs persisted, in part, because the Catholic hierarchy excluded Chinese priests from rising to the status of bishop. Such condescending assumptions blended with a genuine love for the Chinese people, who were viewed as people with great potential. Christian theology required that all humans be treated equally ("There is neither Jew nor Gentile, neither slave nor free, nor is there male and female, for you are all one in Christ Jesus" [Galatians 3:28, New International Version]). However, in addition to a spiritual baptism, Catholic missionaries of this period believed that the Chinese also needed a cultural transfusion from the West. Consequently, thousands of priests, sisters, and brothers went to China, guided by this mentality, which in retrospect now appears more like a Catholic invasion than a religious mission.

Chapter 2

Spiritual Domination by European Catholics in Nineteenth-Century China

HISTORICAL BACKGROUND

The first phase of the Jesuit missionaries' entry into China (1580–1787) is famous for its adaptation to, rather than alienation from, Chinese culture. The return of the Jesuits to China in 1842 was a very different story.[1] The old Jesuits had encountered a sophisticated culture that placed the bar of entry very high for foreign religious teachings. An extremely capable group of Jesuits had met that challenge and established a fledgling Christian Church in China by focusing first on the literati and then shifting to the imperial capital. After Fr. Matteo Ricci established a base in Beijing in 1600, the Jesuits devoted much of the next two centuries to working through the Beijing court. However, this program failed to generate large numbers of conversions in the capital. Whereas the Jesuits had served as imperial advisers and tutors in the seventeenth century, by the eighteenth century they were increasingly reduced to the craftsman status of painting imperial portraits, serving as technicians in the Astronomical Bureau, or building European-style water fountains in the vast imperial garden of Yuanming Yuan. In the provinces, however, the Jesuits had established small but lasting Catholic communities among the patrilineal kinship networks, which remained loyal to the faith of their ancestors.[2]

After the dissolution of the Society of Jesus in 1773 and its reconstitution in 1814, French Jesuits returned to China in 1842, arriving in the wake of Great Britain's military victory in the Opium War (1839–1842). The new Jesuits bypassed Beijing and established their headquarters in Shanghai. The contrast between the old imperial capital and the new commercial and colonialist center reflected the shifting realities of power. With the imperial court removed as an intermediary, European missionaries and Chinese Christians interacted much more directly. Rather than entailing international political relations between Rome and Beijing, the conflicts that occurred pitted local religious authorities against French authorities. The French Protectorate claimed authority over the Catholic Church in China, mixing religion with politics and commerce. Unlike the Portuguese *padroado*, granted by the pope, the French Protectorate grew out of a series of agreements between France and China between 1844 and 1895.[3] Although secular at this time, the French government used the protectorate to advance French colonial interests.

During the anti-Christian movement of the early 1950s, an article appeared in *Renmin ribao* (*People's Daily*), the official newspaper of the Chinese Communist Party, expressing a prominent view of how French Catholics entered China. In the aftermath of the Sino-British Treaty of Nanjing (1842), additional treaties extended to the United States and France the political and commercial treaty rights given to Great Britain. The Sino-American treaty, signed on July 3, 1844, in the village of Wangxia, a suburb of Macau, gave the Americans the right to establish hospitals and churches in the five treaty ports. Using the Wangxia Treaty as a basis, the Sino-French treaty was signed at Whampoa on October 23, 1844, by the Manchu official Qiying (Kiying) and the French ambassador, H. E. Th. De Lagrené.[4] The Whampoa Treaty gave the French the right to establish churches in China.[5] The *Renmin ribao* article stated that the Sino-French Tianjin Treaty of 1858 removed all restrictions against Chinese entering the Catholic Church. In the Beijing Treaty of 1860, the article said, a French missionary serving as interpreter for the French envoy "unilaterally inserted the sentence, 'French preachers are permitted to purchase or lease in all provinces land property and to build houses without restriction.'"[6] The article went on to accuse missionaries of interfering in China's internal affairs; for example, in 1867 "a French bishop named Hung made himself an official of Szechwan Province and ordered an official seal for his own use."

The new Jesuits had a different mentality from the old Jesuits. Whereas the old Jesuits had to build a church from nothing, the new Jesuits encountered a Chinese church that was already becoming Sinified. Whereas the earlier Rites Controversy had involved a mixture of theological and cultural issues, the conflicts between the new Jesuits and the Chinese Christians had far more to do with authority than with theology.[7] The issues were mainly cultural and moral. In essence, Europeans were attempting to reverse a process of inculturation (i.e., Sinification) that had already occurred in the Chinese church. The Chinese Catholics vehemently resisted this reversal. For half a century (1787–1842), mainly Chinese priests had served the church in the prosperous Jiangnan region of the lower Yangzi River. These Chinese priests, led by Fr. Zhang Zhaotai (Simon Perès), CM, and Fr. Wang Ruowang (Jean de Spina), CM, provided the impetus for the return of the Jesuits to China.[8]

The revival of the Catholic Church in postrevolutionary France, after the Napoleonic Wars had ended, made the return of the Jesuits to China possible. However, difficulties in adjusting to the secularization of the state caused them to identify with the old political order. At this point the Catholic clerics in France, including the Jesuits, were extremely conservative, even reactionary. The elevation of Pope Gregory XVI (1831–1846), born Bartolomeo Alberto Cappelari, the son of an aristocratic attorney, reinforced their very conservative viewpoint.[9] He was a reactionary, elected with the aid of conservative Austrian statesman Prince Klemens von Metternich and opposed to both modernization and democratic movements. He banned railroads in the Papal States, famously punning on the French term *chemins de fer* (roads of iron) to call them *chemins d'enfer* (roads of hell). And yet he denounced slavery and the slave trade in 1839. Prior to his election as pope, he headed the Sacred Congregation for the Propagation of the Faith (Propaganda), and as pope he strongly promoted both missions and the development of native clergy.

In September 1834, the Christians of the Jiangnan mission (in the diocese of Nanjing) sent a petition to the pope, lamenting the neglected pastoral conditions in their mission and requesting that the Jesuits return.[10] Their petition elicited vehement opposition from the Portuguese bishop of Nanjing, Gaetano Pirès-Pereira, CM (Bi Xueyuan) (1763–1838), based far to the north in Beijing. Bishop Pirès-Pereira sent a scathing pastoral letter to the Jiangnan Christians, defending the rights of the Portuguese king and the Portuguese Lazarists while denying the possibility that the Jesuits could return to Jiangnan.[11] Led by Frs. Zhang and Wang, the Jiangnan Christians were undaunted and in 1835 sent a second appeal to the pope, along with a copy of the pastoral letter from Bishop Pirès-Pereira. It was signed by fifty-one Christians who represented the lay leadership of the Jiangnan region Catholic Church.

In response to these appeals, Gregory XVI sent Ludovicus, count of Bési (Louis-Marie de Bési) (Luo Baiji or Luo Leisi), as a Propaganda missionary to China.[12] Monsignor Bési was well connected. Much of the nineteenth-century Catholic hierarchy still consisted of an aristocratic old boys' network, and Bési was part of it. Raised in Verona, he was a friend of the pope, with whom he shared aristocratic origins in what was then part of the Austrian Empire (today part of northeastern Italy). He also had good relations with the Jesuit Father-General Jan Roothaan.[13] Unfortunately, Bési was a poor choice for this assignment. His arrogance, rigidity, and abrasiveness produced disagreements with all parties. Still, as long as he had the pope's confidence, his position was secure.

Bési left Rome in 1833, designated as the successor of the elderly Bishop Pirès-Pereira. En route to China, he visited Paris, where he was hosted by the Foreign Mission Society (Société de Missions Étrangères). However, he did not visit the Lazarists (Vincentians), an order that would provide some of his greatest opponents in China.[14] After he arrived in Macau in 1834, the Portuguese Lazarists blocked Bési's original plans of going to Beijing or the northern province of Shandong. A small pension derived from the property of former Jesuits, paid annually from Macau by Portuguese Lazarists, supported the five or six Chinese priests who served the Catholics of Jiangnan. In 1835 Paul Tou, a Jiangnan Christian and former student of the St. Joseph College in Macau, made his annual journey to Macau to carry letters from the Chinese priests of Jiangnan and to receive their pension payment. While there, Tou learned of Bési's presence and went to Huguang province (a Ming dynasty province that was subdivided in the Qing dynasty into Hunan and Hubai provinces) to meet him.[15] Tou mistakenly believed Bési to be a Jesuit, which created a sensation among Catholics in Jiangnan, who believed their prayers for the return of the Jesuits had finally been answered. Later, in 1839, the Chinese priests and Catholics of Jiangnan invited Bési to be their bishop.[16]

Most European priests in China at that time took a very disparaging view of Chinese priests. Bishop Pirès-Pereira expressed this attitude in writing to a fellow cleric: "As you have already been to Macau several years ago, you know the character of Chinese priests who love to live in their own manner, that is, without rules and without obedience. They invent new falsehoods, they lie to the Christians in opposing the Europeans. You are forewarned. You should not receive their letters and you should not believe all that they say, because these are lies."[17] In 1838 the Chinese clergy and laity of Jiangnan invited Bési to come to their mission. On this basis, Bési made an unauthorized trip to Jiangnan, where he obtained a long letter addressed to Gregory XVI, signed by ninety-eight Chinese, informing the pope of the sad state of their mission. They asked the pope to name a bishop for Jiangnan and to send Jesuit missionaries. However, the Lazarists discovered Bési's whereabouts and forced him to leave Jiangnan.[18]

When Bishop Pirès-Pereira died in 1838, Gregory XVI reorganized the China mission. Many of the Portuguese missionaries were members of a group formally called the Society of Missionary Priests, founded by St. Vincent de Paul in 1625 and called the Vincentians or Lazarists. Originally involved with mission work in the French countryside, by the nineteenth century they focused on foreign missions. The Lazarists included a large number of Chinese priests who were very loyal to their old Portuguese mentors in the seminaries in Beijing and Macau. Eager to reduce the nationalistic tendencies of the Portuguese priests, the Holy See subdivided the three dioceses of Macau, Beijing, and Nanjing and created twelve new vicariates, each now under the control of the papal missionary agency Propaganda rather than Portugal. In 1839 Bési was named titular bishop of Canope and vicar apostolic of Shandong. Because he was the closest vicar apostolic to the diocese of Nanjing (Jiangsu, Anhui, and Henan provinces), Bési became the administrator of the diocese and returned to Jiangnan in 1841.

Bési then proceeded to replace the Lazarists in Jiangnan with Jesuits.[19] He wrote numerous letters to Rome, requesting assistance from the latter order. One of these communications involved a long report to the Jesuit father-general on his 1838–1839 visit to Jiangnan, describing the very fond memories the Chinese Catholics there had for the old Jesuits.[20] On January 13, 1840, Cardinal Philippe Fransoni, prefect of Propaganda, wrote to the Jesuit Father-General Roothaan, inviting him to send three or four Jesuits to assist Monseigneur Bési.[21] Because France was then the leading Catholic country in Europe in terms of power and resources, the Jesuit father-general responded by asking the head of the Jesuit province of Paris to select three Jesuits capable of carrying out a mission in China. Thus began the powerful presence of the French Jesuits in modern China.

THE RETURN OF THE JESUITS TO CHINA

Fr. Claude Gotteland (Nan Gelu) (1803–1856) was chosen as the superior of the renewed Jesuit mission.[22] Born at Bossens (Savoy), Gotteland taught physics, chemistry, and natural history at Fribourg in Switzerland.[23] Before departing for China, he prepared by studying with well-known astronomer Charles-Louis Largeteaux, who taught him from missionary manuscripts dealing with China.[24] The Chinese Christians in Beijing and Nanjing wanted to regain the scientific expertise that the old Jesuits had provided to the Chinese imperial court.[25]

Before the Jesuits' departure, Propaganda requested that they swear obedience to the condemnation of the Chinese rites issued by Pope Benedict XIV in 1742.[26] Benedict's ruling had suspended the eight permissions of the papal legate Mezzabarba, which had allowed Chinese Catholics to participate in the all-important rites to ancestors and to Confucius. This restriction was an ominous sign because the rites to ancestors and to Confucius were still a very controversial and unsettled matter in China. The pre-1800 China Jesuits had overwhelmingly supported adopting an accommodating stance toward the Chinese rites, but their nineteenth-century confreres shared the uncompromising viewpoint of most non-Jesuit missionaries. Gotteland obtained free passage to China for the Jesuits and departed from Brest on April 27, 1841.[27] After a two-week layover in Manila, they continued onward and arrived in Macau on October 21.

Chinese Christianity between 1707 and 1839 was in a state of "retarded growth."[28] The Catholic Church in China at the time of the Jesuits' return in

1842 consisted of approximately 250,000 Catholics out of a total estimated population of 413 million.[29] As there had been the same number of Catholics in the seventeenth century, when the population was only 150 million, the church's growth clearly had not kept pace with the increase in China's population. By the time of the former Jesuit bishop Gottfried von Laimbeckhoven's death in 1787, the number of professed Christians in Jiangnan had fallen to thirty thousand.[30] Nevertheless, the seeds for an indigenous church had been well planted in Jiangnan, and growth resumed under native Chinese impulse. In the mid-nineteenth century Jiangnan appears to have contained 20 percent of all Catholics in China. The total population of Jiangnan in 1850 was 81.766 million, with approximately sixty thousand Catholics.[31]

Approximately fifty European and a hundred Chinese priests ministered to the Catholics in China in 1842. The Europeans comprised four groups: (1) Italian missionaries, mostly Franciscans, under the control of Propaganda; (2) Lazarists composed mainly of Portuguese and Chinese; (3) secular priests of the Foreign Mission Society of Paris; and (4) Spanish Dominicans of the Philippines province. Because the number of priests in Jiangnan was insufficient to administer the church, lay people took positions of leadership, mainly as catechists responsible for teaching church doctrine.

The Jesuits arrived in China toward the end of the Opium War (1839–1842). The Treaty of Nanjing, negotiated by the British with the Chinese government, had opened up five Chinese treaty ports to both trade and missionizing. But the forced nature of their opening produced hostility among the Chinese toward the colonialist powers. As the Opium War was concluding, Bési wrote to Gregory XVI that the Chinese hatred of the Protestant English extended, by association, to European Catholics.[32]

Because the Portuguese jealously guarded the monopoly rights given to them by the *padroado*, they insisted that all visitors to Macau possess a visa authorized by Lisbon. When the three French Jesuits arrived there without these visas, they were forced to leave after a short stay. The Jesuits also faced the hostility of the Lazarists in Macau, who knew of Bishop Bési's plans to replace them in the Jiangnan mission with Jesuits.[33] Consequently, on March 12, 1842, the Jesuits left Macau on the English ship *Masden* and traveled to Chusan (Zhoushan), a group of offshore islands between Shanghai and Ningbo. In the aftermath of the Opium War, the Chinese on Chusan were extremely hostile to foreigners, and the Jesuits had to carry pistols to protect themselves when walking in the streets. The Jesuits were well received by the English and met the Protestant missionaries Karl Gutzlaff and William Milne, who were serving as translators for the British military forces.[34] Frs. Gotteland and Benjamin Brueyre (Bruyère) arrived in Shanghai on July 11, where Bési met them.

The Jesuits arrived at Shanghai three weeks after the British took control of the town. The timing of their arrival and their close association with the hated

British conquerors caused the Chinese authorities at Shanghai to view them with hostility as invaders. At first, Propaganda did not give the Jiangnan mission to the Jesuits but ordered all missionaries (Jesuit and Lazarist) to obey Bési.[35] However, in 1844, at the request of Bési, Propaganda separated Henan province from the diocese of Nanjing. This forced the Lazarists to relinquish the Jiangnan mission to the Jesuits. The Jesuits had won through their close contacts with Bési. Over the next two years, sixteen more Jesuits arrived.[36] The Jesuit arrivals included four Massa brothers of Naples, who were sons of the baron of Pescasseroli.[37] Father-General Roothaan had sent Cajétan Massa to serve as a secretary and companion to Monseigneur Bési, who had requested the service of an educated and refined Italian brother. This conveys some idea of the upper-class status of Jesuits of that time. Cajétan was later replaced by his brother Nicolas Massa.

One of the first tasks that Bési assigned to the Jesuits was development of a seminary. New priests were essential to his plan to supplant the Chinese catechists with priests trained more in accord with his point of view and European religious priorities. Fr. Brueyre opened this seminary on February 3, 1843, in Zhangpoqiao (Tsang-pou-kiao) with twenty-three students aged thirteen to eighteen. Eighteen of these students were from Jiangnan province, while the other five were probably from Shandong.[38] In May it was named the Seminary of the Immaculate Heart of Mary.

The English consul was charged with protecting the French Catholic mission and Chinese Catholics in Shanghai until the arrival of the first French consul in 1848. However, Bési was shortsighted in depending so extensively on the military and political power of the British consul in resolving mission problems with the Chinese authorities. These problems included civil matters that had little to do with religion, such as defending Chinese Christians when they refused to pay certain taxes. On December 15, 1844, Bési wrote to Gregory XVI that European priests and Chinese Christians in Shanghai had no fear of persecution because of the English consul's support; consequently, many Chinese were asking to be baptized. Bési appeared oblivious to the fact that Europeans' abuse of their situation was provoking hostility toward Christianity in Jiangnan.[39]

In August 1846 Bési and Gotteland set in motion a plan for the return of former Catholic churches in Shanghai, which included active collaboration with the new British consul at Shanghai, Rutherford Alcock, and the consular agent of Denmark, Alexander Calder. Fr. Mathurin Lemaitre, knowledgeable about legal matters, drafted the petition to the Chinese magistrate.[40] It called for the restitution of a former Catholic church converted into a pagoda dedicated to the Chinese god of war (Guan Yu). The magistrate responded by saying it was impossible to return the former church edifice because the temple was a public facility that could not be relocated. However, he did replace the land. In addition to returning the old cemetery of former Jesuits, the official gave the Catholics three large plots as a form of compensation for the failure to restore the church edifice. The forcible removal of Buddhist monks from a house on this land made a very negative impression on the people of Shanghai. Meanwhile, Chinese officials forced the Chinese Catholics to reimburse them for the costs involved in restoring this land to the European priests.

CONFLICTS WITH THE JIANGNAN CHRISTIANS

Initially the Jiangnan Catholics asked Rome to dismiss the Portuguese clerics and replace them with Jesuits, and they welcomed Bési as their bishop. However, the new Jesuits were so different from the community's nostalgic images of the old Jesuits that the Jiangnan Catholics became disillusioned with them in only five years. They turned to the Portuguese as a force to oppose the Jesuits. Three Chinese priests defended the Portuguese *padroado* and led the campaign against Bési: Shen Bangyan (Matthew de Sequeira), CM; Jin Yiyun (Paul a Costa), CM; and Simon Shen (Monteiro) (d. 1856).[41] The first two, Lazarists of the Macau-based mission, requested that Bési be recalled and replaced with the Portuguese Lazarist Pereira de Miranda, CM (Zhao Fangji). Miranda had personal ties with several Chinese priests in Jiangnan who had been his students at the College of Saint-Joseph in Macau, and he forged secret agreements with them.[42] In May 1845, Miranda informed the Chinese priests of Nanjing of his nomination by Lisbon as bishop of Nanjing. Although the Chinese priests and laity in Jiangnan responded enthusiastically, Miranda did not travel to Nanjing to be consecrated but discreetly waited in Macau because of opposition from Bési and the Jesuits.

Meanwhile, relations between Bési and the Jesuits were deteriorating. When the second group of French Jesuits led by Fr. Stanislas Clavelin had arrived in Jiangnan in 1844, Bési appropriated most of their approximately thirty chests, allowing only the alms for the mission to pass to them.[43] While Bési treated the Jesuits as diocesan clergy under his jurisdiction, the Jesuits claimed that their Jesuit superior (Gotteland) took precedence. In an attempt to resolve this conflict, Bési received Rome's permission to name Gotteland his vicar-general (*famu*), thus placing him under Bési's command. Unable to impose his will on the French Jesuits, he turned to his own countrymen, appealing to the Italian Jesuits and the priests of the Holy Family of Naples.[44]

Bési's relations with the Chinese Catholics became even more difficult than with the Jesuits. He found the Catholic literati and members of old Catholic families particularly troublesome. Never having had good relations with Propaganda, he preferred to work through his friend Pope Gregory XVI, who died in 1846.[45] With the loss of his most powerful protector, Bési felt the need to go to Rome to defend himself against mounting criticism. He laid the cornerstone for the cathedral in Shanghai on November 21, 1847, and on the very same day departed for Europe, accompanied by his personal secretary, the Italian Jesuit René Massa, a fifth aristocratic Massa brother. At the time Bési left China, sixteen European Jesuits (twelve Frenchmen and four Italians) served in the Jiangnan mission.[46] Also serving in Jiangnan were three Italian Franciscans, two members of the Congregation of the Holy Family of Naples, and five Chinese priests who had become elderly and ill. In Rome, Bési advised Propaganda against sending any more French Jesuits to Jiangnan. Propaganda agreed that French influence in Jiangnan should not grow because the region should fall within the Italian sphere of influence. (In 1845 Gregory XVI had accepted the French government's demands that the Jesuits be withdrawn from France.) Consequently, Fr. Massa recruited thirty Italian Jesuits to go to Jiangnan, although funds allowed only nine to depart for China in June 1848.

Although Bési lived for twenty-three more years, the complaints from China were too loud for Propaganda to permit him to return. His lack of humility allowed his bitterness to fester. Just before dying in 1871, he complained, "I have opened China for them and they have dismissed me."[47] Bési's successor in Jiangnan, Fr. Francesco Maresca, possessed a far more genial nature but chose as his coadjutor (assistant) the Italian Franciscan Caelestinus Aloys (Louis) Spelta, whose forceful temperament matched Bési's. In 1848, Fr. Auguste Poissemeux (1804–1854) replaced Gotteland as superior of the French Jesuits. However, the conflict in the Jiangnan mission between the bishops and the French Jesuits continued for twelve years, until 1856, when Propaganda reconstituted the mission of Jiangnan (Jiangsu and Anhui provinces) as a separate vicariate, apart from the diocese of Nanjing. Thereafter Jesuits from the Paris province administered it.

THE JESUIT ENCLAVE ZIKAWEI

In 1847 Fr. Gotteland directed Fr. Lemaitre to purchase property four miles outside the city of Shanghai adjacent to the burial site of the eminent convert Xu Guangqi (1562–1633).[48] A branch of Xu's family had remained faithful Catholics down through the years. They lived on the family property called Zikawei (Xujiahui; literally, Xu family village) and had built a small chapel there. Lemaitre purchased a piece of land adjoining this chapel, and here the first Jesuit residence was built and occupied in July 1848. The Jesuits established their headquarters at Zikawei and proceeded to build an impressive missionary and scholarly complex there (see map 4).

Extensive flooding throughout Jiangnan in 1849, followed by famine in 1850, led to the abandonment of many children. The Jesuits gathered them together in separate orphanages for boys and girls, initially at Siao-tong-yuen (Tsai-kia-ouan, near Ouang-tang) in 1849.[49] Shortly thereafter the orphanages were moved to Zikawei. The Sisterhood of the Presentation was founded in 1855, with its motherhouse at Zikawei.[50] The Helpers of the Holy Souls (1869) established an orphanage, schools for deaf and dumb girls as well as for others, dispensaries, and industrial enterprises.[51] By 1916 fifty-six nuns, including novices, were in residence at Zikawei, and the entire Christian community of Zikawei numbered 3,548 people. The large St. Ignatius Cathedral, with its two prominent spires, capped the 4.5-acre Zikawei site.

Zikawei was an educational and scholarly center providing middle and high schools in St. Ignatius College (1850); Zhendan Xueyuan (Aurora Academy), which later became Zhendan Daxue (Aurora University) (1908); a meteorological, magnetic, and astronomical observatory that issued daily weather reports and forecasts (1872); a museum of natural history (1872); a research library (1847); and a printing press. The Tou-sè-wè (Tushanwan) Orphanage, established at Zikawei in 1864, housed 650 boys by 1937.[52] It was a trade school that, in addition to reading and writing, taught practical crafts, such as brass and gold metallurgy for making chalices, ciboriums, crucifixes, and bells. The boys also learned drawing, painting, and woodcarving for producing religious and practical objects. By the end of 1869, the printing press had already cut the printing blocks for over seventy religious books written by the old Jesuits.[53] Although they began with wood-block printing, in 1874 they added metal type, which enabled them to print books at lower cost.[54] Important Jesuit scholarship was published in the Variétés sinologique series, which included sixty-six volumes, mostly in French, produced between 1872 and 1938.

The Jesuits built two great collections of books in China. One was the Beitang Library, named after the North Church in which it was housed, in Beijing; the other was the Zikawei (Xujiahui) Library in Shanghai. The Beitang Library was assembled between Matteo Ricci's time in Beijing (1601–1610) and 1949. It contained 2,100 Chinese and 4,101 Western-language works collected between the seventeenth century and 1949.[55] The presence of a library from the beginning of the Zikawei complex indicates the priority Jesuits gave to learning. The library was initially housed in three rooms of the Jesuit residence built on this site and occupied in 1848.[56] The increase in acquisitions forced the library to move to a larger facility in 1860. A more permanent twelve-room, two-story stone building was completed in 1906. The eminent scholar Aloysius Pfister (Fei Laizhi) served as librarian from 1867 until 1889.[57] The Jesuits Henri Havret and Angelo Zottoli also developed the collection, assisted by two of Zottoli's students, Ma Xiangbo (1840–1939) and Li Wenyu (1840–1912).[58]

The Zikawei Library is estimated to have grown to approximately one hundred thousand works, of which twenty-five thousand were in English.[59] Although the Western-language books have been catalogued, there are only partial catalogs of the Chinese works. The Chinese collection was arranged according to the five traditional categories of Chinese books: classics (*jing*), history (*shi*), philosophy (*zi*), belles lettres (*ji*), and collections (*congshu*).[60] Sometime between 1953 and 1956, the Communist government appropriated parts of the collection and incorporated them into the Shanghai Public Library.[61] Most of the Jesuit buildings at Zikawei were demolished in the construction of a subway in the 1990s, but the library building was renovated and reopened in 2003. It houses the Western-language collection, while the Chinese-language collection is at the Shanghai Public Library.[62]

CHINESE PRIESTS AND CATECHISTS IN JIANGNAN

The number of Chinese Lazarists in the Jiangnan region when the Jesuits arrived was insufficient to meet the need for priests. They shared a vocational pattern of seminary training in Beijing and Macau, followed by service in Jiangnan. Born in Beijing, Zhang Zhaotai (Simon Pères), CM (1789–1843), studied at the seminary of the East Church (Dongtang) administered by the Portuguese Lazarists.[63] The East Church, also known as the St. Joseph Church (Dongtang Ruose Datang), was the second-oldest church in Beijing, built in 1666 by Fr. Ferdinand Verbiest, SJ, on a site given to Fr. Adam Schall, SJ, by the Kangxi emperor.[64] Located north of Pewter Lane (Xila Hutong) in the southeast quadrant of the old city, it was initially occupied by the Jesuit pair Gabriel de Magalhaes, SJ, and Louis Buglio, SJ, and became associated with Portuguese Jesuits.[65] On the dissolution of the Jesuit order in 1773, the Lazarists occupied the church and established a seminary. The Jiaqing emperor closed and demolished it in 1812, forcing Lazarist seminarians to go to the Portuguese seminary in Macau to complete their training.

Consequently, in 1812 Zhang Zhaotai went to Macau to complete his studies and returned to Beijing in 1817. In 1823 he was sent to the Jiangnan region, where he served mainly at Wuxi for twenty years (see map 2). He and Jean Wang de Spina, CM, were leaders among the Jiangnan Christians in the effort to have Bési recalled. Due to old age, Zhang retired with the Luo family at Qibao, where he died and was buried. The Chinese Lazarist priests in Jiangnan included Zhang's close friend, Matthew Li, CM, who was born in Henan province, entered the Lazarist seminary in Beijing in 1815, and was ordained there in 1820.[66] He was sent to Jiangxi province in 1835 and given charge of the parish in Wuxi. He appears to have left Jiangnan in 1844, when Bési forced the Lazarists out. He died at Dinghai in 1862.

Another very close friend of Zhang Zhaotai who served in this region was Jin Yiyun (Paul a Costa, CM) (1790–1843), born in Weixian, near Beijing.[67] Like Zhang, he entered the Lazarist East Church seminary in Beijing, was sent to Macau in 1812 to finish his studies, and was ordained in 1817. After Jin returned to Beijing, Bishop Pirès-Pereira sent him to Jiangnan, where he worked for thirty years. He ministered to the parishes at Haimen, Chongming, in 1829 and 1830, in Qingpu, Songjiang prefecture, in 1833, and in Pudong from 1834 on. Jin became embroiled in the struggle with Bési but eventually submitted to his authority. He retired to Kaolaojuan, a parish located eight or nine kilometers southwest of Sheshan, where he died in 1847. He was buried with his friend Zhang Zhaotai at Qibao.

Matthew Zhao, CM, was one of the few Chinese Lazarists of the era who spent time in France. Born in 1810 in Hebei province, he entered the seminary at Macau in 1827 and was sent to France between 1830 and 1831.[68] He took his final vows at Macau in 1833 and was ordained at Manila in 1838. He served in Jiangnan for two years before being sent to the Lazarist mission in Mongolia in 1844. He died in Beijing in 1869.[69] Because of the inadequate number of priests, some parishes went for several years without seeing one. Consequently, the vitality of Catholic churches in China depended far more on the catechists and the heads of the local Christian communities than on priests.[70] These individuals gave instruction, proselytized to nonbelievers, distributed religious booklets and calendars, baptized children, and ministered to the sick and dying. They were the first to suffer during anti-Christian persecutions.

Catechetical instruction was a crucial component of pastoral work among Catholics in China.[71] Ignorance of the fundamental teachings of Christianity, rather than persecution, was thought to be the main reason for the falling away of Chinese Christians from the church. Due to the lack of priests, Christian teaching fell mainly to the catechists (*xianggong*). Religious booklets were only a partial substitute for the lack of priests because many Chinese were illiterate. For this reason, neophytes memorized the catechism so that it would not be lost.[72] This practice melded well with Chinese culture in which memorizing the Confucian classics had long been a fundamental pedagogical tool.

Catechists fell into two categories: those who traveled (*chuanjiaoyuan*) and those who had a fixed residence (*huizhang*). Traveling catechists were mainly involved in finding converts. Full-time employees with pay to cover their living and traveling expenses, they often accompanied priests in the capacity of guides and assistants and were required to be celibate because they performed priestly duties.[73] Catechists with fixed residence were elders and headmen. They tended to be older, more literate, and married or widowed. They were responsible for church discipline but also consoled and supported Catholics in need. They instructed catechumens, whom they sometimes took into their homes during the training period. They also held prayer meetings, sometimes gave spiritual readings at Sunday gatherings, baptized infants and adults, and conducted funeral services.

Because of the importance of catechists to the life of the church, the Catholic authorities enhanced the dignity of their office through installation ceremonies. In Sichuan province, seminarians had to serve as catechists for one year before advancing to the priesthood. In Jiangxi province, the Chinese referred to catechists as *jiaotou* (religious headmen).[74] They played a crucial role in the conversion process through a teacher-student relationship and also had the power to expel converts for misbehavior. Sometimes catechists also led their congregations. In the revolt against Bési's and Gotteland's policies in Jiangnan, the catechists played a more prominent role than the Chinese priests.

THE CHINESE CHALLENGE TO EUROPEAN DOMINANCE IN THE *OPEN LETTER*

Bishop Bési and the returned Jesuits lacked the ability to communicate effectively with the Chinese and were obliviously ignorant of Chinese culture. After five years, the Chinese frustration appears to have reached a boiling point, leading to the composition of an open letter. When the Jesuits returned to Jiangnan in 1841, they were forced to deal with Chinese priests and catechists who had been running their own churches for over a half century. Indigenous Chinese traditions had been incorporated into the Jiangnan churches to create a distinctly Chinese church. This involved native confidence on the part of Chinese priests and catechists and among certain Christian literati, along with a reluctance to submit to foreign clerics, particularly in cultural matters not directly related to theology. However, since the end of the eighteenth century, the balance of power in relations between China and the West had been shifting. While China's economy and level of military technology had declined, the forces of European expansion (trade and military) had grown more aggressive, justified by the widely accepted view that nations had a "moral obligation" to participate in commerce. Former American president John Quincy Adams expressed this perspective in an address to the Massachusetts Historical Society in 1840. Adams said that the "*Laws* of Nature" and "Nature's *God*" obliged China to open up to trade.[75] Its self-imposed isolation and refusal to engage in commerce violated the law of nations.

Because of these changes, the new Jesuits were in a far stronger position in China than the old Jesuits. Whereas the latter had to be both flexible and tactful toward the Chinese in order to avoid expulsion, the new Jesuits could be arrogant and rigid. There was little chance that a Chinese government whose weakening powers had little force in the colonialist enclave of Shanghai could expel them. As a result, an intense antagonism eventually manifested itself in the form of a thirty-eight-page pamphlet, titled *Open Letter* (*Zhaoran gonglun*), which voiced ten complaints. This text shows that foreign power was limited in the remote areas of China and that Chinese Christians did not passively accept Western domination.

On Ash Wednesday 1846, the Jiangnan Christians produced this remarkable document, revealing the voice of a seldom heard Chinese church. Not intimidated by the European priests, the Chinese bluntly criticized the manner in which Bishop Bési and his vicar-general, Fr. Gotteland, had administered the Catholic churches in Jiangnan. The *Open Letter* grouped complaints under ten headings: missionaries (*chuanjiao*), confession (*shengong*), issuing mandates (*chuyu*), sages (*xiansheng*), catechism (*daoli*), chanting the liturgy (*nianjing*), building churches (*zao tang*), evangelizing (*guangyang*), foundlings (*yuying*), and the Rainbow Bridge Incident (Hongqiao).[76] These grievances dealt only minimally with theological disputes and mainly with administrative issues and the alleged abuse of authority by Bési and the Jesuits.

The catechist Shen Xizhi, whom the Jesuit Fr. Francois Estève had dismissed from his post, drafted the *Open Letter* anonymously.[77] His name appears in the tenth and last section of the *Open Letter*, linked with the Catholic woman Gu Fenggu of Rainbow Bridge (Hongqiao) in the Punan region.[78] Gu Fenggu appears to have been a forceful woman and possibly one of the Christian Virgins (*Shouzhen guniang*) who vigorously defended the practice of women alone chanting ritual, thus incurring Bési's and Gotteland's enmity. A fellow Christian, Gu Mingguan, testified in front of church members and the Jesuit Fr. Joseph Gonnet that Gu Fenggu had stolen items from the church. When Gonnet informed Bési and Gotteland of the accusation, they punished her and forty other members of the Gu clan by denying them communion and last rites. The catechist Shen Xizhi defended her, saying that the accusations were unjust.[79]

The layout of the printed text of the *Open Letter* indicates that it was probably a collaborative project. A commenter rather than the primary author typically wrote the extensive commentary in smaller characters in the upper margins. In addition, other comments, some in red ink, inserted between the lines of the main body of text indicate yet another possible author. It was printed at Hengtang, approximately fifteen miles north of Wuxi. Congregational complaints appear to have been noted at parish meetings and incorporated into the *Open Letter*.

In section five dealing with the study of doctrine, the writers complained that Bishop Bési and Vicar Gotteland discouraged members of the church from reading scripture and did not allow preaching of the doctrine.[80] These clearly literate Christians resented being told not to read and discuss the sacred texts of their faith. They noted that the writings of the Christian sages recorded acts that many Chinese wished to dispute. Rather than allowing for consideration of these difficult issues, Bési and Gotteland attempted to shut down discussion. The Chinese voiced the suspicion that the real reason behind the refusal was fear that the Chinese might surpass them in understanding scripture.

Part of the problem stemmed from the Europeans' lack of proficiency in Chinese. The *Open Letter* noted that Jesuit attempts to explain doctrine were incomprehensible to the Chinese.[81] The writers of the *Open Letter* stated that they possessed 120 segments in Chinese of the accounts of the biblical prophets (*xian shengxian*) and precepts of Jesus, but many of the passages were confusing.[82] Their desire to study and discuss these passages reflected not only the wish of an intellectually inclined group but also a realization that Chinese laity and priests were far more able to lead the church than Europeans, with their poor understanding of the Chinese language and culture. So this was, at its core, a struggle for control of the Catholic church in Jiangnan.

The Chinese commonly practiced collaborative authorship, and there was precedent for this in the letters the Jiangnan Catholic community sent to the pope, endorsed with multiple signatures. On the last page of the *Open Letter*, a handwritten note (in red ink to distinguish it from the black ink of the printed text) announced a parish meeting to be held at Hengtang on Pentecost. The time between the publication of the *Open Letter* on Ash Wednesday and the parish meeting on Pentecost Sunday was thirteen and a half weeks (the forty-six days of Lent between Ash Wednesday and Easter, plus the forty-nine days between Easter and Pentecost). The announcement read, "On the Day of the Descent of the Holy Spirit [Pentecost] there will be a parish meeting in Hengtang to discuss the pros and cons of publishing a supplementary essay at a later time."[83] The scheduling around these major feast days indicates that these meetings were part of deliberate plan rather than a spontaneous outburst. However, a supplementary essay was probably never published.[84]

The vocabulary in the *Open Letter* appears to blend the vernacular and the literary. The letter's tone reflects great bitterness over European priests' treatment of the Chinese. The style is less refined than traditional literati standards and, unlike writings by some of the more notable Christian literati, makes only minimal use of classical allusions. This impression is reinforced by the use of passages from scripture in support of certain points. The confident interpretation of these biblical passages reflects a catechist's level of familiarity, indicating that catechists were the dominant force among Catholics in that region.

When the *Open Letter* began to circulate in Jiangnan, Bési was in Hong Kong conferring with the Propaganda procurator.[85] In his absence, Gotteland responded by writing a very blunt rebuttal in French, which was translated into Chinese and published as a forty-one-page (nine-thousand-character) essay titled *Wubang lun* ([The Response to] a Slanderous Essay).[86] Gotteland's response was twice the length, in terms of the number of characters, of the *Open Letter*, and the technical quality of its woodcut printing was superior. Its literary style was also more refined, and one finds a quote from the *Book of Rites* on the first page, but as none of the Jesuits in China at that time had the ability to compose fluently in literary Chinese, this would have been due to literati assistance. Gotteland is totally uncompromising and notes that even after two printings and wide dissemination of the *Open* Letter, the authors had still failed to win many church members to their point of view.[87] What he does offer them is forgiveness for their sins, if they make genuine repentance. Threats made in the *Wubang lun* to punish any Catholics who continued to advocate the ideas in the *Open Letter* or to disseminate its contents may have prevented the publication of a sequel.

ATTACKS VOICED IN THE *OPEN LETTER*

The *Open Letter*, from its opening lines, was bluntly critical and made minimal use of the euphemisms that typically tempered literati Chinese critiques:

> To Bishop Bési and his Vicar-General Gotteland:
>   Your two honorable excellencies have caused chaos in the orders you have issued and in the mistakes of your management. The misuse of your servants [in the church] and falsehoods in your words have reached the true believers and disturbed them. There is great sorrow in our hearts. As to the truth of what is fair and just and the illumination of what is real, we are at the point of feeling hopeless. . . . We humble persons have carefully written an essay in ten parts and present them to you.[88]

The commentary in the upper margin opened by accusing Bési of misleading behavior:

> Before the Bishop [Bési] ascended his honorable position in Jiangnan, he was completely humble and loving. And because of this, the people were respectful and looked up to him. Who would have thought that after he ascended to his position, he would be so different than before? He only understands putting himself first in importance, suddenly forgetting the foundations on which he himself depends.[89]

The marginal commentary of the *Open Letter* also expressed anger over the disrespectful treatment of Chinese by Europeans:

The Bishop [Bési] and his grand vicar [Gotteland] rely on Western military forces and treat the Catholic fathers of our country like disposable property, occasionally reprimanding the Chinese priests, but otherwise ignoring them.[90]

The *Open Letter* strongly criticized the new Jesuits' deficiencies in Chinese. Misunderstood by parishioners, their spoken Chinese created problems, particularly in confessions. Their inability to read the Confucian classical texts set them in sharp contrast to the earlier Jesuits, who built their apostolate on a study of these texts and an accommodation between Christianity and Confucianism. Fr. Gotteland responded to this criticism in the early pages of *Wubang lun*. He was impatient with the *Open Letter*'s unfavorable comparisons of the new Jesuits with the old, who, he claimed sarcastically, the Chinese people all revered as "Grand Secretaries" (*daxue shi*).[91] He said that because times had changed and the emphases of the old Jesuits differed from those of the new, such assessments were pointless.

Gotteland said that, unlike the new Jesuits, the old Jesuits did not give priority to learning local dialects, ministering to sick people, or teaching religious fundamentals like the Four Precepts (*Sigui*). They devoted themselves instead to the study of characters and reading Chinese books. Gotteland wrote that when Matteo Ricci arrived in China, he was freed from pastoral duties for seven years to pursue this sort of study and was thus able to "penetrate the meaning of the Chinese classics and histories" (*suoyi neng tong Zhonghua jingshi*).[92]

Gotteland wrote that the original intention was for newly arrived Jesuits to live quietly in one place for one to two, or even four to five, years. During this time they were to devote their effort to learning characters and studying Chinese books. Before this plan was implemented, however, parishioners began requesting assistance from the fathers. Some of these requests involved pastoral duties that were difficult to ignore, such as administering confession and last rights to mortally ill people in the absence of a priest. Because of these requests, Bési and Gotteland ordered that the study of Chinese be deferred until later.

Another unstated reason for deferring the study of Chinese was European arrogance. The new Jesuits did not share their predecessors' respect for the Confucian classics and histories. Of course, times had changed, and China had fallen from its pedestal, no longer a world power whose culture commanded European respect. For Gotteland, who arrived in the midst of China's humiliating collapse before the British military forces, China was a nation in decline, and the deficiencies of its culture contributed to this deterioration and to Europeans' scorn.

The first section of the *Open Letter*, titled "Missionaries" (*chuanjiao*), cited several biblical passages, mostly from the Gospels of John and Matthew, to contrast the teachings of Jesus with the actions of Bési and Gotteland. The first quotation came from John 15:5: "I myself am the vine [trunk] and you all are the branches and leaves. I cause the branches to grow separately from my body while I myself am alive, but if the branches are cut off, they are unable to live."[93] The Chinese author used this passage to say that while Jesus was the trunk in union with the branches (i.e., his followers), Bési and Gotteland had broken that connection. By their frequent agreement with the despised "red-haired people" (i.e., the British), Bési and Gotteland placed the Jiangnan Christians in the difficult position of seeming to collude with the British.[94] This made them objects of attack by other Chinese.[95]

In the third section, dealing with denial of marriage to all those studying to enter the seminary, the catechist criticized Bishop Bési for not keeping his word on a practical matter. When Bési had first established a seminary, he announced that the parents of seminarians would need to supply their sons' food and clothing for only the first year, after which the bishop would cover their expenses. But five years after the founding of the seminary, the bishop's promise remained unfulfilled.[96] In addition, the section accused Bési of imposing alien marriage customs on the Chinese Christians by refusing to allow for traditional marriage contracting. Instead, he had imposed the "barbarian" (i.e., European) custom of contracting marriages in a manner that gave priority to negotiating for the woman over the man.

The *Open Letter* also accused Bishop Bési and the Jesuits of materialism in matters large and small. The catechist criticized their extravagance in food and clothing.[97] Whereas the old Jesuits were said to have normally eaten coarse, homely food and only rarely to have consumed flesh food (meat and garlic), Bési indulged himself, eating the four savory meats (normally used only in sacrifices) on a daily basis. Whereas the old Jesuits had worn poor clothing and gone barefoot, the new Jesuits wore long and expensive-looking robes. Bési was also criticized for favoring large, more affluent parishes over smaller, impoverished ones. The catechist believed this violated what Jesus himself had said in John 10:16: "There is one flock and only one shepherd."[98] The catechist added, "The shepherd understands that they are one flock and he does not divide them into large and small [i.e., treat them differently]. The rich and poor places are all under a single shepherd."

The *Open Letter* accused the new Jesuits, unlike the old, of despising the effort to explain the Four Precepts. In the Roman Catholic catechism, observing the Four Precepts is as obligatory as obeying the Ten Commandments.[99] The precepts include (1) hearing mass on all Sundays and holidays, (2) fasting and abstaining on designated days, (3) making confession and receiving Holy Communion at least once a year, and (4) contributing support to the church according to one's ability. Because of the Jesuits' poor fluency in Chinese and their inability to effectively proselytize the literati, the socioeconomic level of their converts was limited to craftspeople.[100] Furthermore, the Jesuits were unable to understand the confessions of these humble Chinese, whom they had confused about the purpose of confession.

Bishop Bési and the Jesuits were accused of unfairly demanding that poor Chinese Christians contribute to the building of churches. In section seven on building churches (*zao tang*), the *Open Letter* claimed that Bési and Gotteland wrote to new converts, encouraging them to build a church for their branch.[101] When the new converts failed to send contributions, Bési became angry and reprimanded them for disobedience. However, the writers of the *Open Letter* wondered how the bishop could be unaware of the poverty of these Chinese. The upper-margin commentary added that the Jiangnan Christians suffered losses due to bandits and lacked the funds to contribute to the construction of new churches.

Bési and Gotteland were also accused of colluding with the "red-haired [i.e., English] land peddlers, white foreign devils, who are becoming rich" (*Hongmao fan du ke. Bai guize. Fa cai ren*).[102] Unlike the former Jesuits, whom government officials praised and called "Confuciuses from the West" (*Xi lai Kungfuzi*), Bési and Gotteland were faulted with a harshness previously unknown to the church in China.[103]

THE ESTRANGEMENT OF THE CHRISTIAN VIRGINS OF SONGJIANG

One of the most contentious disputes between Bési and the Christians of Jiangnan involved a group of young women in Songjiang. Prior to 1800, the missionaries had consistently honored the Chinese custom of strict separation of the sexes in church. The pioneering Franciscan Antonio Caballero a Santa Maria (Li Andang) (1602–1669) wrote from Jinan in 1656 that the women came to mass on Saturday, while the men came on Sunday.[104] The Jesuits were usually able to generate more funds for church building than the Franciscans and thus to build separate chapels for women. The Dominicans sometimes built a solid partition in the church, dividing the men from the women.[105]

Bési stepped with characteristic insensitivity into this very delicate sphere of Chinese sexual relations. The Songjiang Christians' support of the Portuguese Lazarist priests over Bési and the Jesuits complicated the ensuing dispute. The issue that ignited the clash involved the chanting of prayers during the mass. From the time of his arrival in Jiangnan, Bési had been annoyed by the Christian Virgins and Chinese church administrators who refused to accept his authority in matters that involved Chinese customs and were only indirectly related to theology.[106] The Christian Virgins were very attached to the long prayers they chanted in unison. Many of the Chinese parishes no longer recited these prayers, but the Christian Virgins of certain areas continued to do so.

Bési felt that the recitation was more an exercise in theatrical elocution than an act of piety. In the last months of 1845, he issued an order that prohibited the women from monopolizing these prayers and insisted that the entire church body recite them, singing in two choruses, with men and women alternating. His order created a tempest in the wealthy and sophisticated parishes around Shanghai, particularly in Songjiang, where Bési's action represented an unwarranted interference in the Chinese custom that strictly prohibited public interaction of males and females.

In section six on chanting the liturgy (*nianjing*), the Chinese questioned Bési's command on the grounds that the chanters could not determine any theological basis for it in the 120 segments of scripture from which the chants came.[107] The *Open Letter* noted that their prayer book (*shengjiao rike*), issued under Pope Pius VI (1775–1799) and approved by Archbishop Alexandre de Gouvea (Tang Lishan), included an invocation for contracting a marriage.[108] In this ceremony the male chanted the first part, the female the second part, and the men and women followed respectively in imitation; otherwise, there was no mention of chanting. On one occasion, when a group of Christian Virgins became flustered and failed to chant properly, Bési and Gotteland stopped the mass, causing great embarrassment to these young women. In their rigid demands that the men and women chant together, Bési and Gotteland were accused of treating the Chinese like animals.[109] When they visited the Chinese churches, they commanded the men and women to chant together, oblivious of the Chinese complaint that this mixed-sex chanting violated Chinese propriety.[110]

Gotteland's four-page rebuttal to the Chinese chanting issue in his essay *Wubang lun* was particularly weak.[111] Moreover, he revealed an irritation with the inattentiveness of the Chinese at mass, noting that some people dozed while others carried on distracting private conversations.[112] He felt that having everyone chant together would help to focus the congregation's attention on the mass. Gotteland invoked his priestly authority in issuing a threat. Priests (and here he had the Chinese priests in mind) who supported the rebellion of these parishes would be prohibited from visiting them and saying mass.[113] This would effectively deny the sacraments to these parishioners. Because in Catholic theology the sacraments were the sole channels of grace, prohibiting them would deny the parishioners salvation. In essence, Gotteland tried to treat a cultural matter as a theological one. Not surprisingly, he failed to resolve the issue.

The religious training of women presented special difficulties for the China missionaries. Early in the history of the mission, several Christian women felt called to take vows of chastity in the Dominican missions in

Fujian.[114] Because of the lack of religious congregations with community life in China, Chinese women who preferred to remain virgins rather than marry were forced to live in the seclusion of their family homes. There was a particular enthusiasm for this way of life in Sichuan, which in the late eighteenth century was the most flourishing vicariate in China. In 1744, Monsignor Joachim Enjobert de Martiliat, MEP (Ma Qingshan), created a set of regulations, borrowed from the Dominicans' Statutes for Christian Virgins of Fujian, that organized these individual women into an Institute of Christian Virgins.[115] The regulations emphasized a life of seclusion, simplicity, prayer, obedience, and manual labor; however, their apostolic tasks were initially confined to their own families. Eugenio Menegon has shown that women in Fuan, Fujian, were responsive to the Spanish model of the *beatas*. Based on virginity, the model was modified to fit local circumstances in China by shifting the focus to celibate chastity.[116]

Because of conflict between the aspirations of these Christian Virgins and the established roles for women in the Catholic Church and Chinese society, Propaganda imposed new rules and more control over these Christian Virgins in 1784.[117] In Sichuan, the Christian Virgins educated girls, trained catechumens for baptism, baptized dying infants, and were active in famine relief and medical care. They played a leading role in enlarging the number of Catholics in Sichuan to forty thousand by 1800, while church growth in the rest of China languished.

In Jiangnan, the Christian Virgins presented special difficulties for the Jesuits. Fr. Gotteland wanted very much to import a European order of nuns to organize the religious life of these young women, but he felt that circumstances did not permit it. Fr. Estève praised these Christian Virgins of the Jiangnan church effusively as "the flower of Christendom. . . . [T]hey are a very great aid in instructing the ignorant, in baptizing and rearing abandoned infants, and in exhorting pagans in danger of dying."[118] They appear to have been part of a sodality associated with the Virgin Mary, perhaps a form of the Confraternity of the Holy Mother (*Shengmu hui*) founded in Jiangnan by Fr. Francesco Brancati. Gotteland referred to them as "the Holy Mother and her religious group of holy women" (*Shengmu ji shengnü jiaozhong*).[119] In 1856 in Jiangnan, Fr. Gonnet gathered nine Christian Virgins to live together as a family in order to train them as virgin-catechists who would serve in the formation of other virgins.[120]

This dispute over chanting grew in strife because one of Bési's harshest critics led the opposition. Fr. Shen Bangyan (also known as Shen Jinglun, Shen Jingwei, Shen Zeyu, or Matthew Shen de Sequeira) (1790–1879) stands out as a leader of the Chinese in the Jiangnan church.[121] A Lazarist and very loyal to the Portuguese priests, Shen spent most of his life in southeastern Jiangsu province, within a fifty-kilometer (thirty-three-mile) radius of

Shanghai. Born in Chongming, and probably baptized there, he later traveled to Beijing to enter the seminary run by the Portuguese Lazarists at the East Church. When this seminary closed in 1812, he went to Haimen in Jiangsu. In 1813 he went to the College of Saint-Joseph in Macau to complete his studies and was ordained a priest in 1818. After serving in Jiangxi province for four years, he returned to his hometown of Chongming in 1837.

In 1844 Fr. Shen was placed in charge of the church in Songjiang. Throughout his life, he was quick to utilize letters and petitions to Europe to advance the causes he supported. He wrote numerous petitions to Rome on behalf of the Jiangnan Christians. Several of these petitions, signed by him and Chinese lay leaders, are preserved in the Propaganda archives.[122] Fr. Shen, known by many Chinese with affection as "Old Shen," was one of the leading defenders of the Portuguese *padroado* in the struggle with Bési and particularly in the dispute involving the appointment of Fr. Pereira de Miranda as bishop of Nanjing.[123] On November 7, 1845, he composed an enthusiastic letter to the queen of Portugal in Lisbon, renewing his criticisms of Bési and asking her to send Fr. Pereira de Miranda as soon as possible to assume his seat as bishop of the diocese of Nanjing.[124] The Songjiang Christians even prepared a house to receive Bishop Miranda when he visited.

The disagreement reached a breaking point in 1847 when Bési replaced Shen with the Italian Franciscan Fr. Chérubini Bianchieri (Bai Gelubing) and ordered Shen to leave Songjiang and go to Macau.[125] A crisis erupted when Shen refused, calling on the Christian literati to resist and denouncing Bési to Rome. Bési threatened him with clerical suspension. Finally, Shen agreed to retire to nearby Zhangpoqiao near Sheshan. His break with Bési was so decisive that he no longer wished to have any further contact with European missionaries, even to the point of not wishing to be interred with them. Apparently the Portuguese Lazarists did not share the intensity of his anger, however, and he eventually reconciled with Bési's successor, Monseigneur Maresca. Before dying, he arranged to be buried at the foot of the hill Sheshan. In later years Fr. Shen's tomb became a historical site. His defiant and brave rejection of European authority made him a heroic figure in the long Chinese struggle against foreign imperialism.

Sheshan (pronounced Zo-sè in Shanghai dialect), a low mountain forty kilometers (twenty-six miles) southwest of Shanghai, is the site of the famous Sanctuary of Our Lady of Sheshan. Fr. Joseph Gonnet purchased the land at Sheshan in 1863 for a sanatorium and spiritual renewal center for Jesuits.[126] Divided into the east and west mountains, it is a densely wooded area with winding roads and streams.[127] Once dotted with Buddhist temples and pagodas, which the Kangxi emperor visited in 1720, it predates the Song dynasty. A church was built on top of the mountain between 1871 and 1873, and the Marian Basilica was built from 1923 to 1935. Annual religious pilgrimages from Shanghai to Sheshan date from 1868. Sheshan was also the site of a Jesuit astronomical observatory and a seminary, which reopened in 1982.

The story of the *Open Letter* reveals the great irony underlying the post-1800 Catholic missionary effort in China. Although organized by Europeans at great effort and expense, this mission movement actually had the effect of damaging the indigenous foundations built by the Chinese Catholics and retarding the development of the Catholic Church in China. For nearly a century after the return of the Jesuits in 1842, Europeans rather than Chinese dominated the priesthood in China, most of them operating under the mistaken belief that Europeans were better able to advance the church than Chinese. Not until Fr. Vincent Lebbe came to China early in the twentieth century would European (predominantly French) priests and bishops be forced to recognize the fallacy of their assumptions.

Chapter 3

European Resistance to the Emergence of an Indigenous Catholic Church

VINCENT LEBBE, THE QUIET MARTYR

The Western priest most committed to the empowerment of Chinese clergy was Vincent Lebbe (pronounced Lay-BAH) (1877–1940). He was the closest twentieth-century counterpart to the great missionary model of Matteo Ricci (1552–1610) in terms of reviving the spirit of accommodation. Ricci's accommodative blending of Western Christianity with Chinese culture had not met with acceptance by all missionaries of the seventeenth and eighteenth centuries, but it had served as a guiding model in the mission. By contrast, the different times in which Lebbe lived made him a contrarian, someone who combined submission to superiors with opposition to their missionary policies. He transformed his powerlessness into influence through the dynamics of martyrdom, blending a personal selflessness with a stubborn conviction about the correctness of his views that bordered on self-righteousness. Consequently, unlike Ricci, Lebbe was regarded as a troublemaker by most of the primarily French Catholic missionary establishment.

Lebbe's emphasis on learning the Chinese language conflicted with the practices of many modern missionaries, who, unlike the pre-1800 missionaries, could barely communicate with the people. While Catholic missionaries in the countryside were more likely than Protestants (apart from the China Inland Mission) to adopt Chinese clothing, Lebbe went further, wearing a queue (until the Chinese Revolution of 1911 made doing so reactionary) and smoking a Chinese pipe. Other European priests, who refused to accept Chinese priests as their equals, much less their superiors, rejected Lebbe's advocacy of elevating Chinese priests in the clerical hierarchy. European priests claimed that due to their lowly socioeconomic backgrounds, the Chinese priests lacked sufficient education and were not "ready" to take charge.

Lebbe's love of both China and the Chinese people led to an emphasis on Chinese nationalism that was at odds with the European priests' promotion of Christianity with a European cultural context. For the French priests who converted the Chinese, adopting Christianity also meant adopting French culture.

Lebbe was born Frédéric (called Freddy) in 1877 in Belgium to a middle-class family of mixed French-Belgian-English ancestry.[1] The family was devoutly Catholic, with two sons and a daughter joining religious orders. Physically, Lebbe was unimposing; he was barely medium in height and build. A spiritually sensitive boy, he was inspired at the age of eleven by a book about the Lazarist missionary Jean Gabriel Perboyre (b. 1802). Martyred in China in 1840, Perboyre was the first of the China martyrs to be beatified (1889).[2] He is said to have declared, "I will be a Lazarist and I will go to China to be martyred."[3] At the age of eighteen, Lebbe changed his name to Vincent when he entered the Lazarist motherhouse in Paris.[4]

On January 31, 1898, Lebbe met and began a lifelong friendship with a kindred spirit at the Lazarist seminary, Antoine Cotta (Tang Zuolin) (1872–1957).[5] Cotta, five years older than Lebbe, came from an old Egyptian Catholic family. Lebbe was far more obedient to his superiors than Cotta, but given that Cotta took St. Paul as his spiritual model, his greater intractability was not surprising. Despite their differing styles, they shared a common core of beliefs that set them apart from most Catholic missionaries of the time. Although both ended up equally alienated from the Eurocentric and racist mission establishment, Lebbe had an intensity of focus and a martyr's devotion that combined to make him the outstanding Catholic missionary in China during the early twentieth century. Cotta was ordained in June 1898 and went to serve in Madagascar. Lebbe left for China two years later. On the ship, Lebbe eagerly began language study with a returning missionary who taught him the rudiments of Chinese. Before reaching China, Lebbe adopted the Chinese name of Lei Mingyuan, meaning "the thunder that sounds from afar."[6]

Lebbe arrived in Beijing in March 1901, when many signs of the Boxer catastrophe of the previous year were still visible. When he entered the priests' dining hall, he found the European and Chinese priests seated at separate tables, with no Chinese at the table of honor.[7] The food was generally prepared in a European manner. The missionaries spoke French, even though most Chinese priests did not understand the language. Many of the European missionaries spoke Chinese poorly, and few of them could read Chinese. The latter inability was not regarded as a major problem because the Catholic missionaries' apostolate was almost entirely among the illiterate people in the countryside. Only two Catholic mission groups emphasized learning the Chinese language: the French Jesuits in Shanghai and the Belgian Scheut fathers in Mongolia. Lebbe realized the importance of language study and focused his efforts on speaking and reading Chinese, despite an eye malady that made reading difficult.

Cotta also suffered from visual problems, his brought on by anemia. This and a native uprising in Madagascar caused him to return to Europe, where he visited Lebbe's family. At Lebbe's urging, he had himself assigned to a mission in southern China. He then switched to the north, arrived in Shanghai in May 1906, and was soon united with Lebbe in Zhili province, where both Beijing and Tianjin are located. In 1902 Lebbe had been sent to Wuqing County, located between Beijing and Tianjin. Later he was appointed district director of the Zhuozhou mission forty miles southwest of Beijing.[8]

In 1906 Lebbe was assigned to the difficult post of mission head of Tianjin, the major port in northern China and the second most important city, after Beijing, in the province of Zhili. With the help of tutors, Lebbe very quickly developed an unusual fluency in Chinese. Numerous Chinese remarked on his eloquence. He cultivated a striking simplicity of dress, even by Chinese standards. He stopped his doorman from screening visitors so that he would be more accessible to everyone. He eliminated the Chinese practice of performing the *koutou* (prostration on the floor) before him, although his superior, Bishop Stanislas Jarlin, reprimanded him for unilaterally changing a missionary tradition observed by all forty Catholic bishops in China. He also had his visitors sit, feeling that the practice of having them stand during a meeting with a priest was racist because it was not observed with Europeans.

By 1908 Lebbe opposed the French Religious Protectorate as an impediment to establishing an indigenous Chinese priesthood. The protectorate had no clear basis in either law or formal delegation of power from China or the papacy; rather, it was "extrapolated" by French diplomacy and military power from the Sino-Western unequal treaties.[9] Initially, in 1844 it gave the French rights in the five treaty ports. If missionaries proceeded beyond the five treaty ports and were arrested in the Chinese interior, they were to be sent unharmed to the French consul in the nearest treaty port. In this way, the treaties placed limits on the Chinese officials' power to control the missionaries.

Article 13 of the Sino-French treaty negotiated at Tianjin in 1858 restored an earlier edict of toleration of Christianity issued in 1692 by the Kangxi emperor and added the right of missionaries with special French passports to enter into the interior of China.[10] Article 6 of the Treaty of Beijing (1860) established property rights for the French in the interior of China, although differences between the Chinese and French versions of the treaty gave rise to disputes over its exact meaning. Frequent requests for assistance from different nationalities of Catholic missionaries strengthened the protectorate. Its continued existence depended on perpetuating the organizational weakness of the Catholic mission in China and preventing the creation of an indigenous (Chinese) clergy. Most non-French Catholic missionaries in China, given the

French power to represent them with the Chinese government, preferred to hold French passports.

Although the French Protectorate established by these treaties did not contain an explicitly religious dimension, the French would intervene in decisions about missionary personnel appointed in China, impeding the establishment of direct relations between the Vatican and Beijing. Ironically, the anticlerical governments of nineteenth-century France fostered remarkably enthusiastic Catholic missionaries in China. French wealth and personnel came to dominate the China mission such that by the time of the Sino-French War (1884–1885), more than 70 percent of the Catholic missionaries in China were French. In 1886, French interests won out when Li Hongzhang, the leading figure in foreign affairs, and Pope Leo XIII (r. 1878–1903) tried to bypass the French Religious Protectorate to establish direct relations. Not until the erosion of European colonialist power in World War I and the rise of Chinese nationalism did the papacy finally overcome French resistance to papal leadership of the Catholic Church in China, bringing the protectorate to an end. The watershed event was the consecration of six Chinese bishops by Pius XI in Rome in 1926.

One of Lebbe's most significant achievements in Tianjin was the establishment of ties with local Chinese business and social leaders, notably Ying Lianzhi (1867–1926), one of the most prominent Catholics in China. By joining committees of leading citizens to provide relief to natural disaster victims, to build a hospital, and to oppose Japan's Twenty-One Demands (1915), Lebbe also cultivated the support of non-Christian community figures, such as wealthy businessman Bian Yinchang.[11] Lebbe also became close with the head of police affairs in Tianjin, Yang Yide. However, the Catholic mission hierarchy in China did not trust Lebbe, and when the Tianjin district was elevated to the status of a separate vicariate in 1912, Lebbe was passed over as a candidate to become the first bishop, and the position went to Paul Dumond.[12]

In 1911 Lebbe opened several public lecture halls in Tianjin at which he, Chinese priests, and educated laymen gave talks on religious faith.[13] He followed this with the establishment of a Chinese Catholic weekly newspaper called *Guangyilu*. Lebbe realized the need to follow the Protestants in establishing schools.[14] In order to found primary and secondary schools in Tianjin, Lebbe returned to Europe to recruit teachers and raise the money needed. Ying Lianzhi's son accompanied him in order to study in Europe. They traveled on the trans-Siberian railway, avoiding the deluxe international train and using the cheaper local expresses instead. In Europe Lebbe received a surprisingly responsive reception as he gave numerous lectures on China and spoke on the need for an authentically Chinese church. By the time he departed from Marseilles in January 1914 to return to China, although he had failed to recruit teachers for schools in China and raised an insufficient amount of money, he had laid the groundwork of support in Europe for an indigenous Chinese church.[15]

Lebbe's temporary expulsion from China resulted from his intense involvement with the public aspects of the Tianjin mission, particularly the Laoxikai affair (1912–1917) and the Tianjin Catholic Action movement, which involved an effort to exert a Christian influence on society. The Laoxikai affair arose out of Bishop Dumond's attempt to build a new cathedral in Tianjin and the attempt of the French consul in Tianjin to exploit this cathedral site to enlarge the French concession to include the area of Laoxikai.[16] After indecisive negotiations with the Chinese government, the French consul led a force of French police and Annamite soldiers into Laoxikai and ejected the Chinese from their police station.[17] Most of the Catholic bishops in China were French and uniformly supportive of French political interests. However, this French landgrab generated a great deal of Chinese resistance, and Lebbe sided with the Chinese. The Tianjin Chinese organized a general strike and boycotted French goods. Chinese Catholics began sending complaints to Rome.

The Catholic mission establishment felt threatened. In order to dismantle the Tianjin movement, the vicar-general of the Lazarists disbursed all the priests in Tianjin to other vicariates. In Holy Week of 1917, Lebbe was transferred south of the Yangzi River to Shaoxing, where he was frustrated by his inability to communicate in a southern Chinese dialect. Lebbe's close colleague, Fr. Cotta, was ordered to Quito, the capital of Ecuador, where the extreme climate, as in Madagascar, would likely create problems for his health. Unlike Lebbe, whose obedience to the commands of superiors sanctified his resistance, Cotta refused to go and protested the expulsion on a technicality. Crowds of protective Chinese Catholics frustrated attempts by the French and Chinese police to arrest him. Finally, in 1919, at the request of the pope's vicar apostolic, Monseigneur de Guébriant, Cotta agreed to leave China and returned to France.[18] Eventually he was sent to the United States to teach Chinese to prospective missionaries. However, he left the Lazarists and joined the Maryknoll fathers (Catholic Foreign Mission Society of America). He served on the Maryknoll seminary faculty at Ossining, New York, until his death.

Benedict XV's issuance of the papal encyclical *Maximum illud* suddenly transformed Lebbe's powerlessness in November 1919. Harshly critical of missionary tactics, the document gave formal papal endorsement to the views Lebbe and Cotta had conveyed in their letters to Rome.[19] Believing the pope had been misled, most of the missionary establishment in China tried to bury the encyclical. These clerics were very hostile to Lebbe, who accompanied the pope's vicar apostolic, Monseigneur de Guébriant, back to Paris in 1920 and worked with Chinese students studying in France.[20] The Lazarists and the

French government, as well as the bishops in China, prevented Lebbe from returning to China for several years. However, the leading figures in Rome were sympathetic to Lebbe's point of view. No Chinese bishop had been appointed since the consecration of Luo Wenzao (Gregorio López) (1617– 1691) by the Italian Franciscan Bernardin della Chiesa at Canton in 1685.[21]

In December 1920 Lebbe was called to Rome by Cardinal Désiré Joseph Mercier, who, along with Cardinal Willem Van Rossum, the newly appointed Sacred Congregation for the Propagation of the Faith (Propaganda) prefect, sympathized with Lebbe's views. Van Rossum asked him if any Chinese priests were ready to become bishops.[22] When Lebbe said yes, Van Rossum borrowed his pencil stub and wrote down the names Lebbe gave to him. These names became the basis of the list of Chinese bishops. Soon afterward Lebbe met with Benedict XV, who took from a drawer a bundle containing one hundred thousand lire and gave it to Lebbe for the needy. Lebbe returned to Paris and in 1923 founded the Catholic Association of Chinese Youth, which produced a magazine titled *Le bulletin de la jeunesse catholique chinoise*, issued weekly in Chinese and monthly in French.

When Benedict XV died, his forceful successor, Pius XI (r. 1922–1939), implemented the ideas Benedict had initiated. Six months after becoming pope, Pius XI sent Celso Constantini (Gang Hengyi) to China as his papal nuncio. Constantini nominated one of Lebbe's candidates, Zhao Huaiyi (Philip Tchao), as his first recommendation for a Chinese bishop. In 1926 Pius XI issued his encyclical on missions, *Rerum ecclesiae*, which gave even greater emphasis to the ideas in Benedict's *Maximum illud*.[23] The encyclical stressed that local clergy should not be relegated to a secondary role below foreign missionaries; rather, native priests should be preferred. Constantini arranged for six Chinese to be made bishops. He accompanied the six Chinese to Rome, where Pius XI consecrated them at St. Peter's on October 28, 1926. Lebbe was present at the ceremony, which happened to take place on the twenty-fifth anniversary of his own elevation to the priesthood. He returned to China in April 1927 as an assistant to one of the Chinese bishops in a rural vicariate in the former province of Zhili (now called Hebei).[24]

The missionary establishment in China remained very hostile to Lebbe. Soon thereafter he adopted Chinese nationality and escaped the official oversight of the French Religious Protectorate. Thereafter he signed his name Vincent Lei.[25] He founded two religious societies, one for brothers called Little Brothers of St. John the Baptist (Yaohan Xiaoxiongdi Hui) and one for sisters called Little Sisters of St. Theresa (Delai Xiaomeimei Hui).[26] Lebbe and his Little Brothers and Little Sisters contributed to the Chinese war effort against the Japanese. Although a vocal opponent of communism, Lebbe participated in the Second United Front of the Nationalists and Communists by having the Little Brothers serve as stretcher bearers for the wounded on both the Nationalist and the Communist sides.[27] When the Second United Front began to disintegrate, Lebbe became skeptical of the Communists, who jailed him for thirty-eight days. Upon his release, he was flown to the Nationalist capital in Chongqing, but, suffering from the terminal stages of jaundice, he died on June 24, 1940.

MA XIANGBO AS A LEADING CONFUCIAN CATHOLIC

Ma Xiangbo's long life (1840–1939) was filled with an intense sense of frustration. Born into a wealthy and prominent old Catholic family in one of the most prosperous and literate areas of China, his mind was filled with ambitious goals that he failed to achieve. One of the most prominent Catholic intellectuals and political reformers of his age, he despaired over the situation in China. During the last years of his life, he repeatedly said, "I am a dog who only knows how to bark; I have been barking for one-hundred years, and still have not managed to awaken China."[28]

Ma and Ying Lianzhi (1866–1926) served as leaders in the major reform movements of the late Qing dynasty and early Republic of China. Their learning and status as scholars were comparable to predecessors like the Three Pillars of the early Christian Church: Yang Tingyun (1557–1627), Xu Guangqi (1562–1633), and Li Zhizao (1565–1630). However, the scarcity of such prominent intellectual figures in modern history shows how the Catholic missionaries' converts had declined in stature over three centuries. All twenty-one of the identified Catholic *jinshi* (the highest scholar-official degree holders) lived prior to 1800.[29] The intellectual apostolate of Catholics in China had declined for several reasons. The most intellectual of Catholic religious orders, the Society of Jesus, had been dissolved in 1773. After the society's reconstitution, the Jesuits who returned to China in 1842 were no longer as accommodating of the Chinese and their culture. The balance of power between China and Europe had shifted in favor of Europe, and the mainly French Jesuits who led the return were too colonialist in mentality to be interested in such accommodation. In addition, the rulings of Rome in the Chinese Rites Controversy had forced a straitjacket on permissible Catholic thinking about Chinese culture. Through both the training and the limited funding of missionaries, Rome demonstrated an unwillingness to support an intellectual apostolate in China.

While the term "accommodation" fittingly describes the relationship between the early Jesuits and the Three Pillars, "estrangement" is more appropriate as a description for the long and troubled relationship between the post-1841 French Jesuits and Ma Xiangbo. European interests and the expansion of Francophone influence narrowly defined the vision of nineteenth-century French missionaries. However, Ma Xiangbo's vision for the modernization of China was inspired by the work of his early Jesuit predecessors and the Chinese converts they made. Generationally speaking, Ma represented the last of the traditional Chinese literati.[30] He was born in 1840 into a prominent Jiangnan family that had been Catholic since the time of the founding Jesuit Matteo Ricci. His family traced its genealogical roots to the great Yuan dynasty scholar Ma Duanlin (ca. 1228–1322).[31] In the twenty generations between this ancestor and Ma, the family produced numerous scholar-officials. The Ma family of Dantu County was one of several prominent clans of the lower Yangzi River region that converted to Christianity, including the Shanghai family of Xu Guangqi, the Hangzhou family of Li Zhizao, and the Qiantang family of Yang Tingyun. Ma was baptized with the name of Joseph one month after his birth. The Ma family village in Dantu became Catholic and remained so throughout the Qing dynasty.[32]

Ma's father, Ma Songyan, was a Confucian teacher who later studied medicine and went into business.[33] In 1844 Ma began studying with a classical teacher named Tao in a private school for seven years.[34] The Confucian Thirteen Classics became a formative influence throughout his life. In 1852 he took the first literary exam, and then he shifted his emphasis toward Western studies. In 1851, at the age of eleven, he was sent to Shanghai to enroll in the new Collège St. Ignace (Xuhui Gongxue), or St. Ignatius College, named for the Jesuit founder Ignatius of Loyola. The blending of Chinese culture and Western curriculum at the school was largely the work of the Jesuit Angelo Zottoli (Chao Deli) (1826–1902), a Neapolitan who entered the Jesuit order in 1842 and came to China in 1848. Zottoli became a Sinologist who published a collection of Chinese works in Latin translation titled *Cursus litteraturae sinicae*.[35] He was named principal of St. Ignatius in 1852 and was the master of Ma's novice class, becoming a longtime mentor and friend to Ma. He used Ricci's famous work of Jesuit accommodation, *The True Meaning of the Lord of Heaven* (*Tianzhu shiyi*), as a seminary textbook. He encouraged Ma to continue his classical studies, promoting him at the precocious age of fourteen years to the role of teacher of Chinese classics at St. Ignatius.[36]

Ma's upper-class background reinforced his impetuous and impatient nature. Many of the students at St. Ignatius College came from wealthy commercial and shipping families, a background that freed these sons from pressing mundane concerns, giving them a self-confidence they had never earned. This privileged status enabled Ma to join the first carefully selected group of eleven Chinese allowed to study as seminarians at Zikawei.[37] A tension existed between the French and Italian Jesuits at Zikawei, with the Italians tending to side with the Chinese. Ma favored the Italian priests, two of whom, Zottoli and Francesco Adinolfi, were his closest spiritual mentors. Ma was bitter when in 1871 the French Jesuit August Foucault replaced Zottoli as his spiritual advisor. As head of the mission, Foucault requested in 1875 that the Jesuit headquarters not send any more Italian priests because they were stoking anti-French sentiment among the Chinese.[38] Reinforcing Ma's class background was a driven and idealistic personality that found compromise to be difficult. This led to several painful ruptures in his life that we can only partially attribute to the arrogance and condescension of the French Jesuits.

Ma studied at Zikawei for twenty years (1851–1870), including from 1862 to 1870 as a seminarian. He entered the Society of Jesus in 1864 and was consecrated as a priest in 1870. He served as principal of St. Ignatius College from 1871 to 1875, all the while laying the foundation for his effort to blend Chinese and European cultures. Part of this blending involved the application of natural science to China's practical needs. As he studied with the prominent Jesuit scientist Auguste Colombel, Ma absorbed the Jesuit belief that there was no fundamental conflict between theology and science. As principal of St. Ignatius, he emphasized the study of science as well as of Chinese classics, literature, history, and philosophy. He personally accompanied St. Ignatian students to the official exams. However, in emphasizing Chinese studies, he encountered opposition from European priests who feared this would make the students heretics.[39] Ma's granddaughter, Ma Yuzhang, claimed that he was knowledgeable in seven foreign languages: English, French, German, Greek, Italian, Japanese, and Latin.[40]

Both Ma Xiangbo and his younger brother Ma Jianzhong left the priesthood to protest the racism of the French Jesuits and the unequal treatment meted out to Chinese and foreign novices. In 1873 the Ma brothers had been forced to vacate their two south-facing rooms at Zikawei and move into north-facing rooms so that the more desirable rooms could go to two newly arrived French priests. Jianzhong subsequently left the Jesuits prior to ordination and went to Paris, where he attempted to achieve very high standards in order to win the respect of condescending Caucasians. Ma himself remained in the order until 1876, when the increasing arrogance of the French fathers toward China became unbearable.[41] In addition, his vows as a Jesuit required him to relinquish his private property, the procreation of children, and any unauthorized responsibility. This gave rise to a conflict when his elder brother Ma Jianxun donated two thousand taels of silver to Ma's mission work in Suzhou. The contribution violated the Jesuit ban on private property.[42] Other reasons may have contributed to his leaving the Jesuit order. His father died in 1875, perhaps raising questions of the continuity of the family line or perhaps inheritance.[43] He married after leaving the order. Perhaps he was also motivated to enter politics.

One of the most powerful influences in Ma's life was his mother, a devout woman born into the Catholic Shen family.[44] She was deeply disappointed when her two sons (Ma and his younger brother) left the Jesuit order. Just before dying in Sijing in 1895, she said to Ma, who had rushed to her bedside from Shanghai, "My son was a priest; since you are not a priest, I don't recognize you as my son."[45] The lingering sting of his mother's remark, along with his later grief at his wife's death and his disillusionment with politics, contributed to his return to religious life in 1898.[46]

MA XIANGBO AS A REFORMER

After leaving the Jesuits, Ma joined the reformers of the late Qing period. His older brother, Ma Jianxun, a prominent military officer and member of the Huai faction under the eminent reformer and Self-Strengthener Li Hongzhang (1823–1901), assisted him. His training as a Jesuit priest excluded him from the higher ranks of governmental service. His knowledge of the West, however, augmented by a trip to Europe and the United States in 1887, enabled him to become an influential advisor. He became a private secretary to Li Hongzhang and was sought out as a consultant during the Hundred Days' Reform (1898) and the Revolution of 1911. Republican government cabinets often consulted him. A common nineteenth-century expression stated that every Chinese convert to Christianity meant one less Chinese, but Ma remained authentically Chinese, and his reputation as a patriot peaked during the First Sino-Japanese War (1894–1895).[47]

Ma's attitude toward Western culture blended admiration with disdain. He hated the Europeans' attitude of superiority and condescension toward the Chinese; yet he admired the practical value of Western studies. When the Taiping army of Li Xiucheng appropriated the Zikawei cathedral and school as a soldier barracks, Ma fled with the rest of his family to the Shanghai International Settlement, where European soldiers and weapons protected them.[48] Despite his resentment of French chauvinism, the Ma brothers experienced extensive immersion in French culture through the French Concession in Shanghai. This exposure left its mark in Ma's fluent French and lifelong appreciation for French liquors.[49]

After leaving the Jesuit order, Ma continued to worship as a Catholic. On visiting Europe in 1887, he made a special trip to Rome for an audience with Pope Leo XIII. His wife, children, and family property impeded any return to the Jesuits. In 1894, however, Ma's wife, pregnant with their third child, died in a sea disaster. After the defeat of the Chinese in the First Sino-Japanese War and the collapse of the Hundred Days' Reform, Ma despaired over the political situation in China. He left governmental service in Beijing and returned to Shanghai to pursue his intellectual interests. His former student, the Jesuit Shen Zegong, visited and served as a spiritual mediator in reestablishing Ma's links to the Jesuits. After a month-long retreat at the spiritual center at Sheshan, Ma decided to return to the order. He transferred the care of his two children to the church. His nine-year-old daughter, Ma Zongwen, was sent to the Shanghai Convent of the Holy Mother and told to refer to her father thereafter as "uncle."[50] After a twenty-two-year break (1876–1898), Ma returned to Zikawei and resumed his religious life. During that interval, the European-biased treatment of Chinese religious had eased, and Ma now served as an important link between the Catholic Church and the upper levels of Chinese society. He became a leader of the indigenization of Christianity in China and now had the stature to fight the European chauvinism of the French priests.

During a fifteen- to sixteen-year period at Zikawei, from 1898 to 1913 or 1914, Ma became the first Catholic to translate the New Testament into Chinese. The resulting *Xinshi hebian zhijiang* was a translation into classical Chinese with an emphasis on style. Not completed until 1937, the work was published in 1949 by the Commercial Press in Shanghai.[51] Although Ma submitted to the discipline of the church, he continued to resent the French Jesuits' attitudes of cultural superiority, reflected in their requirement that works written in Chinese by Chinese priests be checked for accuracy by French priests.[52]

Ma based his vision of reform for China not only on Christianity and political reforms but also on education. He was deeply disturbed by the diplomatic failure of the Qing court, which stemmed, in part, from its ignorance of international law.[53] After the disastrous Boxer Rebellion, Qing officials borrowed extensively from the Japanese educational system and employed a number of Japanese educators to work in the fledging Imperial University of Beijing. Ma opposed borrowing from the Japanese and avoided using Japanese educational terminology, believing it to rest on translations of Western learning that were alien to Chinese culture. He believed that China needed an authentically Chinese system of higher education, independent of the Qing government.[54]

When Cai Yuanpei and over a hundred students studying at a government school rebelled against the Qing government's attempt to limit their political activity and forbid the reading of works by Rousseau and Liang Qichao, some of them accepted Ma's invitation to study Latin at a new Aurora Academy (Zhendan Xueyuan), which later became Zhendan Daxue (Aurora University). Ma viewed Zhendan as a new kind of Chinese university comparable to Western universities. He called it an academy rather than a university because he wanted, in part, to emulate the classical tradition of Plato's Academy.[55] Referring to the Greek goddess of dawn, the name Aurora symbolized the rebirth of China. Ma's style of teaching, however, also derived from the *shuyuan* (college, academy) of the Tang and Song dynasties, and he insisted on the translation of Western philosophical teachings into classical Chinese.

So Zhendan developed as a hybrid institution that blended Chinese and European traditions.

From its official founding in 1903, Zhendan was a symbiotic effort between Ma and the French Jesuits. The Jesuits contributed the old observatory at Zikawei for classroom instruction, while Ma contributed three thousand *mu* (one *mu* = approximately 0.167 acre) of Ma family property and forty thousand units of unspecified currency (taels? francs?) toward building costs.[56] Ma sought the participation of the Jesuits in instruction because of their learning and pedagogical experience. However, Ma's vision differed in certain fundamental ways from that of the Jesuits. Because he viewed the school as a re-creation of the traditional Chinese academy (*shuyuan*), more akin to a literati society than a higher-education establishment, Ma gave the students greater freedom to run the institution than was usual for a Jesuit institution. He supported the students' proposal to eliminate religion from the curriculum, which the Jesuits opposed. Tensions ensued, and when illness forced Ma to take a brief leave of absence, the Jesuits sought to change the curriculum, which they felt was too broad and ambitious.[57] The French fathers proposed using a more focused French educational model and increasing the use of French, while cancelling English courses, despite a growing demand for English-language classes. The Jesuits sought to concentrate decision making into a more hierarchical structure and to limit enrollment to younger students in order to avoid political activism.

As a result of these changes, in the fall of 1905 Ma and part of the student body left Zhendan to found a new institution, Fudan Gongxue (New Aurora Private School), which in 1910 became Fudan Daxue (Fudan University). Ma retained a lifelong contact with Zhendan, however, which the Jesuits continued to refer to as "his" university. In return for Ma's financial contribution to Zhendan, the Jesuits paid him a monthly stipend for living expenses. In 1936, when the Jesuits considered moving Zhendan to Vietnam, Ma successfully intervened, arguing that, per the original agreement, Zhendan was to educate Chinese.

Ma was not without his supporters. The urban areas of Jiangsu and Zhili provinces were hotbeds of Catholic criticism of the French priests. The missionaries Lebbe and Cotta supported Ma's views.[58] Ma and Ying believed that the Chinese government needed to establish diplomatic relations with the Vatican, an objective realized in 1922 when the Vatican sent its first official representative, Bishop Celso Constantini.[59]

Ma struggled to promote his vision of Chinese Christianity since even many Chinese in Catholic church bodies had embraced the anti-accommodationist views of the French Jesuits. This may have been an instance of one of the pernicious effects of colonialism in which European racism was absorbed by non-European peoples and expressed as a feeling of inferiority about their own indigenous culture. The Catholic magazine *Jiaowu yuekan* (Church Affairs Monthly) criticized the accommodationism of early Jesuits like Matteo Ricci, which used indigenous Chinese terms like *Shangdi* (Lord-Above) from the Confucian classics and *Tianzhu* (Lord of Heaven) to translate "God." They characterized the translation or transliteration of words like "Christ" or "God" as "pandering to the Chinese."[60]

MA XIANGBO'S COLLABORATION WITH YING LIANZHI

The culmination of Ma's vision of a synthesis of Chinese and Western cultures came through his collaboration with Ying Lianzhi, whose given name (*ming*) was Hua and whose baptismal name was Vincent.[61] Ying's background was very different from Ma's. He came from a Manchu family of banner men of the Plain Red Banner, which was fifth in rank among the eight Manchu banners.[62] He was the second of five brothers and had one younger sister. As the son of a Manchu bannerman, rather than a Chinese, it is not surprising that Ying was both athletic and studious. He lifted weights, was a good swordsman, and could shoot an arrow accurately from horseback. Other than receiving some private tutoring in the Chinese classics, he was self-taught. Like Ma, he had strong spiritual tendencies. He studied Buddhist, Confucian, Daoist, and Islamic texts, though he found them unsatisfying. His conversion to Christianity came through his fiancée's illness. When Chinese physicians could not cure her, Ying sent her to a hospital in Beijing run by the Sisters of Charity. She recovered, and Ying was said to be so impressed by the selfless devotion of the nuns that he became drawn to Christianity and was baptized at the West Church (Xitang) in 1895. Ying eventually convinced his entire family to be baptized, although his father became so enraged by the shame his family's conversion had brought upon him that he nearly murdered his wife before being baptized himself.

Ying was critical of the Manchu government and sympathetic to the Hundred Days' reformers of 1898. Although he did not participate in the reforms directly, he felt the need to flee by steamer from Tianjin when they collapsed. One of his companions on the steamer was the leader of the reform movement, Kang Youwei, although Ying did not recognize him at the time.[63] In 1902, in the treaty port of Tianjin, Ying founded the newspaper *Dagongbao*, also known by its Western name, *L'impartial*, and served as both director and editor in chief for ten years (1902–1912).[64] He became a sharp critic of the Manchu government's resistance to reform and a thorn in the side of Yuan Shikai, then commissioner for northern ports and a rising military star and subsequently the model for later warlords. When the United States passed the Chinese Exclusion Act of 1902 (extended in 1904 until 1943), which limited the immigration of Chinese laborers to the United States, Ying vehemently criticized the law and advocated the boycott of American goods. When Yuan responded by banning the sale of *Dagongbao*, Ying cleverly circumvented the injunction by giving the copies away, free of charge. Ying promoted public literacy by pioneering the use of colloquial Chinese (*baihua*) rather than literary Chinese (*wenyan*) in his newspaper; he also led a campaign against foot binding.

Ying began his relationship with Fr. Lebbe in 1903, when the priest came to Tianjin as a missionary. Ying tutored him in Chinese composition, literature, and history. They shared a common interest in using journalism as a medium to advance reform and in appealing to more educated Chinese in Tianjin. In 1915 Lebbe and a group of Chinese Catholics started the first Catholic daily newspaper, *Yishibao* (*Social Welfare*), which became the most widely circulated publication in northern China. In 1914 and 1915, he and Ying rented the large Canton Guild Hall in Tianjin, where they gave remarkable addresses to crowded audiences. The two collaborated in numerous activities, including charitable work.

Lebbe and Cotta led a group of European priests who vocally criticized the imposition of European Catholicism upon China and the related unequal treatment of Chinese and European priests. This discrimination made it difficult to recruit priests among middle- and upper-class Chinese.[65] Ying, Ma, Lebbe, and Cotta became involved in a lay apostolic movement known as Catholic Action.[66] Shanghai businessman and Catholic benefactor Lu Bohong (Joseph Lo Pa-hong) (1875–1937) gave impetus to the movement's establishment in 1912 and remained active in it until his assassination.

The incursion of Japanese military forces into China marked the last decade of Ma Xiangbo's life. Always cool to the Japanese style of modernization, in 1931 and 1932, in the aftermath of the Japanese invasion of Manchuria, he wrote several articles condemning Japanese aggression.[67] Via radio, he tried to rally the Chinese people in defense of their nation. When the Japanese attacked Shanghai in July 1937, Ma moved to Guilin, where in January 1939 he celebrated his birthday of one hundred *sui* (Chinese reckoning of age). Overtaxed by a journey to Kunming, he died at Liangshan in Indochina the following November.

THE FOUNDING OF FU REN CATHOLIC UNIVERSITY

Ma's desire to create an educational model for reforming China by blending Chinese and Western cultures had motivated his establishment of Zhendan and Fudan. After the collapse of the last dynasty and the establishment of the republic, he began to see the need for a religious component in his educational vision. Previously, Christian character building and the education of priests had played little role in the development of the curricula at Zhendan and Fudan. As the nineteenth century drew to a close, Ma began to incorporate these religious elements into his plans for a new university.[68]

The founding of this new university was a collaborative effort that grew out of the friendship of Ma and the Catholic reformer Ying Lianzhi. Ma and Ying shared the belief that successful reform in China required that the Catholic Church become part of the educational system. In 1912 they sent a petition to Pope Pius X advocating development of a native Chinese priesthood. They reminded the pope that the scholarly tradition of the early Jesuit missionaries had combined faith and natural science, but this tradition had fallen into decline with the arrival of less scholarly missionaries who converted less-educated and lower-class Chinese. Ma and Ying proposed that the founding of a Catholic university could correct this problem. This Catholic university should seek to cultivate a new Christian educated elite (*zhimin*) in China by blending traditional Chinese culture with "Western European culture" (*Ouxi zhi wenhua*).

In the absence of a clear response from the pope, Ma and Ying moved ahead on their own. Ying resigned as head of the *Dagongbao* in 1912 and moved with his wife, Shuzhong, to the Western Hills of Beijing to restore his health.[69] The couple occupied a country house on Xiangshan (Fragrant Hills) with a panoramic view of the countryside.[70] In the style of a traditional scholar-hermit, Ying took the literary name of "Rustic in the Pines" (*wansong yeren*).[71] At Ma's urging, Ying Lianzhi's younger sister, his wife, and the imperial princess Kalaqin obtained permission from the imperial family to establish a school in one of the five imperial parks on Xiangshan. Ying undertook management of the school, and in 1913 they established the Fu Ren Academy (Fu Ren She) in this park. The name *fu ren* (to develop virtue) came from the Chinese classic *Lun yu* (Analects) of Confucius, book 12, chapter 24, which states, "A gentleman makes friends through culture and develops his virtue through friendship."[72] A privately funded initiative by Chinese Catholics without assistance from the Vatican or missionaries in China, Fu Ren Academy was similar to Zhendan but differed in its emphasis on cultural history oriented toward Christian texts and in its exclusively Catholic student body. Ying recruited forty young men from all over China to participate in a study group that largely duplicated the traditional Chinese *shuyuan* (academy). Students selected a topic and studied Chinese classics, as well as seventeenth-century works by China Jesuits. Each day they read books, wrote essays, and developed their public-speaking skills. The academy operated until 1918, when lack of funds forced it to close. Once again, Ma's participation in the Fu Ren Academy involved formative ideas more than direct administration. In any case, his departure from Beijing and return to Shanghai in 1913 limited his involvement.[73]

Meanwhile, the Catholic Church sought a greater role in the educational system in China, a topic discussed in mission conferences held in Hong Kong, Hankou, Jinan, and Shanghai from January to March 1914. A main result of these conferences was the effort to establish a Catholic university in China. Yet the faculty of the Grand Séminaire of Beijing's rejection of Ying's offer to teach Chinese literature and history without compensation demonstrated the missionaries' continued resistance to broadened theological training. Consequently, in 1917 Ying composed his famous forty-six-hundred-word *Quanxue zuiyan* (Exhortation to Study), which became very influential in urging Catholics in China to lay greater emphasis on learning.[74] Ying urged native clergy to study Chinese literature. This essay seems to have marked a turning point in Catholic missionary policy in China as Rome began to respond. Pope Benedict XV's 1919 encyclical *Maximum illud* referred to several points Ying had made. On the basis of a report by the Bishop de Guebriant of Guangzhou (Canton), in which the bishop had queried a number of Chinese priests and on whose behalf Ma Xiangbo had replied, the Vatican decided to establish a Catholic university in China.

In 1919 Rome sent an investigative committee to China and followed up with a visit by Fr. George Barry O'Toole (1886–1944), who taught at the Benedictine Archabby of St. Vincent in Latrobe, Pennsylvania.[75] O'Toole met with Ying, and they decided to found a university. Propaganda assigned the Benedictine order the task of founding a Catholic university in China. Ma and Ying were consulted, and in 1925 a contract was signed for property in Beijing.[76] O'Toole was appointed president of the university, which opened on October 1, 1925. Ying had hoped that Ma would assume a leading administrative post, but Ma declined, ostensibly on the grounds of age but also perhaps because he was more interested in generating ideas than in implementing them through administration. Ma was satisfied with the American Benedictines' administering Fu Ren University because they had no other presence or vested interests in China. Ma's influence on Fu Ren University was more fully manifested than at Zhendan and Fudan, in part through Fu Ren Academy, which the new university absorbed, but also because the new university offered Ma the opportunity to develop his conception of an educational model based on a dialogue between the Chinese and Western worlds.[77] Ying died of exhaustion in 1926 and was replaced by the distinguished scholar Chen Yuan (1880–1971).

By 1933 the Great Depression had overwhelmed the American Benedictines with shortages of personnel and finances, and so the burden of running Fu Ren Catholic University fell to the German Steyler missionaries of the Society of the Divine Word (Societas Verbi Divini, or SVD). With the transition from the Benedictines to the Steylers in 1933, Father Joseph Murphy, SVD, an American, replaced O'Toole as rector.[78] Chen Yuan was appointed vice president in 1927 and president in 1929.[79] The university continued to operate during the Japanese occupation. When war broke out between Japan and the United States in 1941, the American faculty members were interned and replaced with Germans and others from neutral countries.[80]

The Society of the Divine Word emerged in 1875 during the climax of imperialism in Europe. Although founded by Germans, because of the church-state struggle (*Kulturkampf*) between the Catholic Church and the German government of Otto von Bismarck, the SVD was located just outside Germany's borders in the Dutch town of Steyl. One of the society's first missionaries to China, Johann Baptist Anzer (An Zhitai) (1851–1903), embodied the aggressive and chauvinistic attitudes of his age and contributed to the climate that produced the Boxer Rebellion.[81] And so it is remarkable that the next generation of SVD missionaries produced a man like Fr. Franz Xaver Biallas (Bao Runsheng), who had to overcome the narrow missionary perspective of his confreres in China to teach at Fu Ren Catholic University and to collaborate with Chinese scholars in the 1935 founding of *Monumenta Serica*, one of the oldest Sinological journals, predated only by *T'oung Pao* (1890).[82] The new journal sought to evaluate Chinese historical materials according to the newest Western methods, to support the translation of research and reference works by Chinese scholars, and to advance international scholarly collaboration by publishing the latest research. Biallas was the editor, but there was an attempt to balance the list of associate editors between Westerners and Chinese.[83] Later, because of the hostility of the new Communist government, publication of *Monumenta Serica* was suspended in 1949, and the editorial office was moved first to Tokyo (1949–1963), then to Los Angeles (1964–1971), and finally to St. Augustin in Germany.

The Communists took control and closed Fu Ren University on October 12, 1950. At the time of the Communist takeover, the university had twenty-two hundred students and 235 faculty members, of whom 45 were religious. On July 25, 1951, the university rector and his staff were imprisoned in the government's anti-Catholic campaign. Beijing Normal University (Beijing Shifan Daxue) absorbed the Beijing campus of Fu Ren Catholic University.[84]

COMMUNIST PERSECUTION AND CATHOLIC MARTYRS IN SHANGHAI

By 1949 the Shanghai region had blossomed into one of the most vibrant Catholic dioceses in China with 150,000 Catholics. Of the over eight hundred Chinese and foreign Jesuits in China in 1949, 232 of them were in the

Shanghai mission.[85] The strength of the Catholic community in Shanghai was due, in part, to the extended patrilineal kinship networks, many of them Christian since the seventeenth century.[86] Many of the clans had become overwhelmingly Catholic due to the church prohibition against marriage to non-Catholics (*waijiao*). Shanghai rather than Beijing would become the center of Catholic resistance to Communist attempts to control and destroy Catholicism in China. It was an ominous portent of future difficulties when People's Liberation Army (PLA) troops entered Shanghai on May 24, 1949, by way of Zikawei (see map 3).[87] However, the troops met with little resistance there or anywhere in Shanghai. Other than a few bullets piercing windows near the Jesuit seminary, the peasant soldiers were polite and even joked with the Jesuits.

Although the French Jesuits continued to play a prominent role in the Shanghai church, the consecration of Ignatius Gong Pinmei (1901–2000) in the St. Ignatius Church at Zikawei on October 7, 1949, clearly established the shift toward indigenous leadership.[88] His consecration occurred only six days after Mao Zedong proclaimed the founding of the People's Republic of China on October 1 in Beijing. Initially Gong was designated bishop of a smaller Suzhou diocese, but his authority expanded to include Shanghai the following year.

The greatest challenge Gong faced was the campaign of the newly triumphant Communist government to take over and eventually destroy the Christian churches. The vehicle of this takeover, the Three-Self Reform Movement, claimed that it aimed to eliminate foreign influence in Chinese churches. (In 1954, there was a change of emphasis from "reform" to "patriotism," manifested in the formation of the Chinese Catholic Patriotic Association [CCPA] and the Chinese Protestant Three-Self Patriotic Movement.) In 1950 the Communists had launched a reform program that attacked the twin evils of landlords and moneylenders.[89] Initially some prominent Christians supported the land reform movement as a form of the social gospel that emphasized Christian service to the poor. Zhou Enlai led at least three conferences in 1950 and 1951 to define the regulations for Christian churches in the new Communist state.[90] In May 1950, Protestant church leaders drafted a "Christian Manifesto" eventually signed by four hundred thousand Protestants.[91] Catholics followed in November with their own manifesto, criticizing imperialists for having used the church as a tool of colonialist oppression. The Catholic manifesto called for cutting church ties with the forces of imperialism and cultivating the patriotic movement based on the Three Autonomies (*zizhi, ziyang, zichuan*) expressed in the Three-Self Reform Movement. The Three-Self concept of Christian churches in China being self-governing, self-supporting, and self-extending is often traced to the writings of Protestants Henry Venn of England's Church Missionary Society and Rufus Anderson of the American

Board of Commissioners for Foreign Missions in the 1860s.[92] However, the Three-Self principles were already part of efforts to create indigenous Chinese churches in the 1850s.[93] When applied to Chinese Catholicism in the 1950s, the Three-Self Reform Movement referred to the Catholic Church as "self-governing" (creating an indigenous clerical hierarchy), "self-supporting" (rejecting foreign subsidies), and "self-propagating" (serving local rather than foreign interests). The third of these autonomies was the most difficult for Catholics because it involved independence from Rome and the destruction of the hierarchical priesthood of a universal church.

The Korean War, which broke out on June 25, 1950, when North Korean troops crossed the thirty-eighth parallel and invaded South Korea, exacerbated the Three-Self Movement. Foreign forces in the joint United Nations army under the command of the staunchly anti-Communist General Douglas MacArthur counterattacked and moved northward. The threat that MacArthur might cross the Yalu River and invade China generated intense anti-foreign and anti-American feelings in an outburst of Chinese patriotism (*aiguo*), and Beijing sent forces into Korea. Nearly 1 million Chinese, including Mao Zedong's younger son, died in the fighting in Korea, making it a national disaster. In 1951 the Catholic Church, because of its ties to the vehemently anti-Communist Holy See in Rome, became a target of this patriotic feeling. Consequently, Catholic missionaries were persecuted in greater numbers than their Protestant counterparts during the Oppose America, Aid Korea movement.[94]

In Shanghai the Catholic Church owned sixty churches and missions and six thousand rental properties.[95] The Communist government imposed heavy taxes, appropriated church schools, and restricted missionaries. In the early 1950s, however, the Catholic Church underwent a revival, with upper-class youth playing a leading role.[96] The government's limited religious tolerance came to an end when the Korean War began in June 1950. Arrests of so-called counterrevolutionaries began in April 1951. Mass accusation meetings led to executions, mainly at the Canidrome, a greyhound-racing stadium in the French concession.[97] In a nightmare scenario, children sang songs while the crowds shouted for the accused to kneel to be shot. In Shanghai and throughout China, hundreds of thousands either were executed or committed suicide.[98]

Meanwhile, Catholic schools were being nationalized and Communist doctrine was replacing Catholic doctrine. In anticipation of the coming struggle with Communists, the Catholic leadership in Shanghai had begun in the fall of 1949 to mobilize Catholic youth through the Marian Sodalities (*Sheng-muhui*) and the Legion of Mary (*Shengmujun*).[99] These grew to one thousand members and could mobilize twenty-five hundred students at important events. Founded by the Jesuits in the sixteenth century, the Marian Sodalities were introduced to Shanghai by the first missionaries. By 1949, however, they had become dormant, and so prominent Jesuit educator Zhang Boda (Zhang Zhengming) (1905–1951) and a small group of Jesuits at St. Ignatius College revived them.

The second youth movement promoted at that time, the Legion of Mary, had stronger ties to the Vatican than the Sodalities. An international, lay Catholic organization focused on Mary, Mother of God, and founded in Ireland in 1921, the Legion of Mary arrived in China with Irish Columban missionaries in 1937. Vatican internuncio Antonio Riberi (Li Peili) (1897–1967), reassigned from Africa to China in 1946, promoted the legion's devotion to Mary. Riberi assigned the Irish priest Aedan McGrath to organize the league's lowest organizational units, the presidia, which were small groups each with a spiritual director (figure 3.1).[100] The presidia were governed by curia, which were in turn governed by a senatus, which controlled all presidia in a nation. Finally, there was a supreme governing authority called the Concilium in Dublin. Riberi felt a sense of urgency in strengthening the League of Mary because it had a demonstrated ability to perpetuate the Catholic faith even in

Figure 3.1　A Communist anti-Catholic political cartoon depicting the papal internuncio to China, Archbishop Antonio Riberi, recruiting Fr. Aedan McGrath to organize the Legion of Mary in China. "The Many Evils of the 'Legion of Mary'" ('Shengmujun' de wan wu zuixing), *Jiefang ribao* (Liberation Daily) (Shanghai), October 12, 1951.

the absence of a priest. China proved fertile territory for the league, and one thousand presidia were soon established. The strength of this movement is one reason why the Communist Bureau of Religious Affairs was so eager to destroy it. The legion had special appeal to young women in Shanghai and grew rapidly between 1948 and 1951. Several successful retreats stimulated interest. The legion expanded in schools and parishes, and by 1951 there were fifteen hundred members in Shanghai, although a core group of four to five hundred young Chinese students, including many women, demonstrated the greatest courage in their defense of the church. Bishop Gong enthusiastically supported the Sodalities and Legionaires, who returned his support with special affection.

Archbishop Riberi's promotion of the legion made him, along with the Catholic Central Bureau and the Legion of Mary, a target of Communist attacks; consequently, pamphlets berating him, such as *Riberi: Imperialism's Tool of Invasion*, were distributed.[101] Although a Vatican diplomat, Riberi was on weak ground because his official status had been recognized in 1946 by the Nationalist government, which had since fled to Taiwan.[102] The new Communist government, to which he had given great offense, had never recognized his official status. In June 1951 Riberi was placed under house arrest, forced to sit on a backless stool, and interrogated in long sessions, some lasting fourteen or more hours. In September, he was called to a press conference and presented with a list of accusations, which he refused to sign. Consequently, he was expelled. He was sent from Nanjing to Shanghai, where he was placed on a train that carried him south to the Hong Kong border.

Meanwhile, the government stepped up its campaign against the Legion of Mary by arresting the Catholic educators who had opposed the Three-Self Reform Movement.[103] The leading Catholic educator in Shanghai at that time, Zhang Boda (commonly cited in Western style as Beda Chang), would become the first martyr in the Communist campaign against the Shanghai Catholics (figure 3.2). Zhang was born in 1905 into a prominent Shanghai family that had been devout Christians for several generations.[104] The family had a close relationship with the Carmelite sisters, and young Boda had Carmelite spiritual mothers both among the Shanghai Carmelites in Tusewei and in the Abbey Saint-Michel-de-Kergonan in Brittany; he communicated with the latter in French. Two of his sisters and an aunt became Carmelite sisters. From a young age he indicated his desire to become a priest. He studied Latin, French, and classical Chinese at St. Ignatius College in Zikawei and entered the Jesuit novitiate in 1925. In 1932 he went to Europe to study philosophy at the Isle of Jersey, then continued to Paris, where he obtained a doctorate of letters for studies in classical Chinese; he returned to China in 1937.

Zhang was one of twelve Jesuits (seven Chinese, three French, and two American) ordained at the church of St. Ignatius, Zikawei, in 1940.[105] Unlike

**Figure 3.2   Zhang Boda (Beda Chang), SJ (1905–1951), leading Jesuit educator in
Shanghai and first martyr of the Communist anti-Catholic campaign of the early 1950s.
Courtesy of the Ricci Institute for Chinese-Western Cultural History at the University
of San Francisco.**

the French, the American Jesuits were relatively new arrivals in the China
mission. The first five California Province missionaries arrived in 1928; over
the next twenty years, the province sent a total of sixty-four men.[106] Initially
they taught at the Ricci College in Nanjing, but after becoming acclimatized
under the direction of their French confreres, they founded Gonzaga College
in Shanghai in 1931. The newly ordained Jesuits in 1940 composed a souve-
nir booklet to which each priest contributed a chapter in Chinese on a saint
who had inspired him. Zhang's choice of the martyr St. Ignatius of Antioch
foreshadowed his own martyrdom eleven years later.[107] St. Ignatius, the third
bishop of Antioch, is said to have been martyred in Rome in AD 108. Ignatius
faced being eaten by wild animals in the Roman Coliseum but appealed to the
Christians of Rome not to impede his martyrdom. He wrote, "I shall really be
a disciple of Jesus Christ if, and when, the world can no longer see so much
as my body."[108] In his ordination tribute, Zhang described how, according to
an ancient tradition, wild beasts ate Ignatius's flesh, exposing to the Coliseum

spectators his inner organs and bloodied heart, on which was written the name of Jesus.

Zhang was named prefect of St. Ignatius College and then, one year later, rector. St. Ignatius was a Catholic school, but most of the students were non-Christians. Out of two thousand students in 1940, eight hundred were Christians, one hundred were catechumens, and the remaining eleven hundred were non-Christians.[109] Shortly thereafter Zhang was appointed dean of the Faculty of Arts at Aurora University (Zhendan Daxue) and director of the Bureau of Chinese Studies. After the Communists took over Shanghai in May 1949, he attempted to resolve disputes with the new government by compromising on secondary matters while maintaining fidelity to the church on primary matters. In this he tried to recast disputes as matters essentially of religion rather than a mixture of church and politics. He succeeded in dealing with an incident in which Communist students broke some religious statues. However, tensions escalated after the Korean War began in 1950 and the Chinese government called upon students to volunteer to fight with the PLA against the United States and its UN allies in Korea. The Communists accused Zhang of trying to sabotage their enlistment efforts.

Zhang's vocal defense of the church made him a target. The attack against him escalated when the government attempted to force Catholics to join the Three-Self Patriotic Movement (figure 3.3). In February 1951 the government convoked a Congress of Education for all directors and prefects of private secondary schools.[110] Zhang and four other delegates (Fr. Yao, Fr. Louis Wang, Br. Alexander Pai, and a layman named Dr. Tsang) opposed a proposal that all Catholic educators should promote the Three-Self Movement in their schools. When they were attacked for their lack of patriotism, Zhang spoke eloquently and persuasively in defense of the patriotism of the Chinese Catholic Church, referring to the contribution of the Catholic Brigade in fighting the Japanese and the charitable work of the Auxiliary Catholic Corps, as well as the schools and medical assistance Catholics provided throughout China. Because of Zhang's influence, the proposal had to be tabled, but there would be a high price to pay.

In the following months, a public campaign was conducted against Zhang, now branded a "criminal." A document appeared titled "Resolution of the Executive Committee of the Assembly of Students of Xujiawei College on the Zhang Boda Affair" (*Xuhuai zhongxue xuesheng zhiweihui guanyu Zhang Boda shijian de jueyi*). This "executive committee" appears to have been an ad hoc group that supported a resolution drafted by an older student with Communist sympathies.[111] The resolution accused Zhang of "ten great crimes" (*shi da zuixing*), which included collaborating with the Japanese, spying for foreigners, and being an agent of Chiang Kai-shek and the

Figure 3.3 An anti-American Chinese political cartoon from the Korean War advocating a more patriotic stand for Catholics under the leadership of the government-controlled Patriotic Catholic Church. Priests are depicted carrying a banner reading, "The Three-Self Reform Movement Combats America and Helps Korea!" (*Kang Mei huan Chao Zizhi Ziyang Zichuan*), *Jiefang ribao* (Shanghai), October 13, 1951.

Americans. Shortly after the appearance of this resolution, Zhang retired as rector of St. Ignatius College. By August 1951, four of the five delegates who opposed the Three-Self resolution at the February 1951 Congress of Education were in prison.

Zhang anticipated his arrest and prepared a parcel of necessities for his stay in prison. The arrest came quietly on the afternoon of August 9, 1951, as he played a game of mahjong with three other professors of theology at Zikawei. He climbed into the waiting car and was taken to Ward Road Prison (the former name of Tilanqiao Prison). The press made no mention of his arrest, but the news spread by word of mouth. During the next four months, government officials subjected Zhang to intense interrogation, aimed at breaking his resistance. They met with only Zhang's silence.[112] Continual interrogations and lack of sleep brought him to the point of collapse. Two Salésien fathers incarcerated in a contiguous cell heard him repeat the prayer "Jesus, Mary and Joseph, help me."[113] He was moved for several days into a cell in the Lokawei Police Station for extensive interrogations. Fr. W. Aedan McGrath recalls hearing Zhang vomiting violently, day and night, in a cell opposite his own before an ambulance carried him away.[114] When he fell into a coma, he was taken to the Ward Road Prison hospital, where ten days later he died on the morning of November 11. The exact cause of death is not clear. An article in *Jiefang ribao* (Liberation Daily) claimed it was encephalitis (*danao huozheng*);[115] another source claimed it was a blood clot.[116]

On the afternoon of Zhang's death, the police came to the Zikawei presbytery to find an acquaintance of "the criminal" Zhang, whom they would take back to the jail to identify Zhang's body.[117] The police were anxious to have this witness attest to the lack of signs of torture. Word of Zhang's passing spread rapidly, and early the next morning a requiem mass was held in the old chapel of the college, followed on the next day by another requiem mass in the large church of St. Ignatius at Zikawei. Three thousand mourners attended, including many young people, with boys wearing black armbands and girls wearing white ribbons in their hair as signs of grief. The requiem masses were followed by masses for a martyr with red vestments. On November 14, two thousand students filled the Church of Christ the King for a Mass of the Holy Cross with red vestments while the sanctuary was filled with red flowers.

Initially the police had planned to release Zhang's body for burial, but the magnitude of the reaction to his death made them fearful of the potential danger of a mass funeral. Consequently, the body was released to Zhang's parents with the restriction that the burial be private. It took place on November 15 under police surveillance in the Xiangong Mu cemetery outside the city.[118] Zhang's flat slab of a tombstone remained blank because the authorities had insisted that the word "criminal" must accompany any inscription of his name. For a short time, it became a place of pilgrimage by students. One student wrote "¡Viva Cristo Rey!" (Long live Christ the King!) in chalk on the cement slab; others laid flowers on the ground to form a cross. Then the government prohibited grave visits.[119]

Zhang was gone, but his influence grew in the model of the martyr St. Ignatius, whom Zhang had identified with in his ordination tribute: "It is when the world no longer sees my body, that I will be a true disciple of Christ."[120] Zhang's arrest and death moved young people in particular. Several weeks before he died, a number of students had written a letter in blood to the student leaders of the Legion of Mary to strengthen their wavering resistance to police pressure.[121] The symbolism of the blood in this letter differs from the worldly meaning of blood, conveying notions not of violence but of Christian martyrdom.

Newspapers, silent on Zhang's arrest in August, suddenly reported that he had been arrested for criminal activities three months previously but escaped his just punishment by dying. They wrote, "His death was too easy, and his great crimes were left unexpiated."[122] Not all priests matched Zhang in his heroic endurance. Fr. Yao had stood with Zhang and three others the previous February to oppose the motion to promote the Three-Self Movement in schools. Yao was arrested on the same day as Zhang, but under pressure in prison, he signed a confession admitting to criminal activities as spiritual director of the Legion of Mary. After his release, he publicly retracted his confession from the pulpit and asked for penance.[123] He later suffered a nervous breakdown and was confined to a mental hospital.

The most disappointing capitulation among priests was that of the Jesuit Fernand Lacretelle. The history of Christianity is filled with cases of apostasy in which individuals renounce their faith. However, a devout Christian can betray his faith through weakness rather than volition. Such incidents often involve confession of sins never committed and disclosure of church secrets to obtain release from interrogation and imprisonment. Such a confession occurred in Shanghai following the arrest of Fr. Lacretelle, the Jesuit mission superior, on June 15, 1953. The closest confidant of Bishop Gong and the highest-ranking Jesuit in Shanghai, Lacretelle was widely regarded as a saintly figure. But between his June 1953 arrest and July 1954 release, he broke under the strain of 550 hours of interrogation, with demoralizing effects on the Shanghai Catholic community.[124]

During Lacretelle's incarceration at the Lujiawan detention center, the police applied intense physical and psychological pressure, causing his weight to drop to ninety-five pounds. Several times, on the verge of dying, he was taken to the Ward Road Prison hospital, where his health stabilized enough for the interrogations to resume. Eventually he wrote a 769-page statement and made a tape recording in which he claimed that Bishop Gong was an imperialist. In addition, he made specific accusations against other priests, naming names. Lacretelle's confession provided damaging details about the Catholic Church in Shanghai and represented a propaganda coup for the government. French prime minister Pierre Mendés-France dissuaded the Chinese government from putting Lacretelle on display in a Cold War world exhibition, and he was merely expelled from China. He reached Hong Kong in July 1954 in poor physical condition, with a puzzlingly selective recall of events. Jin Luxian, who was arrested in September 1953 partly on information that Lacretelle provided, became one of his sharpest critics.

Pope Pius XII's 1954 encyclical *Ad sinarum gentes* (To the People of China) defended the work of missionaries and rejected an independent church movement (i.e., independent of Rome) in China. The Chinese government's reconstitution of the Catholic Church shifted in emphasis from creating an independent church to creating a patriotic one. By appealing to patriotism, the authorities hoped to weaken Catholics' loyalty to Rome. This led to meetings in 1956 and 1957 of the Religious Affairs Bureau with thirty-six Catholics in Beijing and the beginning of the Chinese Catholic Patriotic Association

(CCPA). This group denounced the Vatican because the pope refused to recognize the candidate named to replace Gong Pinmei as bishop of Shanghai. This gave rise to the heterodox practice in China of locally electing bishops without Rome's approval and created a split between a state-approved church and an underground church in which Rome secretly approved bishops.

As governmental pressure on Catholics intensified, 1955 marked a turning point, when resistance led to mass arrests. On September 8, 1955, in Shanghai, Bishop Gong, seven diocesan priests, fourteen Chinese Jesuits, two Carmelite sisters, and three hundred leading Chinese Catholics were arrested.[125] The fact that this occurred on the church anniversary of the birth of Mary, Mother of God, strengthened the Catholic sense of martyrdom. Bishop Gong was defiant. A Catholic history of martyrdom by oppressive governments shaped Shanghai Catholics, who commonly called on the militant St. Michael the Archangel in prayer to defend them against their enemies.[126] The government held a mass meeting in December to voice accusations by seven seminarians and nuns, but Gong remained calm and silent in the face of three hours of denunciations and screams from the mob. However, other priests broke under the pressure and made confessions that damaged the morale of Shanghai Catholics.

The trial of Gong and thirteen other Catholic priests took place on March 16 and 17, 1960.[127] Gong was accused of leading a counterrevolutionary clique, contacting imperialists, and betraying the motherland. The trial, a carefully staged event attended by five hundred people, transformed the accusation, without deliberation, into the verdict. Gong was sentenced to life imprisonment and sent to the Ward Road Prison in Shanghai. At some point he entered into the Chinese gulag of labor camps aimed at *laodong gaizao* (commonly abbreviated as *laogai*), which means "reform through labor."[128] Even in the camp, Gong had a charismatic presence. Yih Leefah encountered him at the White Grass Mountain camp in southern Anhui, where thirty thousand prisoners from Shanghai were incarcerated.[129] Yih had been a professor of fluid mechanics at the University of Iowa when, in 1963, he returned to Shanghai to visit his dying father. Accused of being an American spy, he was sent to the *laogai* camp, where he was forced to work in a pigsty in his bare feet, shoveling excrement. He was on the verge of committing suicide when Bishop Gong persuaded him to live. Gong prayed constantly, a forbidden activity, when he worked with water buffaloes. The prisoners informed on him, and he was subjected to a struggle meeting, a Communist technique in which group pressure was applied to reform the accused. Yih later confessed that he insulted Gong and called him an old fool for praying to his useless god. Gong looked at him with "loving eyes, like Jesus must have looked at Peter when Peter denied him three times after he had been arrested," and Yih felt terrible. Later Gong told Yih that he forgave him and urged him not to give up hope.

The second most important defendant at the 1960 trial was Aloysius Jin Luxian (1916–2013), who also served many years in prison (figure 3.4). The Catholic Church in China split into two churches, one loyal to Rome and another led by the government-controlled CCPA. In later years, Gong and Jin, although of similar origins, followed strikingly different paths within the Catholic Church, reflecting the division between the official and underground churches. Both Gong and Jin came from landowning families in Pudong, a poor, rural section of Shanghai, just east of the Huangpu River and the famous waterfront Bund.[130] Both became long-lived nonagenarians, Gong reaching the age of ninety-eight and Jin living to ninety-six. Both came from Catholic families and were educated at Zikawei.

The irony of the differences between them lies in the fact that while Gong was more loyal to Rome, he was also more closely identified with Chinese culture. Until forced by the debilitating effects of thirty years in prison to

Figure 3.4   Bishop Aloysius Jin Luxian (1916–2013), who served twenty-seven years in prison. After his release in 1982, he became a controversial figure when he accepted, without Vatican approval, the invitation of the Patriotic Catholic Church to become bishop of Shanghai. Courtesy of the Ricci Institute for Chinese-Western Cultural History at the University of San Francisco.

seek medical treatment in 1988 at the age of eighty-seven, Gong had publicly stated that he had never left China and would die in it.[131] Jin, by contrast, who would become more of a nationalist in supporting the Patriotic Church, had lived in Europe for three years (1947–1950) and received his doctorate in Rome. Gong's family had long Catholic roots. Like Ma Xiangbo, Gong was tutored as a child in the Confucian classics and attended Catholic schools were he learned French and Latin. After being ordained, he worked in Catholic schools in the region and had a good relationship with the Jesuits who were a powerful force in Shanghai-area Catholic institutions. He bonded well with students and evoked great affinity and loyalty from parishioners. He was quintessentially Chinese.

When Jin Luxian's family members either died or abandoned him, he became an orphan. The Catholic Church seems to have provided him with a security that Gong, coming from an established family, did not need. Jin entered St. Ignatius College in 1926 and graduated in 1932. He graduated from the Sacred Heart of Jesus Seminary in 1935 and the Seminary of the Sacred Heart of Mary in 1937.[132] In 1938, against the backdrop of the Japanese invasion, he entered the novitiate of the Society of Jesus and took his first vows in 1940. After completing his theology study (1942–1946), he departed Shanghai for France with Zhu Shude, who had been recommended for study in Europe by Zhang Boda. After visiting Paris, they reported to the Jesuit house in a small town near Lyon to conduct their tertianship, the final stage in the formation of a Jesuit.[133] Afterward, Jin went to Ireland, and then to the Gregorian University in Rome. He completed his doctoral thesis in French and his defense (viva voce) in Latin. He arrived back in Shanghai in January 1951, just as the crisis facing the church was unfolding.[134]

The Hungarian-born Jesuit Lazlo Ladany (1914–1990) was a staunch anti-Communist and a vehement critic of Jin Luxian. Ladany fled China at the time of the Communist victory in 1949 and relocated to Hong Kong, where he published the weekly *China News Analysis* from a student hostel at the University of Hong Kong.[135] Fr. Ladany was a "China Watcher," a category of scholars and journalists created by the restricted access to Communist China, particularly for Americans, between 1949 and 1979. During that time there were no formal diplomatic relations between China and the United States. China Watchers read *China News Analysis* widely during his editorship from 1953 to 1982, and Ladany claimed that it was the "only English newsletter about China based on Chinese sources."[136]

After relinquishing editorship of the *China News Analysis*, Ladany wrote a book on the Catholic Church in China in which he painted a scathing portrait of the "red bishop" Jin Luxian in comparing him to Bishop Gong. In 1984 Cardinal Jaime Sin of Manila visited China and met with Jin, then rector of the Shanghai seminary. However, the visit failed to achieve any reconciliation between Rome and the Patriotic Church. A CCPA publication referred to Sin's visit by saying, "The church in China has got rid of the colonialism imposed by foreign missioners and has established an independent self-ruling church."[137] Scholars typically characterize Bishop Gong as having "moral magnetism," while they describe Bishop Jin as brilliant and shrewd.[138] In his memoirs, Jin criticized Gong for his excessive reliance as bishop on the European Jesuits George Germain and Lacretelle, whom he allowed to control the Shanghai diocese.[139] Jin's subtlety shows in his public condemnation of Rome while he privately presented himself as a "bridge between the Patriotic church and Rome."[140] Ladany described Jin's offer to serve as a bridge as "bait" to deceive non-Chinese priests into thinking that friendship with the Patriotics could lead to a resolution of the conflict in China. While lecturing in Germany in 1985, Jin claimed that the "universal church" was an abstraction and the "local church" (whether regional, national, or continental) was the only real church.[141] Clearly, such a view would truncate the administrative and political authority of the Holy See.

Jin was released from prison in 1982, after serving twenty-seven years, and played a prominent role in building the Patriotic Catholic Church. Gong remained in prison for thirty years, finally being released on parole in 1985 into the custody of the Patriotic Church (figure 3.5). His release occurred only six months after Jin's illicit consecration as a bishop of the Patriotic Church.

Figure 3.5   Cardinal Ignatius Gong Pinmei (1901–2000), the most prominent symbol of Catholic resistance to Communist persecution. He was secretly appointed (*in pectore*) to the College of Cardinals by Pope John Paul II in 1979. After thirty years in prison, he was released on parole in 1985. This photograph was taken on September 8, 1987, one year before he went to the United States for medical treatment. Courtesy of the Ricci Institute for Chinese-Western Cultural History at the University of San Francisco.

Gong had refused to join the Patriotic Church, so he was not "rehabilitated" and was still regarded as a "counterrevolutionary."[142] He took up residence in Zikawei, practically a prisoner of the Patriotic Church.[143] Although still the legitimate bishop of Shanghai, he had no power. In 1988 his nephew received permission to take him to the United States for medical treatment. Gong had secretly been made a cardinal (*in pectore*) by Pope John Paul II in 1979, and in 1989 he flew to Rome to receive a public consecration. He never returned to China but remained at a home for retired priests in Connecticut until his death in 2000.

Chapter 4

Love and Hysteria in Catholic Orphanages in China

FEMALE INFANTICIDE

The helplessness of infants stirs feelings of sympathy in many people, and Catholic religious sisters had a special concern for the abandoned daughters of China. It was a bond born of the humility that the sisters willingly culti-vated in their vows of service to God and that the Chinese girls were forced to bear by their birth in China. And yet misunderstandings and suspicions about activities in the Catholic orphanages provoked a level of hostility and hysteria among the Chinese that was almost equal in intensity to the accusations of sexual seduction of Chinese women by Catholic priests.

The Chinese word commonly used for infanticide, *ninü* (literally, to drown a girl), reflected the fact that girls were the primary victims. The practice was entrenched in Chinese society and has continued in modified form down to the present. The most frequently practiced form of infanticide involved thrusting the newborn infant head first into a jar filled with liquid and drowning it.[1] This was done sometimes by the midwife and sometimes by the mother herself. Often the infant was simply abandoned in the street; occasionally it was left in a garbage dump and devoured by street dogs, rodents, or pigs. Sometimes a live infant was placed in a basket (*lantun*) and wedged into the fork of a tree in the hope that someone would find and raise it. The incidence of infanticide varied greatly by period and region in China. It was less pervasive in the north and more extensive in the lower Yangzi River and Canton regions.

The main reasons for female infanticide—poverty and the inability to care for the child—were reinforced by social custom dictating that females would leave the home to marry and were "goods in which money was lost" (*pei jianhuo*). By the Qing dynasty, dowries were the mark of a respectable marriage, and families went into debt to dower their daughters suitably or to

maintain ("matching doors") or raise (hypergamy or marrying up) the status
of the family. In addition, a large dowry guaranteed sufficient status for the
bride so that she would be treated with respect by the family into which she
was marrying. This would help protect her from a tyrannical mother-in-law
(a common problem new wives faced). Males were also preferred because
the Chinese patrilineal society dictated that only males could carry out the
ancestral ceremonies linking each new generation to past generations in the
family. While both practical and social reasons contributed to the preference
for boys, weak and deformed males were sometimes eliminated. Infants born
to unmarried mothers were also killed. Buddhist temples provided baskets
and baby towers for depositing unwanted infants, though these were primarily for stillborn or deceased babies.[2]

There were laws against infanticide. The Qing dynasty criminal code, *Da
Qing lüli*, issued in 1647, was based on the Ming code of laws established
by the Yongle emperor and modified to include Manchu law. Section 294
declared that anyone who killed his son, grandson, or slave and attributed the
crime to another person would be punished with seventy blows of a heavy
bamboo and a year and a half of banishment.[3] In 1773 the Qianlong emperor
expanded this prohibition to include infanticide.[4] However, the law was rarely
enforced at the local level.

There was no consensus in Chinese society on the practice of infanticide,
and both Buddhists and Confucians voiced strong dissent. Buddhist opposition to infanticide was tied to the notion of karma (the moral quality of one's
deeds) and voiced on the popular level in vividly illustrated broadsheets,
which warned parents of karmic retribution for taking the lives of newborns.[5]
Conversely, this didactic literature emphasized the karmic rewards for those
who helped to save newborn infants from death. Buddhist opposition to
female infanticide was more consistent than that of Confucians, who valued
age over youth and males over females.

The Confucian view of female infanticide was more complicated and less
clear-cut. In Chinese culture the dominant symbols for male and female—the
dragon and the pearl—represent the yang-yin balance. The dragon is a symbol of male sexual vigor and fertility.[6] Unlike the fire-breathing, frightening
dragon of Western culture, the Chinese dragon (*long*) is benign and auspi-
cious. Since the time of the Han dynasty (206 BC–AD 220), the dragon had
been the imperial symbol. By contrast, ancient Chinese believed the pearl
(*zhu* or *zhenzhu*), the female symbol, to consist of the moon's essence, created
through the processes of *yin* (a female force, as opposed to the male force,
yang) in the shell of the mussel.[7] Since the dragon and the pearl represent
complementary forces that create balance in nature, large-scale destruction
of the pearl force through female infanticide would be harmful. The pearl
image served as an affectionate reference to the father-daughter relationship

in the commonly used Qing phrase "a pearl in the palm" (*zhangzhu* or *zhang-zhongzhu*).[8] In the autobiography of Shen Fu (1762–after 1809), his wife, Chen Yun, explains why she has given away her pearls: "Women are entirely *yin* in nature and pearls are the essence of *yin*. If you wear them in your hair, they completely overcome the spirit of *yang*. So why should I value them?"[9]

After 1900 the Chinese basis for opposing female infanticide shifted from morality to a concern for the destruction of a natural resource ("productive female citizens"), which threatened China's ability to survive as a nation.[10] The treatment of female infanticide as a problem of national population control rather than a problem of morality allowed for the eventual creation of the One-Child Policy in 1979, which resulted in the expansion of female infanticide through the use of sex-selective abortions.

Unlike the popularly oriented morality books (*shan shu*), which were syncretic blendings of Confucianism, Buddhism, and Daoism, the purest Confucian arguments against infanticide targeted a more literate audience. Occasionally public proclamations forbidding infanticide, titled "Dissuasives from Drowning Daughters" (*jie'ni nü wen*), were posted.[11] Confucian opposition to female infanticide was expressed in arguments for the necessity of cosmic balance between heaven and earth, yang and yin, and male and female. An official warning against female infanticide, posted on walls throughout Shanghai in 1866, condemned the drowning of girls on the basis of the harm it did to Heavenly Principle (*Tianli*) in violating Heavenly Harmony (*Tianhe*). Other Confucian arguments against female infanticide were framed as part of a criticism of the abuse of females, which violated the second of the Confucian Five Relationships: ruler-subject, parent-child, husband-wife, elder-younger, and friend-friend. Yet other condemnations of female infanticide cited the legendary models of female filial piety in the daughters Ti Ying (ca. 157 BC) and Hua Mulan (ca. AD 501–556). Finally, officials tried to limit the size of dowries (*zhuanglian* or *jiazhuang*) because of their contribution to female infanticide. Local elites (degree-holding gentry and merchants) started to establish foundling hospices (*yuyingtang*) staffed by wet nurses (*naima*) in 1655 or 1656 as a benevolent practice.[12] These hospices were populated mainly by girls.

The growing poverty of nineteenth-century Chinese appears to have increased the numbers of abandoned children and the incidence of infanticide.[13] Stories about the plight of these unwanted children began to circulate in Europe, where they generated a response reminiscent of the famous Children's Crusades to the Holy Land of 1212. A young French seminarian named Charles de Forbin-Janson (1785–1844) became obsessed with the plight of these abandoned children, who were rumored to be eaten by dogs.[14] His repeated pleas to go to China as a missionary denied, Forbin-Janson was appointed bishop of Nancy. He gathered a number of prominent clerics and lay persons in Paris in 1843 and founded the Society of the Holy Childhood (Société de la Sainte-Enfance). In searching for funds to literally buy the abandoned children, baptize them, and raise them as Christians, he appealed to children to help other children as part of a worldwide Christian family. He asked the children of France to break open their piggybanks and make a monthly contribution of one sou (the approximate equivalent of US$1 today). The movement evoked such enthusiasm that critics accused the China missionaries of fabricating horror stories in order to raise funds.[15] Forbin-Janson subsequently extended the appeal to prominent clerics.

Although Forbin-Janson died in 1844, the society distributed 19,500 French francs to China and Southeast Asia in 1845, 42,500 francs to China alone in 1846, and 1.7 million francs to China by 1893. The society produced a popular periodical titled *Annales de la Sainte-Enfance* (vols. 1–32, 1846–1912), with an abridged English version titled *Annals of the Society of the Holy Childhood for the Redemption of Pagan Children*. Pope Gregory XVI supported the group and gave it official sanction in March 1846.[16] By 1943 the society claimed to have baptized a total of 34 million children. Although the society extended its work to other parts of the world, China remained its priority until 1950, when the new Communist government ended all foreign mission contributions to China. Today the blatantly Eurocentric features of the Society of the Holy Childhood have made it an embarrassment to Catholics.

Louis-Marie de Bési and Claude Gotteland were both friends of Forbin-Janson, and the Holy Childhood movement influenced the Jesuits' mission work in China.[17] In April 1843, Gotteland gave a retreat for seven or eight Chinese priests, at which time he presented the rules to follow in saving the souls of moribund children. The *Annales de la Sainte-Enfance* published letters written by the Jesuit Frs. Stanislas Clavelin and Théobald Werner on their ministry to moribund Chinese children. Gotteland recorded in letters his wish to establish orphanages at Shanghai that would become models for all of China, a hope realized with the establishment by 1875 of 101 Catholic orphanages in the country.[18] Orphanages for girls predominated and helped to mitigate the effects of infanticide.

The Jiangnan Christians' *Open Letter* of 1846 reacted defensively to the issue of infanticide in section nine, titled "Foundlings" (*yuying*). Infanticide appears to have been widespread in the Jiangnan region during the mid-nineteenth century.[19] Bési and Gotteland ordered that, in Christian families, when the infant of an unwed mother was discarded in a basket, it should not be suffocated.[20] The *Open Letter* responded quite bluntly that few Chinese Christians would follow this command. Four thousand years of Chinese history had established and justified the practice of a mother smothering a newborn infant she was unable to rear. Not doing so would leave it to a worse fate, since no one would protect an abandoned baby.

Most of the *Open Letter*'s response to Bési's and Gotteland's condemnation of suffocation of infants focused on the European priests' failure to appreciate Chinese culture. They were unable to see that although China lacked knowledge of transcendental truths, it had developed a sophisticated understanding of human nature.[21] As a result, the catechist wrote that the European priests failed to see that Christian scripture and Confucian texts were companion texts of equal validity.[22]

The *Open Letter* applied this same principle of human nature in defending Chinese culture in regard to the propriety of separating the sexes. From seven years of age onward in China, males and females were not supposed to share a bed. The *Open Letter* referred to a passage in one of the Gospels where Jesus spoke of the nurturing of children as akin to the chicken sitting on an egg. (It appears that a Chinese proverb was used in translating this undetermined section of the Gospels.) The point was that human nature, whether in the Christian scriptures or in Confucian texts, was not very different. The implied conclusion was that the Chinese understanding of human nature justified the mother's suffocating an infant because one responsibility of motherhood was knowing when one lacked the means to raise the child properly.

Infanticide in China was a very controversial subject in the nineteenth century. Westerners' declining respect for Chinese culture made them less willing to view the practice from the Chinese perspective. The issue was comparable in its complexity and intensity to the debate over abortion today. Since infanticide was technically illegal, even if rarely prosecuted, it was done quietly, and Chinese sources rarely mentioned it. Westerners received only secondhand information. Given the distorting nature of hearsay, it is not surprising that there were widely differing estimates about the extent to which infanticide was practiced.

Gotteland's response to the *Open Letter*'s criticism reflects how little Europeans knew about infanticide in 1846. Gotteland wrote very little about the details of infanticide, probably because he was unaware of them due to the understandable reticence of Chinese on the matter. Gotteland knew only about the numbers of abandoned children and was concerned primarily with saving them, in both a physical and a spiritual sense. He wrote that those responsible for recovering foundlings should find wet nurses to suckle them and have them baptized, and that the baptism should be entered in the church records.[23] Gotteland showed no awareness of the gender imbalance in infanticide. Whereas the seventeenth-century Christian literatus Li Jiugong had used the term *ninü* (literally, to drown a girl) in condemning infanticide, Gotteland used the gender-inclusive phrase *yasi zinü, zaojue renlei* (to smother a child and cause premature death to a human life).[24] Since Gotteland wrote his response to the *Open Letter* in French, the translators probably rendered a gender-inclusive French meaning in the Chinese version. The China Jesuits' greater awareness of the details of infanticide and the fact that it involved girls far more than boys would develop over the following years and find expression in an 1875 study by Fr. Gabriel Palâtre.

In an attempt to ascertain the extent of infanticide in China, the North China Branch of the Royal Asiatic Society invited written responses from residents throughout the British Empire. It received seventeen replies, nine arguing that infanticide was pervasive in China and eight arguing that it was not. Discussion followed a reading of these responses at an open meeting of the society on May 14, 1885, in Shanghai. The published proceedings included both the seventeen written responses and the subsequent discussion.[25] At the meeting, attended by non-Catholics, the physician R. A. Jamieson referred to the French Jesuit Gabriel Palâtre's book as one of the most authoritative works on the question of infanticide.[26]

Protestant involvement in saving Chinese children was far less active and limited by both the theological rejection of the salvic efficacy of infant baptism and an initial refusal to believe that the Chinese were exterminating infant girls in large numbers.[27] Whereas Catholics established numerous hospices with wet nurses to suckle abandoned infants and orphanages to raise the children who survived, the number of Protestant foundling homes numbered less than a dozen.[28] Perhaps the most substantial was the Bethesda foundling home in Hong Kong run by female Pietist Germans of the Berliner Frauen-Missionsverein für China (BFM) from the 1850s until 1919. Most of the foundlings at Bethesda came from German mission stations in the Pearl River delta in nearby Guangdong province. Unlike the Catholic institutions, which accepted moribund children, most of whom died after baptism, Bethesda accepted only viable infants.[29] Bethesda gave the girls a basic education, taught them household skills, and, after their religious confirmation, arranged for their marriages to Chinese Christian men.

Female infanticide initially declined after 1949 under the Communist government because of an emphasis on expanding the population, but after implementation of the One-Child Policy in 1979, it revived in the form of sex-selective abortions. A debate continues over the number of girls killed through female infanticide.[30] One recently published article on the topic de-emphasizes the number of deaths through female infanticide, claiming that abandonment probably occurred more frequently than infant drowning.[31] However, other studies estimate the ratio of baby girls killed to be one-fifth to one-quarter, an amount that visible abandonments could not account for.[32] While the exact dimensions of female infanticide have yet to be determined, the evidence available in anecdotal, documentary, and demographic form provides a strong case for a cumulative toll in the millions.

THE CANOSSIAN SISTERS IN SHAANXI

Catholic women's orders in China have received far less attention than men's orders.[33] Only in recent years has the Institute of Christian Virgins begun to attract the attention of secular scholars.[34] The Virgins' indigenous pre-1800 origins and exclusively Chinese membership allowed them initially to avoid the taint of colonialism. However, European missionaries soon began to intrude on this indigenous dynamic and to "regularize" the religious life of the Virgins.[35] In 1855 at Zikawei the Jesuit Luigi Maria Sica (Xue Kong-zhao) (1814–1895) opened a school for young girls saved from abandonment or infanticide. Living a life in common and under a rule of discipline, they received instruction from four Virgins. Although they did not take religious vows, these Virgins of the Presentation (Vierges Présentandines) evolved into the Présentandines, or the Association of the Presentation of the Blessed Virgin (Shengmu xian tanghui), under the authority of the French mission superior. The Présentandines established a novitiate in 1869. Other Chinese women entered the novitiate of Auxilaries.

The European Catholic orders of sisters have not escaped the taint of colonialism. Their activities in China between 1842 and 1952 coincided with the high point of European influence. Because the study of these women's orders has attracted few scholars, their own members, rarely professional historians, have tended to write their histories. Nevertheless, these stories are important and deserve to be told, not only because of the sisters' genuine compassion for abandoned girls and poor Chinese but also because of the courage they showed in the face of the life-threatening violence and disease then plaguing China. Their stories also reveal these Catholic sisters to have been a feminist force and to have bonded profoundly with these abandoned girls. Moreover, their service in remote mission fields gave them challenging opportunities to take responsibility and display leadership not available to European lay-women at that time.

The Daughters of the Charity of Canossa (Figlie della Carità Canossiane), a relatively modern religious order, was founded in 1808 in Verona, Italy. Maddalena di Canossa (1774–1835), canonized as a saint in 1988, is regarded as the order's founder. She entered a Carmelite convent at the age of seventeen but sought out a less cloistered path, devoting herself to serving the "beloved poor." Also known as Servants of the Poor, the Canossian sisters continue that service today in thirty-five countries. Beginning in 1860, the Canossian sisters established missions in three Chinese provinces (Hunan, Hebei, and Shaanxi) as well as Hong Kong. At the 1886 synod in Hankou, two vicars apostolic in China sought Canossian nuns for their vicariate and reminded Canossian superior Mother (M.) Paula Vismara of her long-standing promise to supply them.[36] One of these vicars apostolic was Monseigneur Gregorio

Antonucci, OFM (An Dingxiang) (1846–1902), of the southern Shaanxi vicariate. Consequently, when M. Vismara returned from a trip to Italy in December 1890, she brought back fourteen young Canossian sisters with the intention of using them to establish two missions, one in southern Hunan and the other in southern Shaanxi.

Shaanxi province (map 1) is one of the richest historical areas in all of China. The present-day city of Xi'an was the site of capitals of major dynasties—the Zhou, Han, Sui, and Tang—for over a thousand years, longer than any other city in China. In 1936, Shaanxi would return to political prominence when it became the base of the surviving Long March Communists at the Yanan Soviet. Shaanxi province is also the site of the first entrance of Christianity into China in the early seventh century, when missionaries from the Assyrian Church (Nestorianism) appeared around AD 635. Nestorianism was eradicated in the Anti-Buddhist Persecution of 845, but Christianity revived in Shaanxi when the Jesuit missionary Etienne Faber arrived in 1635, ostensibly to verify the Nestorian stone inscription that had been recovered. He established himself at Hanzhong, dying there in 1657. Thereafter the Catholic Church survived in Shaanxi with a continuous history (see map 1).

Franciscan missionaries worked in Shaanxi for two centuries, and in 1885 missionaries from the Milan-based Seminary for Foreign Missions (founded 1850) arrived. This group was modeled on the Foreign Missions of Paris in being an association of secular priests with a center for training missionaries. Pius XI was eager to have prosperous northern Italy share the burden of missionizing, and consequently in 1926 this seminary merged with the Pontifical Seminary of the Apostles Peter and Paul in Rome for the Foreign Missions (founded in Rome in 1871) to form the Pontifical Institute for the Foreign Missions (PIME).[37] The Italian missionaries from these seminaries were crucial in guiding the apostolic vicariate of southern Shaanxi. The vicariate covered an area of slightly more than eighty square miles in southwestern Shaanxi. Hanzhong was the main prefectural city where the bishop was based. At the beginning of the twentieth century, the vicariate contained a population of 5 million inhabitants, of whom eleven thousand were Christians.

Between 1891, when the first six Canossian sisters arrived in Shaanxi, and 1952, when the last European mother left, forty-two Italian sisters served in this vicariate.[38] There were also Chinese sisters, but their numbers are uncertain. The Canossian sisters in Shaanxi dedicated themselves to caring for unwanted children, mostly abandoned girls. They were supported financially by the Society of the Holy Childhood, which was so closely identified with China that during its early years it was nicknamed the "Society of the Little Chinese." However, the Holy Childhood funds did not always arrive on schedule, and so the orphanage had to develop sources of bridge funding to tide their operations over during the delay in the arrival of the Holy Childhood subsidies from Paris and Lyon. In 1901 the sisters placed over five hundred babies with wet nurses, and more than 350 girls lived at the orphanage.[39]

Six Canossian sisters departed from the Canossian motherhouse in Hankou in February 1891 with the aim of establishing a Holy Childhood orphanage in Shaanxi. Fr. Vincenzo Colli accompanied them. They made the three-month journey partly by boat, going north on the Han River despite the danger of bandit attacks. At one point they stopped on the riverbank at the prefecture Hingan-fu (Xingan-fu, today called Ankang).[40] When a suspicious barge approached, Fr. Colli fired his gun four times into the air. After withdrawing for a time, the barge of bandits returned, and Fr. Colli fired again, first four times and then six times, hitting their vessel. He shouted that he was a European and had enough powder to kill them all. His bravado worked, but many times in mission situations such as this, such tactics did not, and Europeans died. These six sisters had volunteered to pioneer this new Canossian mission. Four of them had years of experience at Hubei: Superior M. Teresa Archinti and Mothers Giuditta Bernasconi, Marietta Poglighi, and Luigia Silva. Two of the sisters, Leopolda Benetti and Elena Perego, had just arrived from Pavia with M. Vismara.

A main source of information about what happened after their arrival in Shaanxi comes from the annual letters of M. Archinti, who served as the superior of this new mission for thirty-two years, until her death in 1923. Their first orphanage in Shaanxi was in the village of Jinjiagang (they referred to it as Fun-kia-in). The donation of a house to the Holy Childhood by three Chinese Virgins, blood sisters named Maria, Teresa, and Margherita Ly (Li), indicates the sisters' collaboration with Chinese Christians. For six years (1891–1897) the Canossian sisters operated an orphanage in this house, while the convent at Guluba was being built.[41] In her first letter (1892), M. Archinti wrote that the mission house was very small and the subsidy from the Lyon Society for the Propagation of the Faith completely inadequate. Consequently, Monseigneur Antonucci was forced to suspend receipt of any more babies beyond the two hundred already in the care of Chinese wet nurses.[42] The orphanage had seventy girls cared for by the six sisters and a Chinese Virgin, probably one of the Li sisters. Marriages for seventeen girls in the senior orphanage would soon be arranged, usually into other Catholic families. The sisters were also responsible for training catechists, and sixty-five Virgins from the adjacent villages had been trained to that end in a Sunday school (Oratorio).[43]

In addition to the orphanage, by 1892 the sisters had opened a dispensary where poor people came for medical care and medicines. When no financial subsidy from the Holy Childhood had yet arrived in 1893, the mission had to reduce the number of wet nurses from 200 to 150. A school for catechists had been opened, but a lack of space limited it to seven women. Death diminished the sisters' numbers when one of the six pioneers, Sr. Silva, passed away.[44] The wet nurses cared for the infants in their homes and were paid on a bimonthly basis.

In 1895 Monseigneur Antonucci, a Franciscan, was recalled to Italy, and a remarkably youthful twenty-nine-year-old priest, Pio Giuseppe Passerini, PIME (Ba Shilin) (1866–1918), took his place as vicar apostolic of southern Shaanxi province, based in Hanzhong. The sisters at Hanzhong were particularly fond of him and referred to themselves as his "darlings" (*beniamine*).[45] M. Archinti always described him as "saintly" in her letters and reports.[46] Fr. Enrico Scalzi (Xia Zhiqi), vicar-general of Shaanxi, assisted Bishop Passerini. Three additional sisters arrived at Jinjiagang in 1895: Ms. Consolina Biscardi, Violante Corradini, and Santini Mesina. After six years of construction, the new facility at Guluba, surrounded by a large Christian community, was ready. Its setting on a hill was described as "delightful."[47] In 1897 the sisters and orphans moved into the airy and spacious new structure. They traveled together in a progression and ascended the hill in sedan chairs, preceded by a file of little donkeys and followed by the Legion of St. Francis acting as the rearguard. Their excited voices echoed throughout the beautiful valleys, and one of the sisters was moved to shout out the Canossian slogan: "Love drives us!" (*Caritas urgent nos*).

Whereas only 80 people could be housed at Jinjiagang, the number at Guluba quickly doubled to 160. Some neighboring Chinese, upset by these "foreign devils" (*yanggui*) occupying Guluba, seem to have reacted acrimoniously. A disturbance occurred in which hostile "sectarian" (i.e., Chinese popular religious) figures arrived at Gulaba. Shots from a revolver were heard, though it was unclear whether sectarians or imperial troops called to quell the disturbance fired them. For their protection, the priest in charge ordered the sisters to leave, but they returned several days later.

By 1899, the numbers at Guluba had grown to include 7 Canossian sisters, 3 Chinese Virgins, 180 orphans, 40 boarders, 38 elderly women, 35 neophytes who had finished preparing for baptism, 70 babies, and 163 additional babies in the care of the wet nurses.[48] Clearly Guluba was a refuge for women and girls, although a PIME priest was also present as a director (figure 4.1). There was great need for a ministry to girls because, according to the Canossian sisters, "the culture of the woman was little cultivated in China."[49] The Canossians expressed the need in this way: "The good of so many girls required a place where with the honey of Christian virtue they might have been able to learn diverse domestic work and afterwards to become true angels in their future family." Except for the Christian aspect, the goal was very similar to that pursued by most working-class Chinese families.

For the Canossian sisters, however, others besides girls had great needs at that time. The needy also included those elderly who lacked families to support them. Consequently, the structures at Guluba were expanded to house, on one side, an orphanage supported by Holy Childhood funds and, on the other side, a home for the elderly. A catechumenate for training catechists, fostered by Bishop Passerini and directed by Fr. Scalzi, also developed at Guluba, and yet another ministry, a project of the Virgin of the Poor, served the indigent. Fr. Scalzi directed it as well, with the assistance of M. Archinti. A hospital ward treated invalids: the lame, blind, mute, deaf, and incurable. Monseigneur Passerini established a cemetery for the Canossian sisters within the Guluba premises in 1905, and the bodies of three sisters were disinterred and reburied there.[50] Through Fr. Scalzi's efforts, a hostel for the elderly was built and occupied on November 1 (All Saints Day), 1913. It had two floors and housed a chapel as well as a hospice.

The next great threat to Guluba came from rebel bandits who, although probably not members of the Society of Righteous Fists (Boxers), nevertheless emerged in the lawless atmosphere that fostered Boxer activity to the east in the neighboring province of Shaanxi. For two months in 1900, the Guluba Christians withdrew behind their thick, high walls to survive. This danger was followed by smallpox and typhus epidemics that killed Sr. Santina Mesini, several Virgins, orphans, and boarders at Guluba, and numerous converts. Nevertheless, conversions of Chinese were numerous. The rebel gangs struck again in June and July 1903 in the district of Pin Ling Sing in the prefecture of Xingan, which lay to the east of Hanzhong prefecture. Among their ten Christian victims was the Chinese Sr. Cecelia, one of the newly consecrated Canossian aggregates, who had taken her vows at Guluba.[51]

In 1903 Monseigneur Passerini returned from a trip to Rome with three new Canossian sisters from Pavia. Problems with contagious illnesses continued to plague Guluba. In addition to those afflicted with typhus and smallpox, five of the Chinese residents were diagnosed with leprosy and had to leave to prevent spreading the illness in the crowded premises. In 1905 a Chinese-style crypt was begun in honor of Our Lady of Lourdes. A chapel in honor of Our Lady of Sorrows was built, and a Way of the Cross was constructed all along the walls of the large compound.[52] For the first time, three Chinese students were sent from Guluba to Rome to be ordained as priests.

There appear to have been obstacles to accepting Chinese women as full equals among the Canossian sisters. The basis of this inequality may have been located in unrealistic rules involving theological formation issued in Europe that impeded the Chinese sisters' acceptance. Nevertheless, there was a close working relationship between European and Chinese women who had taken religious vows. The secular priests in the vicariate recruited numerous young Chinese girls for the Institute of Virgins. After receiving instruction in the faith,

Figure 4.1 Orphans found and educated by the Canossian nuns, on the front steps of the cathedral dedicated to Sts. Peter and Paul, Guluba, Shaanxi, ca. 1910. Photographed by Fr. Leone Nani, PIME, Photograph #262, PIME–Milan, Photo Archives.

they returned to their native villages to assist the local missionaries. In 1901 three of the Chinese Virgins in the vicariate became Canossian aggregates, and 116 Virgins attended the annual retreat that year.[53] The number of Chinese sisters grew. By 1921 they were in charge of the orphanages at Jinjiagang and Xingan.[54] The girls at these orphanages were very young, and when they reached a certain age, they were sent to Guluba to be trained as housewives.

Some mild epidemics aside, a period of peace from 1900 to 1912 in the southern Shaanxi vicariate followed the Boxer-related chaos. New sisters arrived to replenish losses through death and to minister to the growing number of dependents (babies, orphans, elderly, and disabled), who had expanded from eighty at Jinjiagang to a total of over a thousand sheltered at Guluba, Hanzhong, and Xingan.[55] Srs. Serfina Battaiola, Cecilia Bertagnoli, and Redenta Motta arrived in 1903; Srs. Carmela Galbarini and Isabella Zetti arrived in 1906; Srs. Maria Buzzacchero, Luigina Frigo, and Teresa Melli arrived in 1909. In 1912 Fr. Capettini returned from Italy with five sisters, who arrived at Guluba early in 1913.[56] The dissolution of the Manchu monarchy and the founding of the Republic of China in 1912 brought diminished xenophobia and improved attitudes toward foreigners in China. In 1911 the growth of the southern Shaanxi vicariate led to the expansion of orphans to 385 spread between Guluba and two other orphanages. Of the 624 infants placed with the outside wet nurses, over half (327) died because they were past helping when received. Guluba hosted 1,614 residents and priests in 1911 and celebrated 463 baptisms. There were nine needlework laboratories on the premises, mainly for adult women.

The Guluba complex was built with thick, fortresslike walls on a hill to protect against bandits and rebels. According to the British diplomat and experienced traveler Eric Teichman, who visited Guluba in 1917, the Catholic complex occupied an entire hill in the Qinling Mountain foothills. Whenever bandits threatened, its gates could be shut and guns taken out.[57] Like other Catholic missions, it owned some of the surrounding land and earned income from its cultivation. Teichman observed the contrast between Protestant and Catholic missionaries. Protestant missionaries were mostly married and, except for the China Inland Mission missionaries, attempted to create a Western lifestyle abroad, which set them apart from the Chinese they were missionizing. Catholic missionaries lived in a manner closer to the Chinese people.[58] In her famous autobiography as told to Ida Pruitt, Ning Lao Taitai described her work for a Protestant missionary family in 1899 and 1901 in Shandong and complained about the additional work imposed by the missionaries' foreign style of living.[59] Conversely, Protestants criticized the conditions in the Catholic orphanages as oppressively institutional.

The remarkable photographs that we have of Guluba during this time are due to the efforts of Fr. Leone Nani, PIME, who was there from 1904 until 1914. He was quite young (arriving at age twenty-three) during these years and filled with youthful exuberance. He described the apostolic vicariate of southern Shaanxi as perennially damp due to the pervasive rice paddies and rainfall.[60] This area was directly south of the Qinling Mountain range, which served as a geographical divide from the dryer terrain to the north. The rice paddies were supplied by the various rivers in the area, including, most notably, the Han River, which allowed for commercial traffic as far south as Hankou. The rivers were also a plentiful source of fish. The vicariate included two prefectural cities (Hanzhong, where the bishop resided, and Xingan) and twenty-eight large villages, with a total population of 5 million. Nani's self-portrait, holding a rifle, indicates that most missionaries at this time had to use guns for defense against brigands and other hostile forces.

Among the sources of bridge funding that the Guluba mission relied on were seventy-two *mu* in dry and irrigated land, which it had purchased. A land measure that varied by province, a *mu* generally equaled 240 square paces, or 0.167 acre. In addition, the Guluba mission owned smaller amounts of land measuring nine *fen* (ten *fen* = one *mu*) and five *li* (ten *li* = one *fen*). In sum, the orphanage was listed as owning almost eleven acres. As intensively cultivated rice land, this produced a greater yield of grain than it would of wheat or corn.

While the Canossian sisters operated from the St. Joseph House at Guluba, the bishop was located about thirty-five kilometers to the southwest at Hanzhong. Monseigneur Passerini made his visitations throughout the vicariate on a mule.[61] Although in 1901 Monseigneur Passerini appointed Fr. Enrico Scalzi director of the female orphanage in the St. Joseph House, it appears that the sisters had a great deal of independence in the daily operation of the large complex. Fr. Scalzi seems to have occupied himself more with managing financial matters, including the investment of Holy Childhood funds in farm property lent out to tenant farmers. This was important because the Holy Childhood funds sent from Paris and Lyon did not suffice to cover all of the operating expenses. Moreover, World War I made the remittances from Europe precarious, delaying their arrival or greatly reducing their amount. Fr. Scalzi had some success in increasing the Guluba funds. By the end of 1906, the acreage had been expanded from almost seventy-three *mu* to eighty-four *mu* and seven *fen*. The needlework of the orphans and adult women had yielded 880.40 taels of uncoined silver (1 tael = 1.1 ounces, or 31.25 grams), plus 125 *diao*, or strings, of cash (1 *diao* = approximately 1,000 copper coins with square holes in their middle and tied together in a string, equivalent to 1 tael). These funds enabled the infirmary to be added to St. Joseph House. Additional funds were raised through offerings made by parishioners for the orphans to say prayers for the donors and for the deceased.

In 1907 the monseigneur authorized Fr. Scalzi to institute charitable work whose collection in money was supervised by the superior, M. Teresa Archinti, and her deputy, M. Leopolda Benetti. The sisters were explicitly excluded, however, from retaining the sums received, ostensibly to prevent the misuse of funds by limiting the number of hands that had access to them. It is not clear exactly what this charitable work involved, but it was apparently done by the orphans. In April 1918 Monseigneur Passerini suddenly fell ill with meningitis and died seven days later.[62] At the time, the southern Shaanxi vicariate had grown to almost twenty thousand Catholics, including the catechumens and fifteen priests.[63] The monsignor's death prompted Fr. Scalzi to compose a summary of funds earned from charitable work during the former's tenure. In a report dated December 31, 1918, Fr. Scalzi stated that between April 10, 1907, when the monseigneur's authorization for the charitable work began, until the end of 1918, chattels and property in the value of 2,597.24 in silver taels and 5,425.088 in copper cash had accumulated. Fr. Scalzi explicitly noted that these things could not be redeemed but remained tied to the benefice of the Holy Childhood in perpetuity.

Church regulations obliged the sisters to present detailed reports on their finances. These reports generated competition between the sisters and the male priestly hierarchy in China and Rome in which the sisters appear to have held their own. It is clear that service as missionaries in distant lands gave the Canossian sisters opportunities for experiences and challenges that far exceeded any they would have found as laywomen in Europe, and this certainly contradicts the stereotypical image of cloistered nuns.

After Monseigneur Passerini's death, the Sacred Congregation for the Propagation of the Faith (Propaganda), the missionary agency in Rome, questioned Fr. Scalzi's handling of the Guluba funds.[64] Because of this, he was removed as vicar delegate in Xingan and transferred to another province. On September 30, 1922, M. Archinti wrote a letter of clarification to the Canossian mother-general, explaining the handling of finances between 1895 and 1922 and defending Fr. Scalzi against accusations of wrongdoing. When the sisters first came to southern Shaanxi in 1891, they handed over several hundred yuan (dollars) to Bishop Monseigneur Antonucci. (Whereas a tael was uncoined silver measured by weight, a yuan was coined silver issued in China from the late nineteenth century.) When Monseigneur Passerini succeeded him as bishop, the sisters handed over the dowries of two sisters, which amounted to 902.11 yuan. In 1903 Monseigneur Passerini invested 1,079 yuan in land and transferred its administration to Fr. Scalzi. With donations and high interest (18–20 percent per annum), the capital grew to 12,899.33 yuan and was used to pay for the novitiate, passages between Europe and China, offerings, scholarships, and so forth. Fr. Scalzi, despairing over his exile and disgrace, spent his last days grieving over the impugning of his honesty. He died early in 1922, and his coffin was shipped by boat on the Han River back to Guluba for burial.

The southern Shaanxi vicariate was subject to violence not only from bandits but also from the civil war. On December 5, 1919, the opposing armies reached Hanzhong, and 150 wounded soldiers from both sides filled the mission hospital to capacity. The twenty soldiers who died there had all been baptized, possibly without their knowledge. When the new monseigneur Massi visited Guluba in 1924, the fruits of Fr. Scalzi's labor were apparent.[65] There were homes for old men and old women, orphanages for the boys run by the fathers and for the girls run by the sisters, and a school for catechists. M. Natalia Piccioni (who had arrived at Guluba in 1920) was named superior in 1927, and her assistant was M. Teresa Melli. Anxious to remove any cloud of doubt about the sisters' honesty, M. Piccioni submitted a financial statement of the mission to the vicar apostolic immediately.

Civil war and famine made the work of saving the abandoned children more difficult. In October 1928 the Communists drove out the Nationalists and established a base at Hanzhong-fu, increasing the threat to the church and foreigners.[66] Communists revived and spread the old rumors that the missionaries were killing babies to remove their hearts and eyes to make medicine. Half of the two thousand babies gathered in 1929 died, and it was difficult to find even suitable wood to make coffins because of deforestation and lack of funds. A devastating blow to Guluba came in November 1930 when an army of over seven hundred bandits attacked with overwhelming force. The residence, seminary, convent, hospices, and three churches were looted and destroyed. M. Piccioni wrote, "Hell broke out, a citadel of charity, which had operated for 34 years, was reduced to shambles and the work of dozens of Sisters, both Missionary and Local, was destroyed and annihilated in a few hours."[67] The bandits claimed to be attacking the foreign devils. The Guluba complex was never rebuilt and in subsequent years remained a deserted ruin.

COMMUNIST CAMPAIGN AGAINST CATHOLIC ORPHANAGES

After the 1949 Liberation, the expulsion of Chiang Kai-shek and the Nationalists to Taiwan, and the beginning of the Korean War in 1950, Communist China saw the United States as a major threat to its existence. Because of the Vatican's power to approve bishops and hence its control of the Catholic Church in China, the institution came under attack. In a public campaign that began early in 1951, the Communist government attempted to link the Catholic Church with the United States under the forces of imperialism and capitalism. The anti-Catholic prejudice that persisted in the United States in the 1950s, which prevented the election of a Catholic president until John F. Kennedy's razor-thin victory in 1960, shows the tenuous basis for linking the Vatican and the United States.

Political cartoons in newspapers and magazines played an important role in this Chinese Communist propaganda campaign. A cartoon captioned "The Religious Invasion of American Imperialism in Asia" from the monthly publication *Shijie zhishi* (*World Affairs*) conveys the line of attack (figure 4.2).[68] Foreign Catholic clerics are presented as spies for capitalistic America working under the guise of priests. Pope Pius XII (1939–1958) is depicted wearing a papal miter with a dollar sign on it to symbolize his support of capitalism. He instructs three different disgruntled Asians in Christianity, while another figure hiding under his religious vestments hands a plaque inscribed *Yazhou qingbao* (Asian intelligence) to an American identifiable by his Uncle Sam top hat. Another cartoon, titled "The Vatican in the Service of American Imperialism," served as a cover illustration for *Shijie zhishi* (figure 4.3). It shows Pius XII wearing a papal miter and glasses, with an American in

Figure 4.2 A Communist political cartoon accusing the Catholic Church of spying for the United States. Pope Pius XII is depicted as a supporter of capitalism (dollar sign on his papal miter) and a spy for the United States. While he instructs Asians in religion, a spy hidden under his robes gives information (the plaque inscribed "Asian intelligence" [*Yazhou qingbao*]) to an American (in striped top hat). *Shijie zhishi* 24 (October 1951) (?).

為美帝國主義服務的梵蒂岡

Figure 4.3   A Chinese Communist political cartoon: "The Vatican in the Service of American Imperialism." Pope Pius XII conceals an American wearing sunglasses (General Douglas MacArthur) inside his robes; a masked cardinal of the church hides behind him. Both figures brandish knives. From a collection of reprinted works from *Shijie zhishi*, in a pamphlet by Tian Wenqun, ca. 1951.

sunglasses, perhaps General Douglas MacArthur, hiding under his robes and brandishing a long knife. Another figure, whose cap indicates a cardinal of the church, hides behind the pope, blindfolded and armed with a knife.

The Communist campaign against Catholic orphanages began early in 1951. Like the campaign against the Legion of Mary, it was part of a broader anti-Catholic campaign. Because most of the abandoned infants Catholics gathered in China were already moribund, they died soon after baptism. To atheistic Communists, the notion that baptism bestowed a saving grace was a superstitious fallacy, but the high rate of infant mortality in the orphanages rendered the Catholic sisters vulnerable to accusations of maltreatment and provided the Communists with a useful tool for political exploitation. The theme of Catholic priests' deceptiveness extended to depictions of the Catholic orphanages, as portrayed in another cartoon dated July 1953 and captioned "The Hypocritical Disguise of Imperialists Who Engage in Criminal Activity" (figure 4.4).[69] The deception involved the Catholic practice of gathering abandoned infants into foundling homes. Under the guise of baptizing a baby who will soon die and join the other skeletons in the children's cemetery, the priest is actually working as a spy gathering intelligence (*qingbao*), which he hands to an American wearing an Uncle Sam top hat. The smaller figure beside him appears to be the Nationalist (Guomindang) leader Chiang Kai-shek, at the time supported by an American defense agreement that prevented a Communist invasion of Taiwan.

The campaign against orphanages made for sensational theater. In Daxian two jugs supposedly filled with a solution made from the dead children's marrow were presented to an audience of three thousand in the city theater as proof of Catholic abuse of Chinese children.[70] The sisters were accused of the cannibalistic practice of cooking this soup from dead orphans' bones and eating it for nourishment.

On February 28, 1951, the Canton newspaper *Nan Fang* published the first allegations against a local Holy Childhood orphanage. On March 17, five Canadian sisters of the Immaculate Conception were accused of mistreating children there and were detained. This was the beginning of a politically sponsored wave of hysteria over foreign Catholic abuse of Chinese children that swept across the entire nation. The campaign ignored the reality of the original Chinese abandonments and moribund condition of these children. The Hong Kong newspaper *Dagongbao*, on April 23, 1951, used screaming headlines to report, "The Nanking Heart of Jesus Home killed our children!" The skeletons of over a hundred children were exhumed from graves in the orphanage yard and offered as "proof" of maltreatment by seven Catholic sisters, who were imprisoned. Orphanage records indicated that from January 1948 until June 1950, out of 557 children received, 372 had died. The Communist press claimed the high mortality rate was evidence of maltreatment

Figure 4.4 A Chinese Communist political cartoon: "The Hypocritical Disguise of Imperialists Engaged in Criminal Activity" by Zhang Wenyuan. A priest, in the guise of baptizing an abandoned infant, soon to join the others in the children's cemetery, hands an intelligence report to an American with a striped top hat. The smaller figure beside him, with the bandaged face and military cap, appears to be the Nationalist (Guomindang) generalissimo Chiang Kai-shek, whose territory on Taiwan the United States was defending militarily from mainland Communist attacks in July 1953.

rather than of the hopeless condition of these children, many of whom were abandoned because of illness. On August 4, 1951, the Shanghai *Jiefang ribao* (Liberation Daily) reported that in the thirty-four months before the Liberation, the records of the Catholic orphanage in Wenzhou indicated that of the 1,392 children received, 302 had been placed with families, while only four of the remaining children survived.[71]

As the campaign against the Catholic orphanages intensified, claims about the number of children who had died through maltreatment grew. The public was encouraged to observe the spectacle of exhuming infants' bodies. Suddenly, through the irrational logic of Chinese Communist propaganda, these infants, who had died through the neglect of the Chinese populace, became objects of outrage directed at the nuns who had tried to save the abandoned children. Eighty thousand people gathered in Wuchang to examine five large caskets of skeletons and to hear claims that maltreatment by Catholic sisters had caused the deaths of over sixteen thousand children in twenty-five years.[72] The Catholic orphanage in Shenyang was said to have killed 13,485 of the 14,193 children it had received since its founding in 1935.[73] The sixty-three children who remained when the Communist state assumed control of the orphanage were in poor health. The most spectacular accusation of Catholic infanticide was levied against the Chengdu orphanage: forty thousand people gathered in a Chengdu park on April 2, 1952, to hear five Franciscan Sisters of Mary charged with responsibility for the deaths of 120,000 Chinese children. The sole witness who testified at this judicial proceeding was a sixteen-year-old girl who had previously lived in this orphanage.[74]

The Communist newspaper campaign against the large Zikawei orphanage in Shanghai began relatively late, in June 1953, and coincided with the campaign against the Legion of Mary.[75] Although old records had been burned and were thus unavailable, the Catholics were nevertheless accused of running, in league with the imperialists, a "concentration camp of death" for Chinese children. The Shanghai Politburo organized a mass funeral on behalf of the parents of children whose skeletons were recovered. The Shanghai newspaper *Xinwen ribao* reported that these parents had been fruitlessly searching for these remains for many years![76] The sad reality was that these children (mostly girls and mortally sick or disabled boys) had been abandoned.

Chapter 5

Sexual Domination by Catholic Priests in China

ACCUSATIONS OF SEXUAL ASSAULT AND THE 120 MARTYRS

Invasion is often linked with rape: both are aggressive acts that violate law and order. Invasion often unleashes rape because together they represent an ascending scale of violence that penetrates a protected and personal sphere of human experience. The threat of such violence often produces hypersensitivity and sexual fantasies that are generated by the vulnerability of potential victims. The Catholic invasion of China produced bizarre rumors about Western missionaries that spread throughout Chinese society, especially among the common people. These rumors were a blend of fantasy and reality engendered by fear and the vulnerability of Chinese females, especially unmarried girls who might be subjected to abusive male priests with spiritual authority over them. The fact that these priests were supposed to be celibate only increased their fear because Chinese were very aware of the lapses in the vows of celibacy of Buddhist monks and they suspected similar lapses from Catholic priests.

The rumors about priestly sexual abuses ebbed and flowed, depending on events, becoming a barometer of Chinese anxiety about the growing power of foreigners in China. The spread of Christian missionaries into the interior after the Treaty of Beijing in 1860 increased the flow of such reports. Kidnapping of children was frequently mentioned. Catholic orphanages were suspected of collecting abandoned (overwhelmingly female) babies for gruesome uses, such as removing their eyeballs for use in Western medicine or photography. Foreign missionaries were also accused of removing fetuses from pregnant women for other uses.

The relationship of Catholic priests to female parishioners was one of the most sensitive areas in the history of Christianity in China. Because of the strict separation of the sexes practiced in China since the Song dynasty (960–1279), Catholic churches tended to have a separate sanctuary for men and women, or else they held male and female masses at different times. When the administration of certain sacraments, such as the oil of confirmation, required the male priest to touch the female confirmand, parish elders were usually present to confirm that nothing unseemly occurred. Despite the opposition of Dominicans, the Jesuits also omitted several secondary rituals when baptizing women, such as applying saliva to the ears, salt to the mouth, and oil to the head and the breast.[1]

Due to this strict separation, sexual relations between a Catholic priest and a woman not only violated priestly celibacy but also provoked serious scandal. Yet priests were constantly rumored to have sexual relations with parishioners. While such reports were obviously exaggerated, they cannot be totally dismissed because we know that some were true.[2] Although modern Chinese society has greatly relaxed the rules and customs separating the sexes, sexual seduction remains a volatile issue, viewed in modern times as a form of aggression and domination associated with Western imperialism. Its volatility lends itself to political exploitation, while the element of fantasy, an inseparable part of human sexuality, complicates our attempt to understand the historical reality.

Historical allegations of rape continue to play a role in hostile relations between the Chinese government and the Holy See in Rome.[3] In September 2000 the Vatican revealed its plans to canonize 120 Catholics killed in China between 1648 and 1930.[4] Eighty-seven of these martyrs were Chinese, and thirty-three were European missionaries. The protomartyr in this group, the Spanish Dominican Francisco de Capillas (Liu Fangji), OP, was beheaded in Fujian province in 1648, followed by five other Spanish Dominicans killed in 1747 and 1748. Twenty-six Chinese and European martyrs were killed between 1814 and 1862, the first being the catechist Wu Guosheng (baptized Petrus) of Guizhou province in 1814. Most of the Chinese martyrs (sixty-six) died during the Boxer Rebellion in 1900.

Pope John Paul II canonized more saints (447) than all the popes of the previous five hundred years combined.[5] However, the origins of this list of 120 martyrs predated his pontificate by many years, and the process formally began with the first beatification (a step preceding canonization) in 1889. The entry "Martyrs of China" in the *New Catholic Encyclopedia* published in 1967 included 119 names, of which 118 also appear in the list of 120 martyrs.[6] The procedures of the Catholic Church for canonizing saints are elaborate and time-consuming.[7] As a result, all of the names on the list appear to have received intensive scrutiny to establish the facts of each individual's martyrdom.

And yet controversy arose. In late September 2000, when the Vatican's intentions became known, hostile articles began appearing in prominent

Chinese newspapers. Spokesmen for the Chinese Foreign Ministry and the Chinese Catholic Patriotic Association (representing the Chinese state-recognized church as opposed to the underground Catholic Church loyal to Rome) criticized this "canonization of so-called saints" (*ce feng sowei shen-gren*) on the grounds that the Vatican was misrepresenting the facts.[8] Rather than martyrs and saints, these 120 individuals had been, according to the spokesmen, criminals allied with Western imperialists then exploiting China. The official Chinese position held that most of these so-called martyrs were in fact justly executed for violating Chinese laws.

Ren Yanli, director of the Christian Studies Section (*Jidujiao yanjiu shi*), a government think tank within the Chinese Academy of Social Sciences, expressed a more nuanced criticism of the canonization of the 120 martyrs of China. In an article, he complained that while the Roman Curia had admirably eliminated anti-Semitic ideas and asked for the forgiveness of the Jewish nation for its failure to forcefully defend the Jews during the German Holocaust, it had shown no corresponding repentance for its failure to defend the Chinese people against Japanese aggression during World War II. Ren believed this revealed that the Vatican was applying a double standard in its relations with China. In fact, instead of repentance, Ren saw just the opposite in Rome's canonization of the 120 martyrs of China, which he viewed as an attempt to obscure the unflattering reality of past imperial injustices toward China and to "encourage contemporary Catholic clergy and believers to follow the model of these saints" in opposing anti-Vatican policies of the Chinese government.[9] Ren believed that such actions by Rome signaled its insincerity about claiming to encourage the Chinese to be both good citizens and good Christians, a crucial sticking point that had impeded the establishment of formal relations between Beijing and Rome

The list of the 120 martyrs had, for the most part, been established years before, and their canonization had been urged for many years by Cardinal Paul Shan Guoxi, SJ (Shan Kuo-hsi), president of the Taiwan Chinese Regional Bishops' Conference (Tianzhujiao Taiwan diqu Tianjiaotuan). In 1996 Cardinal Shan commissioned a painting commemorating the 120 martyrs. The result, measuring 3.9 × 2.6 meters and created over eighteen months by a Taiwan artist, is currently preserved in the Vatican museum (see cover). The list of 120 martyrs, along with their individual descriptions, was published in both Chinese and French editions in Taiwan in 2000.[10] The unfortunate and offensive choice of October 1, the anniversary of the founding of the People's Republic of China (PRC), for the announcement of the canonizations appears to have been made in Rome rather than in Taiwan. In response the Chinese Catholic Patriotic Association in mainland China issued a condemnation of the Taiwan Chinese Regional Bishops' Conference for its contribution to the canonization.[11] Mainland critics of the canonizations claimed that Taiwan

Catholics who sought to hinder the establishment of official relations with the PRC had misled the Roman Curia.

ACCUSATIONS AGAINST FR. FRANCISCO FERNANDEZ DE CAPILLAS, OP

Although most attacks applied generally to all 120 martyrs, an article by Shi Yan, titled "Unmasking the True Colors of the So-Called 'Saints,'" appeared in *People's Daily* (*Renmin ribao*) on October 3, 2000, and focused on three names.[12] *People's Daily* was the mouthpiece of the Central Committee of the Chinese Communist Party, and its articles reflected varying degrees of official backing. The article divided the 120 martyrs into three categories: (1) foreign missionaries who were tools of modern colonialism and the imperialist invasion of China, (2) Chinese Christians who were accomplices and followers of these tainted, wrongdoing foreign Christians, and (3) foreign missionaries who relied on the authority of the unequal treaty regulations, ran roughshod over native villages, bullied and humiliated the common people, caused the people to revolt and die violent deaths in the wars of imperialist invasion, and sacrificed Chinese Christians to gain power for the colonialist nations' religious societies. Shi's article assigned the three martyrs of its focus to this third, most egregious category. In chronological order, the three so-called saints were Fr. Francisco Fernandez de Capillas, OP; Fr. Auguste Chapdelaine, MEP; and Fr. Alberico Crescitelli, PIME.

The most incendiary of the accusations against foreign priests involved sexual seduction and rape. It appears that these three priests were singled out from among the 120 martyrs because they were vulnerable to sexual accusations. In each case the Chinese employed a similar pattern of attack on the behavior of these missionaries.

The earliest of the three, Fr. Francisco Fernandez de Capillas, OP (Liu Fangji) (1607–1648), predated the full-blown period of Western imperialism, which began with the Opium War (1839–1842). According to the Catholic official list of the 120 new saints, Capillas was born in Valencia, Spain, in 1607. He entered the Dominican order in 1632 and was sent to Manila, where he was ordained. Following the typical entry route of Spaniards into China, Capillas went to Taiwan in 1641 and reached the coastal province of Fujian the following year. An active proselytizer, he was accused of assisting a Christian rebel in a local revolt, apparently connected with the Manchu conquest of southern China; he was arrested in 1647 and decapitated in January 1648.[13]

The *People's Daily* article by Shi Yan accused Capillas of crimes that were almost entirely sexual in nature. Capillas is said to have built a large and powerful congregation in Fuan by means of deceiving converts, especially women. The author paints a dramatic contrast between the foreign priests' dominance and the Chinese women's powerlessness. Capillas is accused of creating disharmony in Chinese families by leading women to abjure marriage to become "chaste women" (*shouzhen nü*), a concept idealized in Confucian philosophy since the Song dynasty (960–1279). However, the Christian missionaries were introducing a slightly different variation on chastity in which a woman would remain a virgin and either delay or avoid marriage in emulation of the virginity of Mary. The Dominican missionaries modeled this form of virginity on the Christian *beatas* in Spain and elevated Christian virgins over Confucian chaste widows as a higher form of chastity.[14]

In the village of Xiapi in Fuan there lived a woman named Petronilla Chen, who had been formally betrothed in a marriage contract. Capillas is accused of convincing her to withdraw from the contract and become a Christian Virgin. He is also said to have abducted the woman and fled with her. Shi Yan implies, but does not explicitly state, that Capillas sexually seduced her. Shi is more explicit when he quotes from a Qing government document dated November 13, 1647, which accuses Capillas of evil behavior and inciting the common people by convincing a virgin not to marry, swindling married women through licentious behavior, sexually abusing widows, and fathering an illegitimate child. Shi implies that Capillas was caught and executed for this behavior, but the priest also stood accused of other crimes (inciting the common people to riot against the authorities), which Shi does not mention.

Drawing from Vatican documents complied after Capillas's death and Chinese hagiographical accounts, Anthony E. Clark describes the patterns of martyrdom.[15] Capillas was arrested on his way to administer extreme unction to a Chinese Christian. His body was tortured and his ankles crushed during long interrogations. He was flogged, starved, and exposed to freezing cold, but he continued to preach. He was beheaded, and his body was abused. Miracles, necessary for the process of beatification, were cited: his body did not corrupt, a Dominican friar living in Manila was released from his compulsive sexual desire, and two other friars in Manila were cured of a life-threatening bladder infection that blocked urination. It is not necessary to doubt that these things occurred, but did they constitute a complete account of Capillas's life? The evidence is inconclusive but provides only weak support for the more extreme claims of Capillas's accusers.

ACCUSATIONS AGAINST FR. AUGUSTE CHAPDELAINE, MEP

The second of the new saints under attack was Auguste Chapdelaine (Ma Lai), MEP (1814–1856),[16] a leading figure in the Xilin Religious Incident (*Xilin Jiaoan*), which was a contributing cause of the Second Opium War

(also known as the Arrow War or Anglo-French War) (1856–1860).[17] That
conflict was among the more humiliating experiences in modern Chinese
history, and its memory still has the power to rankle. Anglo-French forces
captured Beijing, causing the emperor to flee, and plundered and burned
the magnificent Yuanming Yuan (Garden of Perfect Clarity). In the earlier
Treaty of Huangpu (Whampoa) (1844), France had gained all the privileges
(except for territory and indemnities) previously acquired by Great Britain
in the Treaty of Nanjing. This permitted the French to conduct business,
to construct buildings and cemeteries, and so forth, but only in Shanghai,
Guangzhou (Canton), and other treaty ports; they could not push into the
interior of China. Despite these limitations, the missionaries felt sufficiently
backed by imperialistic forces to begin penetrating the remoter areas of
Hunan, Guizhou, and Guangxi provinces, which bordered on the French colonialist base in Annam (later part of French Indochina) (map 1). This illegal
movement extended to the Xilin district, in the far western part of Guangxi,
in the 1850s. In this manner Fr. Chapdelaine had illicitly entered Xilin.

Zhen Shi's *People's Daily* article criticized Chapdelaine not only for
entering Chinese territory illegally but also for destroying and interfering
with local customs in the Xilin district. He supposedly denied baptism to
those who refused to destroy their ancestral tablets and to stop going to the
cemetery to revere their ancestors. In addition, he imposed certain marriage
restraints on Christians. Chapdelaine is also accused of collaborating with
forest outlaws (*lulin*) and corrupt officials to promote the spread of Christianity. Finally, Chapdelaine allegedly engaged in illicit sexual activity and
violated the Christian Sixth Commandment, which forbids adultery.

According to the same *People's Daily* article, rumors circulated widely
in Xilin that Chapdelaine displayed a special fondness for women and for
using his priestly power to exploit the helplessness of Chinese females. He
allegedly lured an inordinate number of attractive women into the church and
disregarded the strict prohibition against the intermingling of the sexes in
China. Oftentimes he was the only male in a gathering of married women and
was in a position to take advantage of the situation to rape female Christians.
On occasion, when celebrating the wedding mass for Christians, Chapdelaine
allegedly exploited the opportunity to seduce or rape (*jianwu*) the new bride!
This rumor is apparently a variation on the belief that priests in China practiced the *jus primae noctis* (right of the first night), said to be a European
feudal custom, known in French as the *droit de seigneur* (right of the lord),
by which a feudal lord had the right to have sexual intercourse with every
bride in his domain on her wedding night. There is little evidence, however,
that the *jus primae noctis* was actually practiced in Europe. Moreover, it was
claimed as a feudal right of lords and not as a religious right of priests, whose
rights were defined by membership in a different one of the three feudal

estates (nobility, clergy, and peasantry). The *People's Daily* article accused Chapdelaine of being accompanied in his journey from Guizhou province to Xilin by a very attractive widow with whom he was having an adulterous relationship. This woman was Agnes Cao Guiying, another of the 120 names on the list of martyrs canonized as saints in 2000.

Can we sort out fact from fantasy? We cannot simply dismiss the charges out of hand as politically motivated on the part of the Chinese government because the Vatican's canonization of these 120 martyrs was not without its own political motivation. Also, this dispute cannot be cast as one of Chinese versus Europeans, since 87 of the 120 martyrs were Chinese. In addition, although the *People's Daily* account did not indicate as much, the church viewed the martyrdom of Fr. Chapdelaine as a group martyrdom involving three saints, two of whom were Chinese: Agnes Cao Guiying and Laurence Bai Xiaoman.[18] Pope Leo III had beatified all three on May 27, 1900.

Born into a pious farming family in the hamlet of Métarie in the district of Rochelle (Manche), France, on January 6, 1814, and ordained in 1843,[19] Fr. Chapdelaine served as a vicar at Boucey for seven years, then entered the Foreign Missions of Paris (MEP). He departed for Hong Kong from Antwerp on May 5, 1852. Because of the importance of Guangxi province as a route of passage for French missionaries traveling to Yunnan and Sichuan provinces, Sacred Congregation for the Propagation of the Faith assigned Guangxi to the French-based MEP. However, the area was extremely dangerous in the 1850s because of the Taiping Rebellion.

After spending six months in Hong Kong, Frs. Chapdelaine and Payan departed for Guizhou province on October 12, 1853. After leaving Canton and being robbed of all their possessions while traveling by boat on the West River, they had to turn back.[20] In November they departed again, this time in a boat armed with four cannon manned by twenty-five sailors, and the same group of thieves on the West River allowed them to pass. After a long journey through the mountains of Hunan and by riverboat, they reached Guiyang, the capital of Guizhou province, in February 1854. Chapdelaine began studying the local dialect and was placed under the supervision of Fr. Lyons (Lions) (Li Wanmei), superior of the Guizhou mission. Chapdelaine was instructed in the apostolic methods used by the missionaries Fr. Paul Hubert Perny, MEP, and Fr. Louis Faurie, MEP.[21]

Soon Chapdelaine received a visit from Jerome Lu Tingmei (1811–1858), an enthusiastic neophyte who had converted in 1852 and would also become one of the 120 martyrs. A member of the Miao (Hmong) people, Lu had been active in the community of approximately three hundred Miao Christians who lived in the region of Maokou, bordering on Guangxi province to the south. As a member of the Miao ethnic group in Yunnan and Guizhou, Lu represented an outreach to a people traditionally despised by the Chinese.[22]

A visit from Lu's Christian kinsmen from Guangxi provided the opportunity for Chapdelaine to enter that province. These kinsmen had been traveling in Guizhou on business and were returning to the Xilin district in Guangxi. They informed Chapdelaine that there were Christians in the villages of Baijiazhai and Yaoshan in the Xilin district.[23] Consequently, in December 1854, Chapdelaine, accompanied by Lu Tingmei and his two kinsmen, traveled south into Guangxi. At Yaoshan, on December 8, 1854, he said his first mass in that province.

Trouble soon erupted when a family squabble led the father of the neophyte Bai San (Pe-san) to denounce Chapdelaine as a Muslim rebel. Coincidentally, Chapdelaine had chosen a surname, Ma, used by many Chinese Muslims because of its similarity to the first syllable of the name of the Prophet Muhammad. The magistrate of Xilin district, surnamed Tao, sent government runners (*yayi*) to arrest Fr. Chapdelaine and Lu Tingmei. Chapdelaine's first official encounter with Chinese authority turned out surprisingly well because Tao was familiar with the Christians in Beijing and favorably disposed toward the religion. But he warned that harm might come if Chapdelaine remained in Xilin because a higher official might make difficulties for him.[24] After a brief incarceration, Chapdelaine and Lu were released. Zhen Shi's *People's Daily* article claimed that Tao was a corrupt official. It accused Chapdelaine of negotiating with Tao over a payment to secure the release of a forest outlaw charged with murder and of collaborating with these forest outlaws.

Chapdelaine went back to Guizhou, but because he felt called to minister to the neophytes and catechumens he had converted in Guangxi, he returned to Xilin. On March 19, 1855, the Day of St. Joseph, patron saint of the China mission, Chapdelaine baptized eight or nine people in Guangxi.[25] One of these neophytes, a former Buddhist named Laurence Bai Xiaoman, would meet martyrdom with Chapdelaine less than a year after his baptism. Chapdelaine returned to the MEP base in Guizhou in April and remained there until December 17, when he traveled to Guangxi for the last time.

Sometime between the fall and winter of 1855, Chapdelaine met Agnes Cao Guiying. She was born in 1833 in Guizhou to Christian parents; her father was a poor physician. Cao acquired a reputation for piety at an early age. When orphaned at fifteen, she was given shelter by missionaries who sent her to school, where she acquired a rudimentary literacy. She married a Christian who died three or four years later, leaving her a destitute widow. Fr. Lyons sent Cao to Chapdelaine and recommended her as a catechist to women.[26] Chapdelaine invited her to come to Xilin, where she could apply her apostolate among the thirty or forty families in that region. She agreed and late in 1855 established herself in Baijiazhai in the Xilin district.[27] There she taught Miao Christian women the catechism, as well as Chinese domestic arts, such as cooking, house building, and child care.

THE HISTORICAL CONSEQUENCES OF CHAPDELAINE'S ARREST AND EXECUTION

When Chapdelaine returned to Xilin in December 1855, Zhang Mingfeng of Yunnan, a man very hostile to Christianity, had replaced the friendly magistrate Tao.[28] The close proximity of the Taiping Rebellion probably intensified both Zhang's perception of the Christians as rebels and his harshness toward them. Fr. Chapdelaine himself commented on the unsettled nature of Guangxi in a letter of the previous year: "I think that this is the haunt of the worst bandits of China. It is also here that the great insurrection [of the Taipings] which presently devastates the empire began, and which makes the throne of the Manchu dynasty totter."[29]

When news of the priest's presence in Yaoshan became known, the new magistrate sent out runners to arrest him. At this point, a Christian neophyte surnamed Luo, a lower-ranking literatus with the title of *gongsheng* (tribute student), helped Chapdelaine. Luo's status typically meant that he was a nominee for advanced study at the local Confucian academy and possible admission to scholar-official status.[30] Luo sent a hasty message to Yaoshan to warn Chapdelaine and offer him refuge in his home.[31] As Chapdelaine fled, the Christians hid religious objects and Latin books. The magistrate's runners arrived in Yaoshun and proceeded to confiscate the Christians' oxen, hogs, goats, hens, clothes, bedcovers, and cotton cash as booty.[32] They arrested fifteen of the Christians, including Agnes Cao Guiying. After evading arrest, Laurence Bai Xiaoman led five or six mothers and wives of the arrested men to the magistrates' yamen to ask for the release of their sons and husbands. The magistrate Zhang responded harshly to their pleas and had them whipped and bound in chains.

Luo's home was quite close to the magistrate's court in Xilin. During his night of hiding there, Chapdelaine considered fleeing to Guizhou, where his confreres Frs. Perny and Lyons would have offered him support. Although the Xilin Christians had urged him to flee, he was unable to abandon his neophytes. Chapdelaine's spiritual transformation to martyrdom was portrayed as a dramatic moment in a letter dated July 8, 1856, by Monseigneur Zéphirin Guillemain (Guillemin) (Ming Jijiang), MEP. This transformation typically involves total surrender to the cause, including the sacrifice of one's life, along with an intense energizing due to that surrender, which enables the martyr to endure incredible suffering without apostatizing. It appears that the spiritual dynamics of martyrdom blot out much of the suffering, much as an anodyne might temporarily relieve pain, enabling the martyr to carry on. While the martyr's pain threshold may be raised, however, the physical damage to the body is unmitigated and often leads to death. Guillemain describes Chapdelaine's capture as follows: "Seeing the heaven already opening before

his eyes, he forgot the earth and threw himself on his knees in order to begin
a prayer that he finished only when the runners arrived to seize him."[33]

A wondrous sign is said to have appeared in the sky over Yaoshan on the
day of the fifteen Christians' arrests. Both Christians and non-Christians saw
a crown with a cross in the middle.[34] Whereas the nonbelievers interpreted
it as an evil omen, the Christians understood it to signify that the crown of
victory would come to them later only by means of suffering. Many characteristics of martyrdom similar to those of the Chapdelaine incident had previously manifested themselves among Christian missionaries between 1650
and 1735 in Shandong and southern Zhili, where similar wondrous signs were
sighted.[35]

The runners eventually came to Luo's house, but in deference to his literati
status and venerable age, they did not pillage his property as they had with
the Christian peasants at Yaoshan. Fr. Chapdelaine and Luo's son, also a neophyte, were bound in chains. Prisoners accused of major crimes wore three
sets of irons—on the neck, wrists, and ankles.[36] Chapdelaine and Luo's son
were taken, along with the literatus Luo, to the yamen and reunited with the
other incarcerated Christians. The date was February 26, 1856. The next day
the magistrate first interrogated Laurence Bai Xiaoman. When Bai refused to
renounce his faith, he was beaten with split bamboo canes. When he continued to resist, he was decapitated.

Agnes Cao Guiying was interrogated next. She was equally steadfast in
refusing to apostatize. During the interrogation, the magistrate Zhang Mingfeng
asked if she had been cohabiting with Fr. Chapdelaine in a state of adultery.
(*Tongjian* [illicit sexual relations] and *hejian* [adultery by mutual consent]
were official crimes.[37]) Cao responded with an indignant denial, saying that
she had not even known Fr. Chapdelaine before coming to Xilin. Zhang then
"hurled at her one of the rudest curses offered by the Chinese language."[38]
The magistrate apparently believed the rumor that she and Chapdelaine were
having an affair. Zhang told her that if she refused to renounce her faith, she
would be put to death. When she refused, he supposedly asked her how she
wished to die, and she answered, "With the same punishment as my master
Ma [Chapdelaine]." Did her reply stem purely from her religious conviction,
or could it have also had a romantic basis? Was Chapdelaine only her spiritual
master, or was he lover as well? The evidence is inconclusive.

In any case, the magistrate appears to have granted her wish, for she was
placed in a wooden cage (*zhanlong*) used to strangle criminals condemned for
rebellion and betrayal.[39] The cage used for this slow and painful form of exe-
cution was typically six to seven feet tall. The prisoner stood inside on planks
or bricks, his or her head extending through a round hole in a plank near
the top of the cage. The planks (or bricks) on which the condemned person
stood were gradually removed, causing the victim's feet to be suspended and

unable to touch the bottom. This created a strain in the muscles of the neck, leading to a very slow and painful death from suffocation that could take five or six days.[40] Cao's cage was only a short distance from Chapdelaine's. They were able to see one another, though not to speak. She was placed in the cage on February 28 and survived for four days, dying on March 3, 1856.

Guillemain's letter contains the most complete description of Fr. Chapdelaine's final hours, pieced together at Canton from accounts of Chapdelaine's martyrdom coming out of Guizhou. On the first day of the interrogation (February 26), when Zhang accused Chapdelaine of teaching a religion that fomented rebellion, Chapdelaine denied the charge.[41] When Zhang asked how much silver he possessed and why he had allowed his followers to persuade him to escape, Chapdelaine did not answer. Perhaps he did not understand the questions or perhaps he was imitating Jesus, who remained silent in response to the Jewish high priest's hostile questions prior to the Crucifixion (Matthew 26:62–63; Mark 14:60–61). In any case, the magistrate ordered that he be given three hundred blows with a split bamboo (*zhupian*) on the backside, although one hundred blows represented the official limit for flogging (*manzhang*).[42] The priest's flesh was torn and bloodied, and possibly he went into shock, for he was unable to move. His hands and feet tied to a bamboo frame, he was left on the floor of his cell during the night. The magistrate appears to have largely administered the punishments prescribed in the *Da Qing lüli* (Penal Code of the Qing Dynasty), albeit with excessive severity.

The next day, February 27, the interrogation continued, and Chapdelaine was obliged to kneel on iron chains throughout the day.[43] When Chapdelaine continued to cling to his faith, Zhang ordered that he be given one hundred blows on his cheeks with a leather thong. The last punishment mutilated his face and lacerated his jaw, causing some of his teeth to fly out. At this point, he collapsed on the ground, lying on his stomach. During all of this, Chapdelaine is said to have uttered no groans or cries. Christians believed that he was able to endure the pain of these beatings without crying out by meditating on the flagellation of Christ described in Matthew 27:26 and Mark 15:15.[44] Puzzled by his endurance, however, the magistrate attributed it to some sort of magical art. To counteract the power of the magic, Zhang had a dog butchered and its blood sprinkled over Chapdelaine's body. Too weak to stand on his own, the prisoner was carried back to his cell.

On February 28 Chapdelaine was placed in a cage where he spent the whole day and the following night.[45] During his agony, the magistrate sent an assistant with the offer to release him for the payment of 400 taels; when Chapdelaine said that he had no money, the offer was reduced to 150 taels, but Chapdelaine continued to claim that he had no money. During the night of February 28, a loud death rattle was heard, and his body convulsed, shaking the flimsy wooden cage so violently that it collapsed.[46]

The next morning, February 29, the magistrate ordered the runners to cut off Chapdelaine's head, although he was already dead.[47] Guillemain regarded this as an unnecessarily vindictive act, but actually it was standard practice in China to behead the corpse (*lushi*) of a prisoner found guilty of a major crime if he died before being executed.[48] The mutilation of the body was, in Chinese eyes, an additional punishment because most Chinese sought to keep their bodies intact for the reunion with their ancestors after death.

Chapdelaine's treatment was equivalent to the beheading a thief at the scene of the crime, followed by public exposure of the severed head on a high pole.[49] Whereas the severed head was normally hung in a cage, Chapdelaine's was hung by its hair on a tree outside town.[50] Children were said to have thrown stones at it until it fell to the ground, after which the dogs and hogs fought over it. As for what happened to the rest of his body, accounts differed. One group said it was buried in the criminals' graveyard; others claimed (and Guillemain believed it more plausible) that it was chopped to pieces and thrown in the garbage dump, where animals mauled it. Perhaps the most gruesome of the accounts held that Fr. Chapdelaine's heart was removed from his body, chopped up, stir-fried with pork fat, and then eaten.[51]

Whether this act of cannibalism actually happened is difficult to determine. Although cannibalism (anthropophagy) was not a prominent practice in China, incidences of it have been recorded throughout Chinese history, and a gruesome fascination with the practice appears in many novels and short stories. The most common cause has been famine, but human flesh has also been consumed out of vengeance, from culinary taste, and for medicinal reasons.[52] In nineteenth-century southern China, the executioner of a criminal had the prerogative of selling the warm blood of the victim as a medicine for curing illnesses, such as tuberculosis; eating the gall bladder of famous bandits was believed to increase one's own courage.[53] Moreover, instances of cannibalism have been documented as recently as the Cultural Revolution (1966–1976) in Guangxi, the province where Chapdelaine was executed.[54]

A backlash followed. According to the Abbé Adrien Launay, when Tao, the former magistrate of Xilin, learned of Chapdelaine's death, he wrote a critical letter to his successor, Zhang Mingfeng, claiming that the foreign priest was innocent of the charges against him (presumably those of fomenting rebellion).[55] Guillemain, in his role as prefect apostolic of the missions of Guangdong and Guangxi, filed a complaint with the chargé d'affaires M. de Coucy, protesting the treatment of Chapdelaine on the grounds that it violated article 23 of the Treaty of Huangpu (Whampoa) (1844), which stated, "It is forbidden to strike or to mistreat imprisoned French citizens."[56] When the governor of Guangdong and Guangxi did not respond to the French request that those responsible for Fr. Chapdelaine's death be punished, the incident became a causus belli that, along with the *Arrow* incident shortly thereafter, led Great Britain and France to declare war on China.[57] The result was the Second Opium War (Arrow War) and further defeat and humiliation for the Chinese.

ACCUSATIONS AGAINST FR. ALBERICO CRESCITELLI, PIME

The third person from the list of 120 martyrs singled out for attack by the *People's Daily* article of October 3, 2000, was Fr. Alberico Crescitelli, PIME (Guo Xide) (1863–1900). His death was linked with the powerlessness and frustration of the Chinese peasantry. Born in Altavilla in the southern Italian province of Avellino, the fourth of eleven children, he entered the Pontifical Seminary of the Holy Apostles Peter and Paul in 1880 and was ordained in Rome in 1887. Crescitelli arrived in southern Shaanxi in 1888, where for twelve years he devoted himself to serving the villagers in the vicariate. Fascinated by natural science, he wrote several papers on local Shaanxi fauna and flora unknown in Italy. He ministered to the poor and was particularly concerned with the plight of abandoned baby girls, making special efforts to save them. He was obsessed with counting the numbers of converts and, in his zealousness, may have contributed to his martyrdom.[58] In March 1900, at Bishop Masserini's order, he traveled to the remote western area of Yanzibian in the Ningqiang district of Shaanxi province, where local lords held considerable power. On July 20, he was captured and tortured. The following day he, a catechist, and an uncertain number of others (estimates say as many as twenty catechumens) were killed.[59]

Fr. Crescitelli's martyrdom has become controversial, in part because of the strained political relations between the Vatican and Beijing, and in part because of a misunderstanding about who actually killed him. The Society of Righteous Fists (Boxers), a peasant secret society, advocated combining spiritual forces and martial arts to expel foreigners from China. The group originated in Shandong province and provoked the death of a number of missionaries. When driven northward out of Shandong in 1900, Dowager Empress Cixi secretly encouraged the Boxers to occupy Beijing. However, they were a regional movement focused in Shandong, Zhili, and Shaanxi provinces but less active to the west in Shaanxi province.[60]

Neither the report of the twenty-five years of the Canossian apostolate (1891–1916) nor Mother (M.) Ida Sala's history of the Canossian missions claim that the Boxers killed Crescitelli, although they do note that the xenophobic upheavals in Shaanxi occurred in the same year as the Boxer Uprising.[61] The booklet on the 120 martyrs by the Taiwan Chinese Regional Bishops' Conference, however, does claim that the Boxers murdered Crescitelli.[62] This is unlikely, since the viceroy of Shaanxi, a Manchu named

Duan Fang, opposed the Boxers as well as the imperial edict of July 5, 1900, which sanctioned the Boxer Rebellion.[63] Duan appears to have effectively discouraged their appearance in Shaanxi, although other secret societies in the region had, like the Boxers, underclass origins and a martial arts emphasis.

A combination of Western intrusion and Chinese resentment caused Crescitelli's martyrdom. In northern China during the late nineteenth century, the local temple served as the institution that integrated local social and religious activities. Temple revenues financed important festivities, such as theatrical performances and drought-induced processions for rain.[64] The characters embodied in these performances had a strong influence on the people's imagination and became role models for local youths. However, the Christian missionaries viewed these performances as superstitious and their moral teachings as pernicious. Prior to 1800 missionaries were powerless to control them. Their weakness had the positive effect of forcing the missionaries to be more accommodating to the Chinese. However, after 1800, the European military victories, beginning with the Opium War and the Treaty of Nanjing (1842), gave Westerners the ability to insert certain demands into this series of "unequal" treaties, which gave Christian missionaries prerogatives that disempowered and antagonized many Chinese. The Treaty of Tianjin (1858) exempted Chinese Christians from paying the tax to the local temples, engendering enormous resentment among Chinese who accused Chinese Christians of adopting foreign ways and becoming alienated from their own culture. In addition, missionaries were often quite aggressive in demanding that the local magistrate recognize the treaty rights of Christians.

The Beijing government provided relief funds during the famine of 1900 that afflicted northern China. In far-southwestern Shaanxi in the Ningqiang district, a man identified as Teng Shengxian was responsible for distributing these funds.[65] A *gongsheng* (tribute student) who had purchased a literary degree, which gave him lower-ranking status in the scholar-official class, Teng had an unsavory background. According to Crescitelli, he was a moneylender who had resorted to murder and was feared by both the people and the authorities. He had rented a rice field to a Christian who refused to contribute to temple festivities and was beaten by Teng's hired thugs. Teng provoked a confrontation with Crescitelli by refusing to distribute famine relief to local Christians on the grounds that they did not contribute to temple festivities. Crescitelli appealed to the Ningqiang magistrate, who was obliged to honor the treaty rights of Christians. In an effort to antagonize Teng as little as possible, the magistrate delayed issuing his edict and did not publicize it widely, so few people were aware of it. Teng sought his revenge against the Christians by contacting a gang known ominously as "the Nail."[66] At the same time, Li Chaodong and Li Rongdong, brothers and members of the gentry in Yanzibian, became aware of the imperial edict supporting the Boxers' anti-Christian revolt. All of these forces contributed to making July 20, the day the magistrate had established for distributing the previously withheld famine assistance, the occasion of Crescitelli's death.

Both Chinese and missionary documents support the view that Crescitelli died over a dispute involving the distribution of governmental famine relief. They also support the narrative in which Crescitelli's local enemies, including Teng Shengxian, Li Rongdong, and Yang Hai, stirred up an enraged mob of three hundred people, which included members of the Nail gang. Carrying torches, long swords, and spears, they went in search of Crescitelli, who fled for his life to the office of a local official in Yanzibian.[67] When the official advised him to flee out the back door, Crescitelli was captured, attacked with knives and sticks, and stripped naked.

Accounts of Christian martyrdoms typically compare the plight of the martyr to the passion of Christ.[68] When dawn broke, a hard core of drunken, bloodthirsty thugs returned to finish off Crescitelli. When he asked for a drink of water to quench his thirst due to blood loss, the assassins had a group of boys urinate into his mouth. At high noon, a drunken executioner grasped a large blunt blade, commonly used for cutting straw for cattle, to decapitate him—a prolonged process because of either the bluntness of the blade or the intoxication of the executioners. In addition to his head, Crescitelli's arms and legs were hacked off, and his remains were thrown into the Jialing River. Other Christians were also killed.

Shi Yan's *People's Daily* article does not deny the details of Crescitelli's death but focuses on his acts that provoked the murder. Since the author's motivation was more political than scholarly, the article's veracity is difficult to evaluate. Whereas missionary sources tend to be sympathetic to Crescitelli and emphasize the harsh and brutal treatment he received, they do not explore his human flaws, which might have contributed to the harsh Chinese reaction. However, the *People's Daily* accusations are so extreme that one questions their relationship to reality. For example, the article presents Crescitelli as a totally evil figure who tyrannized the common people, forced them to make contributions to the church, appropriated their lands and possessions, and engaged in sexual debauchery. The apparent source of Shi Yan's charges is a work published in 1987 in Chinese titled *Zhongguo jiao'an shi* (A History of Missionary Cases in China).[69]

The *People's Daily* article claims that Crescitelli required young women who were about to marry church members to go first to the church for baptism. This would be quite plausible for Catholics of that period, but the *People's Daily* revives the same rumor applied to Chapdelaine—namely, that these baptisms were in fact a variation on the European feudal custom of *jus primae noctis*, the right of the lord to have sex with any woman in his domain who was about to marry. In fact, the *People's Daily* article appears to be a mixture of fact and fantasy. It claimed that Crescitelli had raped the fiancées of Christians Fan Zhangfu, Zheng Ganren, and the *juren* degree holder Yang Hai, as well as others—all within the space of the three months (May to July 1900) when he was in Yanzibian.

Is it possible that Crescitelli seduced Chinese female parishioners? Yes, and premarital counseling sessions and baptism would have given him an opportunity to exert his priestly power over any victims, a common feature of sexual abuse. However, the specific accusations lack credible evidence. Consequently, we should regard them as belonging more to the realm of sexual titillation than reality. The exotic fantasy of having sexual relations with someone of a very different culture or race has an enduring power in human history, and this appears to have been as much the cause of these rumors as any actual facts. Resentment of Crescitelli more likely derived from his investments in farmland and other property on behalf of his church and his aggressive use of treaty rights to advance the profits of members of his church.

Chapter 6

The Misreading of the Missionary "Débâcle" in China

The Catholic invasion of China began with the Jiangnan Christians' 1834 invitation for the return of the Jesuits to China and ended with the Vatican's canonization of the 120 Catholic martyrs in 2000. This invasion cannot be understood simply as a physical incursion into China; nor can it be viewed in completely negative terms. The actual migration of thousands of priests and brothers and sisters to China was only one visible manifestation of a highly organized effort. A crucial part of this invasion involved a Western mental conception of China and the Chinese as in desperate need of the material things and the faith that Europe had in abundance. While the physical incursion of China ended with the expulsion of the missionaries in 1951, the mental framework that gave rise to the incursion persisted until the end of the century. The effects of this mental framework extended beyond Catholics and China to shape and distort the views of Chinese history held by foreign scholars and journalists.

This image of the desperation of the Chinese, particularly of children, drove the effort to help them. The pervasiveness of this effort is apparent in the formation of the Society of the Holy Childhood to collect pennies from European children to help save abandoned Chinese children from dying—both through creating orphanages that cared for their physical needs and through catechism instruction that would foster their spiritual salvation. The new Chinese Communist government cut off foreign missionary funding in 1950. In 1982, when post–Cultural Revolution contacts with foreign nations began to increase, the Central Committee of the Chinese Communist Party issued a policy statement to define the relationship of Chinese with foreign churches and the acceptance of foreign funds.[1] Foreign donations could entail no stipulations limiting their use. Any sum larger than ten thousand renminbi (approximately US$1,925 in 1988) required government approval.

The mental framework of the Catholic invasion of China can best be understood through the changing views of the Jesuits during their apostolate in China from the late sixteenth century until 2000. Prior to 1800, the accommodative views of Fr. Matteo Ricci predominated. The realities of the time forced European Jesuits to respect China. During their initial period of work in China, from the time of the first Jesuit's arrival in 1579 in Macau until the papal dissolution of the order in 1773, the Jesuits generally portrayed China as a leading world nation in most senses (geopolitically, demographically, economically, and intellectually), with the notable exception of its incomplete spirituality, which lacked a knowledge of salvation. No single nationality dominated the approximately nine hundred Jesuits who served in China during this first period, although because of the Portuguese *padroado* (royal monopoly on European trade routes to East Asia), the Portuguese monarch exerted a large degree of influence on mission policy. When the Jesuits returned to China in 1842, French influence dominated overwhelmingly, in terms of both membership and policy.

In the aftermath of the victory of an aggressively atheistic communism in 1949 and the expulsion of most Christian missionaries in 1951, the assumption spread widely that the missionary effort to introduce Christianity into Chinese culture had failed. Even former missionaries felt a sense of despair over what David Macdonald Paton (1913–1992), an Anglican priest, called "the débâcle of Christian missions in China."[2] The size of the expulsions indicated the dimensions of Catholic participation in this debacle. By December 1954, only sixty-one out of twenty-five hundred foreign priests who had been in China in 1949 remained, and twenty-one of these were in prison.[3] One missionary, Bishop James E. Walsh, remained in prison until 1970, when he was finally released from Ward Road Prison in Shanghai.[4] Paton's "débâcle" article, appearing in the *International Review of Mission* in 1951, was one of the most troubling critiques of the Christian missions in China published during that time. Paton expanded it into a book that appeared two years later, titled *Christian Missions and the Judgment of God.*[5]

Paton, who published the initial article anonymously because of the intensity of his criticism, excluded Catholicism from his discussion because the "Roman Catholic world and the Protestant world hardly meet in China," but the Chinese Communist government did not accept that strict sectarian separation and expelled both Catholic and Protestant missionaries for similar reasons.[6] Clearly, in voicing despair over the missions' apparent failure, Paton's comments applied to the entire Christian missionary movement of that time. In his book, Paton elaborated on his view of the "débâcle" as God's judgment on the missionaries' work. He wrote, "Our mandate had been withdrawn; that the time for missions as we had known them had passed; that the end of the missionary era was the will of God. . . . [T]he foreign mission that the writer has known and has been in a very small measure responsible for, is now not only out of date, but was in important respects wrongly conceived."[7]

Was the Catholic invasion of China from 1834 to 2000 a "wrongly conceived" "débâcle"? For thirty years (ca. 1950–1980), most historians viewed it in this way. In fact, historian Joseph R. Levenson quoted from Paton's 1951 article in describing this failure.[8] Levenson was one of the most articulate advocates of this point of view, although he placed it in the context of "the Christian failure to succeed a dying Confucianism."[9] In Levenson's view, Matteo Ricci's attempt to construct a "Christian-Confucian syncretism" failed because, in the seventeenth century, Chinese viewed it as alien and "untraditional."[10] Later, in the twentieth century, when Confucianism had declined in Chinese esteem, Levenson argued that the Chinese rejected Christianity as "unmodern." Levenson most eloquently expressed a viewpoint shared by many others.

The theme of Christianity's alien nature to China was developed in greater depth by Jacques Gernet. His *Chine et Christianisme: Action et réaction* (1982) represents the culmination of the view that seventeenth-century Chinese rejected Christianity on the grounds of cultural incompatibility.[11] Gernet made an intensive effort to gather numerous seventeenth-century Chinese texts critical of Christianity in an attempt to explain the causes of Chinese hostility. For him, the Chinese language contained a logic and view of the world irreconcilable with the Indo-European languages of Christian scriptures. While scholars highly praised Gernet's use of Chinese texts, his theory of the linguistic basis for anti-Christian hostility attracted criticism. Moreover, developments of Christianity in China since the book's publication have undermined much of his argument. Like Levenson, Gernet allowed himself to be drawn too much into the present and vested too much significance in developments that turned out to be transitory.

Many historians mistakenly viewed the intense anti-Christian hostility of mid-twentieth-century China as a continuation of long-term historical developments, when in fact it was more a temporary aberration in the historical continuum. In retrospect, mid-twentieth-century Chinese history seems more akin to the brief regime of the Qin dynasty First Emperor Qin Shi Huangdi (221–210 BC), whose revolutionary totalitarianism and hostility to tradition were reproduced in the regime of Mao Zedong. Contrary to widespread belief at the time, Christianity (along with Confucianism) had not died out in communist China.[12] Much like Confucianism during the anti-Confucian campaign and destruction of the classics of the Qin dynasty, Christianity went underground and continued to develop in the hidden layers of China's society and culture. When Christianity began to reemerge in the 1980s, it was far more Sinified than prior to 1951, when dominated by Western missionaries and mission boards. During the intervening years, it had deepened its roots in Chinese culture.

The history of Buddhism in China presents a comparable model to the history of Christianity there. Putting aside earlier unsuccessful beginnings, such as the entry of Nestorian Christianity in the early seventh century, the continuous history of Christianity in China can be dated from the missionary trip to Canton of the first China Jesuit, Michele Ruggieri, from Macau in 1580. This means that the history of Christianity in China had attained approximately four hundred years by the time Gernet wrote *Chine et Christianisme* in 1982. At that time, the religion appeared to have been eradicated from China. If, however, by way of comparison, one assumes that Buddhism entered China in the first century, by AD 400, it was, chronologically speaking, still three centuries away from attaining its full development in the Tang dynasty. If one applies the same time frame to Christianity, Gernet's judgment in 1982 that Christianity was unadaptable to Chinese culture was premature. In fact, Christianity was then on the threshold of reemerging from its underground existence and growing far beyond previous levels among the Chinese. In the second edition of *Chine et Christianisme*, Gernet tried to temper his thesis by changing the subtitle from "Action et réaction" to "La première confrontation."[13] The implication was that instead of claiming that Chinese culture was inherently unreceptive to Christianity, he was modifying his argument and limiting it to only the first encounter of Christianity and Chinese culture in the seventeenth century. However, later scholarship would contradict his thesis with regard to both the first historical encounter and the long term.[14]

Prominent Harvard historian John King Fairbank, under whom Levenson had studied, encouraged his students to examine the history of Christian missions in China. In the 1950–1966 period, seventeen Harvard students produced research papers as either senior honors theses or graduate seminar papers on China missionary subjects. Seven of these papers were published in a volume edited by K. C. Liu.[15] A recurring theme of interest among the papers was the timely topic of anti-Christian movements in Chinese history. One of these papers developed into a doctoral dissertation by Paul A. Cohen, titled "Chinese Hostility to Christianity: A Study in Intercultural Conflict, 1860–1870" (1960). The first chapter of the published version of Cohen's dissertation has remained one of the clearest descriptions of the anti-Christian tradition in Chinese thought.[16]

In retrospect, an attempt to explain the Christian "débâcle" in China clearly drove this interest in anti-Christian movements in Chinese history during the 1950s and 1960s. Many viewed Chinese anti-Christian movements as symptomatic of China's broader rejection of the West. The fallacious assumption that the "débâcle" of Christianity in China would be long-lasting rather than transitory undermined the significance of these explanations. One of the first signs of reversal came in 1979, twenty-eight years after the expulsion of the missionaries from China and three years after the death of Mao Zedong.

It took the form of an article in the official Communist newspaper, *Renmin ribao* (*People's Daily*), extolling the Jesuit Matteo Ricci as "a pioneer of East-West cultural exchange."[17] In light of the radical anti-imperialist and anti-Christian program of the Cultural Revolution (1966–1976), the appearance of this article praising the most famous Christian missionary to China marked the beginning of a significant change in Chinese official policy.

It is one of the ironies of history that during the years when Levenson was writing his postmortem on the failure of Christianity in China in *Confucian China and Its Modern Fate*, the anti-Catholic campaign of the Communist government was peaking in intensity and creating the circumstances for developments that would contradict Levenson's analysis. These developments, for the most part, escaped attention because they were underground in several senses: they were out of public view and occurred in secret meetings of small groups, and they also entailed inner trials of the soul in many individuals, particularly those who suffered through imprisonment. Public prayer could be contained, but private prayer was beyond the control of the state apparatus.

In 1955 Bishop Gong Pinmei, along with the bishops of Baoding, Guangzhou, Hankou, and Taizhou, as well as over a thousand Catholics, were arrested and imprisoned for long terms. Gong remained incarcerated for thirty years, becoming the archmartyr for Catholics, although many other Christians (Protestants as well as Catholics) suffered a similar fate. Gong Pinmei's Protestant counterpart in uncompromising commitment and willingness to suffer years in jail for his Christian conviction was Wang Mingdao (1900–1991).[18] Wang was harshly critical of both the missionaries and liberal theology.[19] His courageous resistance to the Japanese occupiers in the 1940s and later the Communist authorities came at enormous personal cost. He was arrested and imprisoned for almost twenty-three years, from 1958 until 1980.[20] These Chinese Christians became martyrs, and their martyrdom sustained and transformed the Christian churches in China from foreign grafts into an indigenous religion. In the process, they reinvigorated a church that many historians and even former missionaries believed had died.

There were many Christian martyrs, some of whom have remained obscure, such as the Jesuit Zhang Boda. Another was the Jesuit Franciscus Xaverius Zhu Shude (1913–1983), who left the safety of Hong Kong when he felt called to return to his religious community in Shanghai in 1949. Before boarding the plane to Shanghai, Zhu wrote the following in a letter to his brother:

Every day many people are escaping from China to Hong Kong. Yet I cannot find any one, apart from myself, who is preparing to leave Hong Kong for China. Everyone laughs at me for being a fool. In the eyes of the world I am indeed the biggest fool ever born! When a merchant cannot make a profit in one place, he will move somewhere else. Yet I am a priest, and the life of a priest is to serve his flock. As long as there are Christians left in Shanghai, I must return there. Even if there is not a single Christian left in Shanghai, I must still return there. Because I am a priest. I represent Christ and his Church. Wherever I am, the Church is. I am willing to stay in Shanghai, to let the Communist Party know that the Catholic faith is still alive.[21]

After returning to Shanghai, Zhu was imprisoned in 1953 and sent to a labor camp, where he died in 1983.[22]

The establishment in 1978 of the Institute for the Study of World Religions (Shijie Zongjiao Yanjiusuo) reflected the changing Chinese Communist attitude toward religion. This institute, part of the Chinese Academy of Social Sciences in Beijing, was created to study world religions from an atheistic, Marxist point of view.[23] Unlike previous Communist treatments of religion as an ideological deception (as in the oft-quoted Marxist view of religion as "the opium of the people"), this new institute sought to engage with world religions on a more intellectual level. Of course, the institute's official role as a government-sponsored agency distorted any attempts at objectivity. This distortion is evident in its attempt to treat the more vital indigenous Chinese forms of Christianity, unlike the six "world religions," as "popular" superstition, which the Communist government views as a socially destabilizing force and a political threat.

Today, this institute's official annual Chinese directory of religions (*Zhongguo zongjiao baogao*)—called the *Blue Book of Religions* for the color of its cover—lists Catholicism and Protestantism, along with Buddhism, Daoism, Confucianism, and Islam, among the six major religions of China, while it groups the indigenous churches under the category of *minjian xinyang* (folk religions).[24] This is misleading because the true heart of indigenous Christianity in China, both Catholicism and Protestantism, lies in popular culture. Recent scholarship attributes the seventeenth- and eighteenth-century Rites Controversy's preoccupation with orthodoxy versus heterodoxy to the attempt to blend Christianity and Confucianism.[25] The early attempt of Ricci, working with certain scholar-officials, such as Xu Guangqi, to construct a Confucian-Christian synthesis caused an overemphasis on the orthodoxy of Confucianism as a state ideology to avoid the taint of heterodoxy, the usual basis of imperial condemnation of religions. This effort met with limited success, as only a small minority of Chinese literati accepted this blending of Confucianism with Christianity. (Only twenty-one baptized Chinese Christians have been identified as holding the highest scholar-official degree of *jinshi*.[26]) Although Catholicism gained only limited acceptance among the urbanized literati, however, it flourished in a number of rural villages, where it absorbed elements of Chinese folk religion, including popular Buddhism, particularly of the White Lotus sect.[27] Consequently, Chinese Catholicism developed as a blending of world religion and folk religion.

Since Zhou Enlai's initial meetings with Christian leaders in 1950 and the attempt to develop an official policy toward religion, the Chinese government has attempted to control Christian churches through state agencies, such as the Religious Affairs Bureau, which handled the affairs of all five officially sanctioned religions (Buddhism, Daoism, Islam, Catholic Christianity, and Protestant Christianity).[28] The Three-Self Patriotic Movement (Zhongguo Jidujiao Sanzi Aiguo Yundong Weiyuanhui), founded in 1951 and placed under the control of the Religious Affairs Bureau in 1954, was an umbrella organization for all Protestant churches. The government founded the Chinese Catholic Patriotic Association (CCPA) (Zhongguo Tianzhujiao Aiguohui) in July 1957 as an extension of the Anti-Rightist Campaign that was taking retribution against those critics outed when they accepted the invitation of the Hundred Flowers Movement to criticize the government.[29] The creation of the CCPA represented an attempt to control the Catholic Church, but many Catholics refused to participate and chose instead to pray at home.

Early in 1958 the Religious Affairs Bureau consecrated the first Catholic bishops without authorization from the Holy See. This created a fundamental split and led to a division between the pro-government, or patriotic, church and the pro-Rome, or underground, church.[30] The officially recognized Catholic Church in China claims to accept the spiritual but not the political and administrative authority of the Vatican. This is a difficult position to justify theologically. A similar division emerged in Protestantism between the officially recognized (Three-Self Patriotic Movement) and unregistered Protestant churches. However, Protestant theology enabled these house churches, or "autonomous Christian communities," to be largely independent and separate from any organization, whereas the Catholic underground churches felt more obliged by Catholic theology to be more integrated with and loyal to the Holy See. Consequently, unlike the Catholics of the Patriotic Church, the underground churches sought the Holy See's sanction for the ordination of its bishops.

One of the earliest leaders of the underground Catholic Church in China was Bishop Fan Xueyan of the Baoding diocese in Hebei province.[31] Jailed in the 1950s, he was released in 1979, whereupon he began to train clergy and ordain bishops. Although his ordinations were not sanctioned by Rome, Fan argued that canon law allowed such ordinations in extraordinary circumstances, a view eventually supported by the pope. Bishop Fan was arrested in 1982 for maintaining contact with foreign powers and released on parole in 1987.

This brings us to the question of the ultimate historical effect of the Catholic invasion of China. Typically, an invasion is seen as a hostile and harmful incursion, with all its negative connotations. However, if we view an invasion in the less pejorative ecological sense of a plant or animal species moving into and colonizing a formerly unknown area, then the Catholic invasion of China may be seen more positively as one of enrichment. (Of course, this type of ecological invasion can also involve the importation of undesirable species.) It turns out that the Catholic invasion of China from 1842 to 2000 was both negative and positive. Viewed from a short-term historical perspective, it was highly negative—a debacle—but viewed from a long-term perspective, it generated consequences that helped to transform a mission church into an indigenous religion. In the process, the Catholic invasion has enriched Chinese culture, and Chinese Catholicism has, in turn, enriched Catholicism and made it more universal.

The division between the patriotic and underground churches is partly a consequence of the Catholic invasion, which instilled in Chinese Catholics the principle of a universal church guided by a Holy Father in Rome. In theory, that Holy Father might be Chinese. If that possibility seemed very far removed from reality in the 1842–2000 period, the election in 2013 of a South American pope (Francis I) certainly makes it more plausible today. In fact, one could realistically argue that the elevation of a Chinese as pope in the near future is a likelihood.

The division between the patriotic and underground churches, driven not only by foreign forces but also by internal tension, is partly a consequence of a Chinese political system that has a long history of suppressing religious freedom. But just as Chinese have resisted foreign control of Chinese internal affairs, they have also resisted an intrusive state that attempts to control the practice of religion. Given the history of relations between the Chinese government and the Vatican dating back to the sixteenth century, it is unlikely that either the patriotic or the underground church will achieve an unmixed victory. Some degree of compromise will probably be necessary to achieve an accommodation. Once both the government in Beijing and the Holy See in Rome reach an accommodation, the demand of Catholic theology for a united, universal church will likely drive the reunification of the Catholic churches in China.

Appendix A

List of the 120 Martyrs in China Canonized by John Paul II in 2000

Names are arranged according to the years of martyrdom; surnames are in capital letters.

1648   Fr. Francisco Fernandez de CAPPILAS, OP
1747   Bp. Pietro SANS I JORDA, OP
1748   Fr. Francesco SERRANO Frias, OP
1748   Fr. Francisco DIAZ del Rincon, OP
1748   Fr. Gioacchino Royo PEREZ, OP
1748   Fr. Giovanni Alcober FIGUERA, OP
1814   Pietro WU Guosheng, catechist
1815   Bp. Gabriele Taurin DUFREESE, MEP
1815   Fr. Agostino ZHAO Rong
1815   Giuseppe ZHANG Dapeng, catechist
1816   Fr. Francesco Maria LANTRUA (Giovanni da Triora), OFM
1817   Giuseppe YUAN Zaide
1819   Fr. Paolo LIU Hanzuo
1820   Fr. Francesco Regis CLET, CM
1823   Fr. Taddeo LIU Ruiting
1834   Pietro LIU Wenyuan, catechist
1839   Gioacchino HE, catechist
1856   Agnese CAO Guiying
1856   Fr. Augusto CHAPDELAINE, MEP
1856   Lorenzo BAI Xiaoman
1858   Agata LIN Zhao
1858   Girolamo LU Tingmei, catechist
1858   Lorenzo WANG Bing, catechist
1861   Giovanni Battista LUO Tingying

1861	Giuseppe ZHANG Wenlan, seminarian
1861	Mrs. Marta WANG née Luo, widow
1861	Paolo CHEN Changpin, seminarian
1862	Fr. Giovanni Pietro NEEL, MEP
1862	Giovanni CHEN Xianheng, catechist
1862	Giovanni ZHANG Tianshen, catechist
1862	Lucia YI Zhenmei, catechist
1862	Martino WU Xuesheng, catechist
1900	Andrea WANG Tianqing
1900	Anna WANG
1900	Bp. Antonino FANTOSATI, OFM
1900	Bp. Francesco FOGOLLA, OFM
1900	Bp. Gregorio GRASSI, OFM
1900	Bro. Andrea BAUER, OFM
1900	Bro. Flilppo ZHANG Zhihe, OFS, seminarian
1900	CHI Zhuze, catechumen
1900	Fr. Alberico CRESCITELLI, PIME
1900	Fr. Cesidio GIACOMANTONIO, OFM
1900	Fr. Elia FACCHINI, OFM
1900	Fr. Giuseppe Maria GAMBARO, OFM
1900	Fr. Leone Ignazio MANGIN, SJ
1900	Fr. Modesto ANDLAUER, SJ
1900	Fr. Paolo DENN, SJ
1900	Fr. Teodorico BALAT, OFM
1900	Francesco ZHANG Rong, OFS
1900	Giacomo YAN Guodong
1900	Giacomo ZHAO Quanxin
1900	Giovanna Maria KERGUIN (Maria di Santa Natalia), FMM
1900	Giovanni Battista WU Mantang
1900	Giovanni Battista ZHAO Mingxi
1900	Giovanni Battista ZHU Wurui
1900	Giovanni WANG Kuixin
1900	Giovanni WANG Rui, OFS, seminarian
1900	Giovanni WU Wenyin
1900	Giovanni ZHAN Jingguang, OFS, catechist
1900	Giovanni ZHANG Huan, OFS, seminarian
1900	Giuscppe MA Taishun
1900	Giuseppe WANG Kuiju
1900	Giuseppe WANG Yumei
1900	Giuseppe YUAN Gengyin
1900	Lucia WANG Cheng
1900	Maddalena DU Fengju

1900	Marco JI Tianxiang
1900	Maria AN Linghua
1900	Maria CHI Yu
1900	Maria DU née Tian
1900	Maria FAN Kun
1900	Maria FU Guilin
1900	Maria ZHAO
1900	Maria ZHENG Xu
1900	Mattia FENG De, OFS
1900	Mrs. Anna AN née Jiao
1900	Mrs. Maria GUO née Li
1900	Mrs. Anna AN née Xin
1900	Mrs. Barbara CUI née Lian
1900	Mrs. Elisabetta QIN née Bian
1900	Mrs. LANG née Yang
1900	Mrs. Lucia WANG née Wang
1900	Mrs. Maria AN née Guo
1900	Mrs. Maria DU née Zhao
1900	Mrs. Maria WANG née Li
1900	Mrs. Maria ZHAO née Guo
1900	Mrs. Maria ZHU née Wu
1900	Mrs. Teresia ZHANG neé He
1900	Paolo GE Tingzhu
1900	Paolo LANG Fu
1900	Paolo LIU Jinde
1900	Paolo WU Anju
1900	Paolo WU Wanshu
1900	Patrizio DONG Bodi, OFS, seminarian
1900	Pietro LI Quanhui
1900	Pietro LIU Zeyu
1900	Pietro WANG Erman
1900	Pietro WANG Zuolung
1900	Pietro WU Anbang, OFS
1900	Pietro ZHANG Banniu, OFS
1900	Pietro ZHAO Mingzhen
1900	Pietro ZHU Rixin
1900	Raimondo LI Quanzhen
1900	Remigio ISORÉ, SJ
1900	Rosa CHEN Aijie
1900	Rosa FAN Hui
1900	Rosa ZHAO
1900	Simone CHEN Ximan, OFS

1900   Simone QIN Cunfu
1900   Sr. Anna DIERK (Maria Adolfina), FMM
1900   Sr. Anna MOREAU (Maria di San Giusto), FMM
1900   Sr. Clelia NANETTI (Maria Chiara), FMM
1900   Sr. Irma GRIVOT (Maria Ermellina di Gesu), FMM
1900   Sr. Maria Anna GIULIANI (Maria della Pace), FMM
1900   Sr. Paola JEURIS (Maria Amandina), FMM
1900   Teresia CHEN Tinjie
1900   Tommaso SHEN Jihe, OFS
1900   ZHANG Huailu, catechumen
1930   Bp. Luigi VERSIGLIA, S.D.B.
1930   Fr. Callisto CARAVARIO

Appendix B
Chinese Character Glossary

aiguo	愛國
An Dingxiang	安廷相
An Zhitai	安治泰
Ankang	安康
Ba Shilin	拔士林
Bai Gelubing	白格路並
Bai Risheng	白日升
Bai San	白三
Bai Xiaoman	白小滿
baihua	白話
Baijiazhai	白家寨
Bao Runsheng	鮑潤生
beile	貝勒
Bi Xueyuan	畢學源
Bian Yinchang	卞蔭昌
Cao Guiying	聖曹桂英
Caoxilu	漕溪路
ce feng sowei shengren	冊封所謂聖人
Chan Kim-kwong	陳劍光
Chao Deli	晁德蒞
Chen	陳
Chen Yuan	陳垣
Chen Yun	陳芸
Chongming	崇明
chuanjiao	傳教
chuanjiaoyuan	傳教員
Chuci	楚辭

chuyu	出諭
congshu	叢書
Cui Huajiao	崔华杰
Da Qing lüli	大清律例
Dagongbao	大公報
Dahua jian zazhi	大華間雜誌
danao huozheng	大腦火症
daoli	道理
daxue shi	大學士
Delai Xiaomeimei Hui	德來小妹妹會
Dideman	狄德滿
Ding Meili	頂美麗
Dongtang Ruose Datang	東堂若瑟大堂
Du Dingke	杜鼎克
Duan Fang	端方
famu	伐牧
Fang Hao	方豪
Fei Laizhi	費賴之
Fu Ren She	輔仁社
Fu sheng liu ji	浮生六記
Fudan Gongxue	復旦公學
Gang Hengyi	剛恆毅
Gaoqiao	高橋
Gong, Prince (Yixin)	恭新王 (奕訢)
Gong Pinmei	龔品梅
Gonghang	公行
gongsheng	貢生
Gu Fenggu	顧鳳姑
Gu Hongming	辜鴻銘
Gu Mingguan	顧明官
Guan fu, zongzu yu Tianzhujiao: 17–19 shiji Fuan xiangcun jiaohui de lishi xushi	官府，宗族与天主教：17–19 世纪福安乡忖教会的历史叙事
Guan Yu	關羽
Guangping-fu	廣平府
guangyang	廣揚
Guangyilu	廣益錄
Guluba	古路壩
Guo Shila	郭施拉, 郭實臘
Guo Shili	郭士立
Guo Xide	郭西德
Haimen	海門

Haiyan tang ximian	海晏堂西面
He Qingtai	賀清泰
hejian	和姦
Hongmao fan du ke. Bai guize. Fa cai ren.	紅毛販土客。白鬼子。發財人。
Hongqiao	虹橋
Hua	華
Hua Mulan	花木蘭
Huabei de baoli he gonghuang: Yiheduan yundong de qianxi jidujiao chuanbo he shehui chongtu	华北的暴力和恐慌：义和团运动的前夕基督教传播和社会冲突
Huang Liushuang	黃柳霜
Huang Xiaojuan	黃曉鵑
Huang Yilong	黃一農
Huang Zhiwei	黃志偉
Huangpu	黃浦
Huayi xuezhi	華裔學志
hui	諱
huizhang	會長
ji	集
jianwu	奸污 or 姦污
jiaotou	教頭
Jiaowu yuekan	教務月刊
jiazhuang	嫁妝
Jidujiao	基督教
Jidujiao yanjiu shi	基督教研究室
Jidutu Huitang	基督徒會堂
Jidutu Juhuichu	基督徒聚會處
jie'ni nü wen	戒溺女文
Jiefang ribao	解放日報
Jiefang yihou	解放以後
Jiefang yiqian	解放以前
Jiekai sowei "shengren" de mianmu	揭开所谓'圣人'的面目
Jin Luxian	金魯賢
Jin Shida	金世達
Jin Yiyun	金逸雲
Jin Ze	金泽
jing	經
Jing Dianying	敬奠瀛
Jinjiagang	靳家崗
Jiushi fuyin	救世福音
Kalaqin	咯拉沁

Kang Mei huan Chao Zizhi Ziyang Zichuan   抗美換朝自治自養自傳
Kaolaojuan   栲栳圈
lantun   籃囤
Lao She   老舍
laodong gaizao   勞動改造
laodong jiaoyang   勞動教養
Laoxikai   老西開
Lei Mingyuan   雷鳴遠
Li Andang   利安當
Li Jiugong   李九功
Li Peili   黎培理
Li Pengju   栗鵬舉
Li Wanmei   李萬美
Li Wenyu   李問漁
Li Xiucheng   李秀成
Ling Shuhua   凌叔華
Liu Fangji   劉方濟
Liu Guangjing   劉光京
Liu Jiantang   劉鑒唐
long   龍
Lu Bohong   陸伯鴻
Lu Tingmei   盧廷美
lulin   綠林
Luo   羅
Luo   駱
Luo Baiji   羅伯濟
Luo Leisi   羅類思
Luo Wenzao   羅文藻
Luotuo xiangzi   駱駝祥子
lushi   戮尸
Ma   馬
Ma Aosiduo   馬奧斯多
Ma Duanlin   馬端臨
Ma Fangji   馬方濟
Ma Jianxun   馬建勛
Ma Jianzhong   馬建忠
Ma Lai   馬賴
Ma Lai yu Di'er Yapian Zhanzheng   馬賴與第二次雅片戰爭
Ma Qingshan   馮青山
Ma Songyan   馬鬆岩
Ma Xiangbo   馬相伯
Malixun   馬禮遜

manzhang	滿杖
Ming Jijiang	明稽將
minjian xinyang	民間信仰
naima	奶媽
Nan Gelu	南格祿
Ni Tuosheng	倪柝聲
nianjing	念經
Ningqiang-xian	寧強縣
ninü	溺女
Ouxi zhi wenhua	歐西之文化
pei jianhuo	賠賤貨
Ping-yi Chu	祝平一
Pudong	浦東
Qibaozhen	七寶鎮
qingbao	情報
Qinghe	清河
Qingpu	青浦
Qiu Yonghui	邱永輝
Qiying	耆英
Qu Yuan	屈原
Quanxue zuiyan	勸學罪言
Ren Yanli	任延黎
Renmin ribao	人民日報
Rui junwang	瑞郡王
Sai Zhenzhu	賽珍珠
Shan Guoxi	單國璽
shan shu	善書
Shao Xunmei	邵洵美
Shen	沈
Shen Bangyan (Jinglun, Jingwei, Ziyu)	沈邦彥, 經綸, 沈經緯, 子漁
Shen Congwen	沈從文
Shen Fu	沈復
Shen Jianshi	沈兼士
Shen Xizhi	沈席之
Shen Yunhui	沈韞輝
Sheng mujun' de wan wu zuixing	聖母軍'的萬惡罪行
shengjiao rike	聖教日課
Shengjing zhi jie	聖經直解
Shengmu hui	聖母會
Shengmu ji shengnü jiaozhong	聖母及聖女教眾
Shengmu xian tanghui	聖母獻堂會
shengong	神工

Shensi lu	慎思祿
Sheshan	佘山
shi	史
shi da zuixing	十大罪行
Shi Yan	史岩
Shijie zhishi	世界智識
Shijie Zongjiao Yanjiusuo	世界宗教研究所
Shouzhen guniang	守貞姑娘
shouzhen nü	守貞女
Shu Qingchun	舒慶春
Shuku	書庫
shuyuan	書院
Shuzhong	淑仲
Siding	思定
Sigui	四規
Song Shangjie	宋尚節
Songjiang-fu	松江府
suoyi neng tong Zhonghua jingshi	所以能通中華經史
Tang Lishan	湯立山
Tang Zuolin	湯作霖
Tao	陶
Teng Cunye	滕村爺
Teng Shengxian	滕尚賢
Ti Ying	緹縈
ti-yong	體用
Tian Genghua	田耕莘
Tian Yongzheng	田永正
Tianhe	天和
Tianli	天理
Tianzhu shiyi	天主實義
Tianzhujiao	天主教
Tianzhujiao Huaming Shuju	天主教華明書局
Tianzhujiao Taiwan Diqu Tianjiaotuan	天主教台灣地區天教團
Tongjian	通姦
Tushanwan	土山灣
Waibaidu	外白渡
waijiao	外教
Wang Mingdao	王明道
Wang Ruowang	王若望
Wang Yi	王逸
wansong yeren	萬松 野人
Wei Baoluo	魏保羅

Wei Enbo	魏恩波
Wei Tsing-sing	田耕莘
Weixian	威縣
Wen Yiduo	聞一多
Wen You	溫優
Wenhui ribao	文彙日報
wenyan	文言
Wu Guosheng	吳國盛
Wubang lun	誣謗論
Wuqing	武清
Xi lai Kungfuzi	西來孔夫子
Xia Zhiqi	夏芝畦
xian shengxian	先聖賢
xianggong	相公
Xiangshan	香山
Xiangyang-fu	襄陽府
xiansheng	先生
Xiapi	下邳
Xila Hutong	錫鑛衚衕
Xilin Jiaoan	西林教案
Xilin-xian	西林縣
Xinan Lianhe Daxue	西南聯合大學
Xing dao ribao	星島日報
Xingan-fu	興安府
Xinghua	興化
Xinshi hebian zhijiang	新史合編直解
Xinwen ribao	新聞日報
Xinyue she	新月社
Xinyue yuekan	新月月刊
Xiyang Lou	西洋樓
Xu Baida	徐伯達
Xu Leisi	徐類思
Xu Zhimo	徐志摩
Xuanhua-fu	宣化府
Xue Kongzhao	薛孔昭
Xuhui Gongxue	徐匯公學
Xujiahui	徐家匯
Xujiahui cangshulou	徐家匯藏書樓
Xujiahui cangshulou: Ming-Qing Tianzhujiao wenxian	徐家匯藏書樓明清天主教文獻
Yan Dingen	燕鼎恩
Yang Guangxian	楊光先

Yang Manuo   陽瑪諾
Yang Xianyi   楊憲益
Yang Yide   楊以德
Yang Yilong   楊意龍
yanggui   洋鬼
Yangzipu   楊子浦
Yanzhou   兗州
Yanzibian   燕子砭
Yaohan Xiaoxiongdi Hui   耀漢小兄弟會
Yaoli wenda   要理問答
Yaoshan   窰山 (堯山)
yasi zinü, zaojue renlei   壓死子女，早絕人類
yayi   衙役
Yazhou qingbao   亞洲情報
Yesu Jiating   耶穌家庭
Yesuhui Luoma danganguan Ming-Qing   耶穌會羅馬檔案館明清天
   Tianzhujiao wenxian   　主教文獻
Ying Lianzhi   英斂之
Ying Qianli   英千里
Yishibao   益失報
Yizong   奕
Yuanming Yuan   圓明園
Yuanyou   遠游
Yuyi yu Zhimo   幼儀與志摩
yuying   育嬰
yuyingtang   育嬰堂
Zaiyi   載漪
zao tang   造堂
Zaoyang-xian   棗陽縣
Zhang   張
Zhang Boda   張伯達
Zhang Jiasen   張嘉森
Zhang Li   張力
Zhang Mingfeng   張明鳳
Zhang Xianqing   張先清
Zhang Xinglang   張星烺
Zhang Xun   張勳
Zhang Youyi   張幼儀
Zhang Zhaotai   張紹臺
Zhang Zhengming   張正明
Zhangpoqiao   張浦橋
zhangzhongzhu   掌中珠

zhangzhu	掌珠
zhanlong	站籠
Zhao	趙
Zhao Fangji	趙方濟
Zhao Huaiyi	趙懷義
Zhao Zichen	趙紫宸
Zhaoran gonglun	昭然公論
Zhen Shi	甄實
Zhen Yesu jiaohui	真耶穌教會
Zhendan Xueyuan	震旦學院
zhenzhu	珍珠
zhimin	知民
Zhong Mingdan	鐘鳴旦
Zhongguo jiao'an shi	中國教案史
Zhongguo jiaoli jiangshou shi	中國教理講授史
Zhongguo Jidujiao Sanzi Aiguo Yundong Weiyuanhui	中国基督教三自爱国运动会
Zhongguo Tianzhujiao Aiguohui	中国天主教爱国会
Zhongguo Tianzhujiao Aiguohui Zhongguo Tianzhujiao Zhujiaotuan fabiao shengming	中國天主教愛國會中國天主教主教團發表聲明
Zhongguo Tianzhujiao shi renwu chuan	中國天主教史人物傳
Zhongguo Xundao Shengren chuan	中華殉道聖人傳
Zhongguo zongjiao baogao	中国宗教报告
Zhonghua guangrong	中華光榮
Zhonghua shuju	中華書局
Zhonghua Xundao Shengren Tuxiang	中華殉道聖人圖像
Zhoushan	舟山
zhu	珠
Zhu Baohui	朱寶惠
Zhu Shude	朱樹德
zhuanglian	妝奩
Zhuozhou	涿州
zhupian	竹片
zi	子
zizhi, ziyang, zichuan	自治自養自傳

Notes

CHAPTER 1

1. Erik Eckholm with Mark Landler, "State Bidder Buys Relics for China," *New York Times*, May 3, 2000, E1, E5.

2. D. E. Mungello, *The Great Encounter of China and the West, 1500–1800*, 4th ed. (Lanham, MD: Rowman & Littlefield, 2013), 80–85.

3. Samuel Couling, *The Encyclopedia Sinica* (Shanghai: Kelly and Walsh, 1917), 532.

4. James L. Hevia, "Loot's Fate: The Economy of Plunder and the Moral Life of Objects 'From the Summer Palace of the Emperor of China,'" *History and Anthropology* 6 (1994): 319–21.

5. D. E. Mungello, *Curious Land: Jesuit Accommodation and the Origins of Sinology* (Stuttgart: Franz Steiner Verlag, 1985), 13–14.

6. Mark Landler, "China Asks Auction Houses to Withdraw 4 Relics," *New York Times*, April 29, 2000, B11, B18.

7. Young-tsu Wong, *A Paradise Lost: The Imperial Garden Yuanming Yuan* (Honolulu: University of Hawaii Press, 2001), 63–64.

8. Geremie R. Barmé, "The Garden of Perfect Brightness, a Life in Ruins," *East Asian History* 11 (1996): 126–27.

9. Ines Eben v. Racknitz, *Die Plünderung des Yuanming yuan. Imperiale Beutenahme im britisch-französischen Chinafeldzug von 1860* (Stuttgart: Franz Steiner Verlag, 2012), 87.

10. Racknitz, *Die Plünderung*, 167, 174–75.

11. Racknitz, *Die Plünderung*, 189–90.

12. Racknitz, *Die Plünderung*, 202–4.

13. Racknitz, *Die Plünderung*, 305–6.

14. Mark Landler, "Christie's Auctions Relics Despite China's Objection," *New York Times*, May 1, 2000, E3.

15. Eckholm with Landler, "State Bidder Buys Relics for China," E1, E5.

16. Erik Eckholm, "Bringing Treasures Back to China," *New York Times*, July 16, 2000, TR18.

17. Howard L. Boorman, ed., *Biographical Dictionary of Republican China*, 5 vols. (New York: Columbia University Press, 1967–1971), 2:250–52.

18. Joseph R. Levenson, *Confucian China and Its Modern Fate: A Trilogy*, Vol. 1: *The Problem of Intellectual Continuity* (Berkeley: University of California Press, 1958–1965), 59–60, 65–69.

19. Fang Chao-ying, "I-tsung," in *Eminent Chinese of the Ch'ing Period*, ed. Arthur Hummel (Washington, DC: Government Printing Office, 1943), 393–94.

20. Chester C. Tan, *The Boxer Catastrophe* (New York: Octagon Books, 1983), 69.

21. Eric Reinders, *Borrowed Gods and Foreign Bodies* (Berkeley: University of California, 2004), 56–61.

22. Boorman, *Biographical Dictionary*, 1:71.

23. Gu Hongming (Ku Hong-ming) first presented this work as a lecture in English for the Oriental Society in Beijing. It was eventually published as part of a work titled *The Spirit of the Chinese People: With an Essay on "The War and the Way Out"* (Beijing: Peking Daily News Press, 1915). The book was regarded as important enough to justify a wartime German translation published as *Der Geist des chinesischen Volkes und der Ausweg aus dem Krieg*, trans. Oscar A. H. Schmitz (Jena: Eugen Diederichs, 1917).

24. Ku, *Geist*, 13–15.

25. Ku, *Geist*, 43–44.

26. Ku, *Spirit of the People*, 16–17.

27. Ku, *Geist*, 47.

28. Ku, *Geist*, 50–53.

29. Ku, *Geist*, 55–57.

30. Ku, *Geist*, 97–101.

31. Ku, *Geist*, 161–62.

32. Ku, *Geist*, 26–27.

33. W. Somerset Maugham, *On a Chinese Screen* (1922; New York: Paragon House, 1990), 150.

34. Noel Annan, foreword in Goldsworthy Lowes Dickinson, *The Autobiography of G. Lowes Dickinson and Other Unpublished Writings*, ed. Dennis Proctor (London: Gerald Duckworth, 1973), 2–5.

35. Keith Hale, ed., *Friends and Apostles: The Correspondence of Rupert Brooke and James Strachey, 1905–1914* (New Haven, CT: Yale University Press, 1998), 12, 53n.

36. D. E. Mungello, *Western Queers in China: Flight to the Land of Oz* (Lanham, MD: Rowman & Littlefield, 2012), 84–85.

37. Raymond Dawson, *The Chinese Chameleon: An Analysis of European Conceptions of Chinese Civilization* (London: Oxford, 1967), 209; Dickinson, *Autobiography*, 9.

38. [Goldsworthy Lowes Dickinson], *Letters from a Chinese Official, Being an Eastern View of Western Civilization* (New York: McClure, Phillips, 1904), 12–13.

39. William Jennings Bryan, *Letters to a Chinese Official, Being a Western View of Eastern Civilization* (New York: McClure, Phillips, 1906), viii.

40. Bryan, *Letters to a Chinese Official*, 47–48.

41. Bryan, *Letters to a Chinese Official*, 56.

42. Bryan, *Letters to a Chinese Official*, 97.

43. Dickinson, *Autobiography*, 184.

44. Mungello, *Great Encounter*, 135–41.

45. D. E. Mungello, "Reinterpreting the History of Christianity in China," *Historical Journal* 55 (2012): 534–35.

46. The *Zhongguo zongjiao bangao 2013*, ed. Jin Shi and Qiu Yonghui (Beijing: Shehui Keshui wenxian chubanshe, 2013), was produced by scholars mainly from the Institute of World Religions, Chinese Academy of Social Sciences, Beijing, and reflects the view of government-approved orthodoxy in Chinese scholarship.

47. Murray A. Rubenstein, "The Protestant Missionary Enterprise, 1807–1841," in *Handbook of Christianity in China*, Vol. 2: *1800–Present*, ed. R. G. Tiedemann (Leiden: Brill, 2010), 133.

48. Rubenstein, "The Protestant Missionary Enterprise," 144.

49. *Records of the General Conference of the Protestant Missionaries of China Held at Shanghai, May 10–24, 1877* (Shanghai: Presbyterian Mission Press, 1878), 480–87. For a chart summarizing the statistics presented at the Shanghai conference, see S. Wells Williams, *The Middle Kingdom: A Survey of the Geography, Government, Literature, Social Life, Arts, and History of the Chinese Empire and Its Inhabitants*, 2 vols. (New York: Charles Scribner's Sons, 1898), 2:366.

50. Statistics of Roman Catholic missions in China taken from *Bulletin des missions catholiques* for 1870, cited in *Records of the General Conference of the Protestant Missionaries*, 488.

51. Tiedemann, *Handbook*, 2:958–61.

52. Tiedemann, *Handbook*, 2:915–37.

53. Katharina Wenzel-Teuber, "Statistisches Update 2013 zu Religionen und Kirchen in der Volksrepublik China," *China heute* 33, no. 1 (181) (2014): 23. One must emphasize that the number of Protestants in China is subject to dispute; for example, the Pew Forum on Religion and Public Life (Washington, DC) made a study in December 2011 that estimated the number of Protestants in China at over 58 million.

54. Karl Marx, "Persia—China," *New York Daily Tribune*, June 5, 1857, in *Marx on China: Articles from the New York Daily Tribune, 1853–1860* (London: Lawrence & Wishart, 1951), 45.

CHAPTER 2

1. D. E. Mungello, "The Return of the Jesuits to China in 1841 and the Chinese Christian Reaction," *Sino-Western Cultural Relations Journal* 27 (2005): 9–46.

2. Several studies of local Catholic communities in China have appeared recently. These include (in chronological order): D. E. Mungello, *The Forgotten*

Christians of Hangzhou (Honolulu: University of Hawaii Press, 1994); Allen Richard Sweeten, *Christianity in Rural China: Conflict and Accommodation in Jiangxi Province, 1860–1900* (Ann Arbor: University of Michigan, 2001); D. E. Mungello, *The Spirit and the Flesh in Shandong, 1650–1785* (Lanham, MD: Rowman & Littlefield, 2001); Eugenio Menegon, *Ancestors, Virgins, and Friars: Christianity as a Local Religion in Late Imperial China* (Cambridge, MA: Harvard University Asia Center, 2009); Zhang Xianqing, *Guan fu, zongzu yu Tianzhujiao: 17–19 shiji Fuan xiangcun jiaohui de lishi xushi* (State, Lineage, and Catholicism: A Narrative of the History of the Church in Seventeenth- to Nineteenth-Century Rural Fuan) (Beijing: Zhonghua shuju, 2009); Henrietta Harrison, *The Missionary's Curse and Other Tales from a Chinese Catholic Village* (Berkeley: University of California, 2013).

3. Ernest P. Young, *Ecclesiastical Colony: China's Catholic Church and the French Religious Protectorate* (New York: Oxford University Press, 2013), 24–33, 255.

4. S. Wells Williams, *The Middle Kingdom: A Survey of the Geography, Government, Literature, Social Life, Arts, and History of the Chinese Empire and Its Inhabitants*, rev. ed. (New York: Charles Scribner's Sons, 1898), 2:567, 571.

5. Hsieh Hsing-yao (Xie Xingyao), "How Did Imperialism Use Religion for Aggression on China? A Historical Survey of Missionary Work in China," *Renmin ribao* (Beijing), in *Current Background*, April 18, 1951, in *Religious Policy and Practice in Communist China: A Documentary History*, trans. Donald E. MacInnis (New York: Macmillan, 1972), 134.

6. Hsieh, "How Did Imperialism Use Religion," 135–36.

7. The Chinese Rites Controversy involved debate over the Chinese name for the Christian God and the interpretation of rites in honor of familial ancestors and Confucians. See D. E. Mungello, ed., *The Rites Controversy: Its History and Meaning* (Nettetal, Germany: Steyler Verlag, 1994). George Minamiki, SJ, presents the Jesuit view in *The Chinese Rites Controversy from Its Beginning to Modern Times* (Chicago: Loyola University Press, 1985), while the dissenting Dominican perspective is presented by J. S. Cummins in *A Question of Rites: Friar Domingo Navarrete and the Jesuits in China* (Aldershot, UK: Scholar Press, 1993).

8. Fang Hao, *Zhongguo Tianzhujiao shi renwu chuan* (Hong Kong: Xianggang Gongjiao Zhenlinxue hui, 1973), 3:244; Shen Xizhi et al., *Zhaoran gonglun* (Hengtang, 1846), reprinted in *Xujiahui cangshulou: Ming-Qing Tianzhujiao wenxian* (Chinese Christian Texts from the Zikawei Library), ed. Nicolas Standaert (Zhong Mingdan) et al. 5 vols. (Taipei: Faculty of Theology, Fujen Catholic University, 1996), f. 18a (V, 2074).

9. Richard P. McBrien, *Lives of the Popes: The Pontiffs from St. Peter to John Paul II* (New York: HarperCollins, 1997), 336–39; P. G. Maxwell-Stuart, *Chronicle of the Popes* (London: Thames & Hudson, 1997), 217; Louis Wei Tsing-sing (Tian Genghua), *La politique missionnaire de la France en Chine, 1842–1856* (Paris: Les Nouvelle Éditions Latines, 1960), 87.

10. Wei, *La politique missionnaire*, 84.

11. Wei, *La politique missionnaire*, 85–86.

12. Joseph de Moidrey, SJ, *La hiérarchie catholique en Chine, en Corée et au Japan (1307–1914)* (Shanghai: Zikawei, 1914), 31.

13. Bési is thought to have been a secular priest, although his close association with the Italian Franciscans has led some historians to regard him as a Franciscan of the strict order. Yet another historian (Wei, *La politique missionnaire*, 112n362) has regarded him as a member of the Congregation of the Holy Family of Naples.

14. Wei, *La politique missionnaire*, 88.

15. Fr. Colombel, "Ch. VI. Le Kiang-nan," in *Les missions catholiques françaises au XIX° siècle*, ed. Jean-Baptiste Piolet, SJ (Paris: Librairie Armand Colin, 1902), 173–74. Joseph de la Servière, SJ, *Histoire de la mission du Kiang-nan*, 2 vols. (Shanghai: T'ou-sè-wè Orphanage, 1914), 1:16, gives the year of Paul Tou's visit to Macau and meeting with Bési as 1837.

16. In 1837 Frs. Zhang and Wang composed a letter signed by other Chinese priests and influential Catholics of Jiangnan. This letter was addressed to Bishop Pirès-Pereira at Beijing and requested that Bési be given the powers of vicar general for Jiangnan. Servière, *Histoire*, 1:17.

17. Letter of Pirès-Pereira to Raphael Umpierres, January 15, 1835, at Beijing, Scritture riferite in Congresso, Cina e Regni adiacenti (Prop. S.R.), Archives of the Sacred Congregation of the Propaganda, Rome, viii, 314–15, cited in Wei, *La politique missionnaire*, 90.

18. Wei, *La politique missionnaire*, 90–91.

19. Wei, *La politique missionnaire*, 91.

20. Wei, *La politique missionnaire*, 92.

21. Samuel Couling, *The Encyclopedia Sinica* (Shanghai: Kelly and Walsh, 1917), 260.

22. The other Jesuits chosen were François Estère (1807–1848), who was born in Paris, and Benjamin Brueyre (Bruyère) (b. 1810), who later founded the first seminary in Jiangnan.

23. Carlos Sommervogel, SJ, *Bibliothèque de la compagnie de Iésu*, 12 vols. (Brussels and Paris, 1890–1932), 3:1621.

24. Wei, *La politique missionnaire*, 92.

25. Wei, *La politique missionnaire*, 253.

26. Minamiki, *Chinese Rites Controversy*, 69–76.

27. Two French Lazarists, Laurent Carayon and Jean Combelles, accompanied the three Jesuits on their journey on *l'Erigone*. Wei, *La politique missionnaire*, 92.

28. Kenneth Scott Latourette, *A History of Christian Missions in China* (London: Society for Promoting Christian Knowledge, 1929), 156.

29. Ping-ti Ho, *Studies on the Population of China, 1368–1953* (Cambridge, MA: Harvard University Press, 1959), 282.

30. Servière, *Histoire*, 1:11.

31. Based on church figures compiled by priests in Jiangnan, the number of Catholics there in 1847 was 60,963; however, a Jiangnan catechist in 1846 gave a higher figure of 80,000 (Shen Xizhi et al., *Zhaoran gonglun*, f. 7b [V, 2053]). Servière, *Histoire*, 1:356, states that the number of Catholics in Jiangnan in 1847 was 60,963 and grew to 74,296 by 1857. Ho, *Studies*, 283, breaks the total Jiangnan population of 1850 down into 44.155 million in Jiangsu and 37.611 million in Anhui.

32. Wei, *La politique missionnaire*, 156.

33. Wei, *La politique missionnaire*, 184–86.

34. Wei, *La politique missionnaire*, 186.

35. Wei, *La politique missionnaire*, 187.

36. The first of these Jesuit brothers arrived on May 24 under the leadership of Fr. Auguste Poissemeux (1804–1854); the second group arrived on August 20 led by Fr. Mathurin Lemaitre (1816–1863). Servière, *Histoire*, 1:82–83.

37. Of the Massa brothers, Augustin (1813–1856) and René (1817–1853) were priests, while Cajétan (1821–1850) and Nicolas (1815–1876) were frater coadjutors (brothers) who later concluded their studies and were ordained as priests in Jiangnan. A fifth brother, Louis Massa (1827–1860), joined his siblings in China at a later date. The Jesuit arrivals also included Louis Sica (1814–1895) and Louis Hélot (1816–1867). In addition, two Italian Franciscans, Frs. Chérubini Biancheri (Bai Gelubing) and Caelestinus Aloys (Louis) Spelta (Xu Leisi; Xu Baida) (b. 1818), moved from Huguang province to Jiangnan province in 1848. Daniel Van Damme, OFM, *Necrologium Fratrum Minorum in Sinis*, 3rd ed. (Hong Kong: Tang King Po School, Kowloon, 1978); 1st ed. compiled by Joannes Ricci, OFM (1934); 2nd ed. compiled by Kilian Menz, OFM (1944), 133, 141.

38. Colombel, *Les missions catholiques françaises*, 176.

39. Wei, *La politique missionnaire*, 190–92.

40. Wei, *La politique missionnaire*, 452–55, 513.

41. Servière, *Histoire*, 1:107.

42. Wei, *La politique missionnaire*, 467–68.

43. Wei, *La politique missionnaire*, 470.

44. Bési consecrated one of the priests of the Holy Family of Naples, Francesco (François-Xavier) Maresca (initially Ma Fangji, later Zhao Fangji) (1806–1855), as brother on Pentecost 1847.

45. Wei, *La politique missionnaire*, 471–72.

46. Wei, *La politique missionnaire*, 518.

47. Wei, *La politique missionnaire*, 473.

48. American Jesuits of Gonzaga College, *Portraits of China* (Shanghai: Tou-sè-wè Press, 1936), 63–64.

49. Colombel, *Les missions catholiques françaises*, 180.

50. Latourette, *History*, 234.

51. Couling, *Encyclopedia Sinica*, 62.

52. American Jesuits of Gonzaga College, *Portraits of China*, 34–36.

53. Jos. Jennes (Yan Dingen), CICM, *Four Centuries of Catechetics in China* (*Zhongguo jiaoli jiangshou shi*), trans. Eng. Albert Van Lierde (Li Pengju), trans. Chinese T'ien Yung-cheng (Tian Yongzheng), CICM (Taipei: Tianzhujiao Huaming Shuju, 1976), 174–75.

54. Servière, *Histoire*, 2:277.

55. Adrian Dudink, "The Chinese Christian Books of the Former Beitang Library," *Sino-Western Cultural Relations Journal* 26 (2004): 46; H. Verhaeren, CM, *Catalogue de la Bibliothèque de Pé-t'ang* (Beijing: Imprimerie des Lazaristes, 1949), vi.

56. Huang Zhiwei, "Xujiahui Cangshulou" (The Xujiahui [Zi-ka-wei] Library), trans. Norman Walling, SJ, *Tripod* (July–August 1992): 22–24.

57. Henri Cordier, "Nécrologiè. Aloys Pfister," *T'oung Pao* 2 (1891): 460–64.
58. Huang, "Xujiahui Cangshulou," 23–25.
59. Mungello, "The Return of the Jesuits to China in 1841," 42. See also Noël Golvers, "The Provenances of the Western Books in the Former (and Current) Xujiahui (Zikawei) Library, Shanghai," *Sino-Western Cultural Relations Journal* 36 (2014): 24–42.
60. Huang, "Xujiahui Cangshulou," 26–27.
61. The latest entry I found in the Zikawei foreign-language catalog during my visit to Shanghai of 1986 was dated 1952.
62. Although the Shanghai Public Library absorbed the Chinese portion of the Zikawei Library, most of the collection is currently not accessible at the new Shanghai Library building (opened in 1996) and rather is housed in a separate room at the Shanghai Library Book Storage (Shuku) near the Botanical Gardens. See Adrian Dudink, "The Chinese Texts in the Zikawei Collection in Shanghai: A Preliminary and Partial List," *Sino-Western Cultural Relations Journal* 33 (2011): 1–41. The foreign-language section of the Zikawei Library is housed in the renovated Zikawei Library building at 80 N. Caoxilu in Shanghai.
63. Joseph van den Brandt, *Les Lazaristes en Chine, 1697–1935. Notices biographiques* (Beiping: Imprimerie des Lazaristes, 1936), 25–26; Fang, *Zhongguo Tianzhujiao*, 3:242–44.
64. L. C. Arlington and William Lewisohn, *In Search of Old Peking* (Beijing: Henri Vetch, 1935), 142.
65. Jean Charbonnier, MEP, *Guide to the Catholic Church in China* (Singapore: China Catholic Communication, 2013), 40–42.
66. Brandt, *Les Lazaristes*, 24.
67. Jin Yiyun's *hui* (private name) was Jin Shida. See Fang, *Zhongguo Tianzhujiao*, 3:246–48; Brandt, *Les Lazaristes*, 26.
68. Brandt, *Les Lazaristes*, 32–33.
69. In addition, Paul Zhang, CM, was born in the town of Xuanhua-fu in Zhili province in 1814 (Brandt, *Les Lazaristes*, 50–51). He entered the seminary at Macau in 1835. In order to test his vocation, he asked to go to the mission in Jiangnan, where he served for five years before returning to Macau in 1843 to complete his seminary training. He served as a missionary in Beijing and died in 1858.
70. Jennes, *Four Centuries*, 106–9.
71. Jennes, *Four Centuries*, 102–3.
72. Jennes, *Four Centuries*, 105.
73. Sweeten, *Christianity*, 27.
74. Sweeten, *Christianity*, 28–29.
75. James L. Hevia, *Cherishing Men from Afar: Qing Guest Ritual and the Macartney Embassy of 1793* (Durham, NC: Duke University Press, 1995), 233.
76. Shen Xizhi et al., *Zhaoran gonglun*, f. 1a–19b (V, 2039–2077).
77. Servière, *Histoire*, 1:91–92. Just before publishing the article "The Return of the Jesuits to China" (2005), I was put into contact with Huang Xiaojuan, who was writing a doctoral dissertation on Chinese Christians in the years 1780 to 1860. Using fragments of the Zikawei Archives preserved at Vanves, France, she identified Shen

Xizhi as the primary author of *Zhaoran gonglun*. Huang found the identification in an incomplete copy of the catalog of the Zikawei Archives titled "Extrait du catalogue des Archives de Zi-ka-wei, 1902," preserved in the Jesuit archives at Vanves, France. The identification is made in section B 15 of the Zikawei Archives (cf. Servière, *Histoire*, 1:92n1). Seized by the Communist regime, the complete archives are not part of the Zikawei Library currently housed at the Shanghai Municipal Library. Huang Xiaojuan later included the results of this discovery in "Christian Communities and Alternative Devotions in China, 1780–1860" (PhD diss., Princeton University, 2006), 126n235. In my article ("The Return of the Jesuits to China in 1841," 29), I mistakenly identified the catechist Shen Xizhi as the Lazarist priest Shen Jingwei (Ziyu, Bangyan).

78. "Punan" means "south of the Pu River" and is juxtaposed with "Pudong," which means "east of the Pu River."

79. Shen et al., *Zhaoran gonglun*, f. 15b–16a (V, 2069–2070).

80. Shen et al., *Zhaoran gonglun*, f. 7b–8a (V, 2053–2054).

81. Shen et al., *Zhaoran gonglun*, f. 8b (V, 2055).

82. Shen et al., *Zhaoran gonglun*, f. 9a (V, 2056). In Sichuan, Jean Basset, MEP (Bai Risheng, ca. 1662–1707), made a partial translation of the New Testament before dying, though it is unclear to what extent his manuscript may have circulated throughout China. See Jost Oliver Zetzsche, *The Bible in China* (Nettetal, Germany: Steyler Verlag, 1999), 28–29.

83. Shen et al., *Zhaoran gonglun*, f. 19b (V, 2077).

84. Scholar Louis Wei Tsing-sing writes in his published doctoral dissertation for the University of Paris that he found a work in the "Fonti cinesi" section of the Biblioteca Nazionale Centrale in Rome that he dates to 1847. However, he gives no Chinese title, and his description of the work could easily fit the *Zhaoran gonglun*. See Wei, *La politique missionnaire*, 574. At my request, the librarian of the China Mission material in the Biblioteca Nazionale Centrale, Dr. Marina Battaglini, searched the collection for such a title, but without success. Since the *Zhaoran gonglun* was printed twice, it is possible that the second printing was done in 1847—that is, in the year following the first printing in 1846. Consequently, Wei may have found a copy of the second printing.

85. Servière, *Histoire*, 1:92.

86. [Nan Gelu (Claude Gotteland)], *Wubang lun*, reprinted in *Xujiahui cangshulou*, f. 1a–21a (V, 2079–2119).

87. Nan (Gotteland), *Wubang lun*, f. 1a (V, 2079).

88. Shen et al., *Zhaoran gonglun*, f. 1a (2040).

89. Shen et al., *Zhaoran gonglun*, f. 1b (V, 2041).

90. Shen et al., *Zhaoran gonglun*, f. 13a (V, 2064).

91. Nan (Gotteland), *Wubang lun*, f. 3b (V, 2084).

92. Nan (Gotteland), *Wubang lun*, f. 4a (V, 2085).

93. Shen et al., *Zhaoran gonglun*, f. 1b–2a (V, 2041–2042). The Chinese translation of John 15:5 is very close to the Revised Standard Version translation: "I am the vine, you are the branches. He who abides in me, and I in him, he it is that bears much fruit, for apart from me you can do nothing."

94. Shen et al., *Zhaoran gonglun*, f. 2a–b (V, 2042–2043).

95. The source of the catechist's knowledge of the Gospels was likely to have been *Shengjing zhi jie*, a commentary on the Gospels by Portuguese Jesuit Manuel Dias Jr. (Yang Manuo) (1574–1659). It is a lengthy work (14 *juan*) of translation and commentary on the Gospel readings used in Sunday masses and on major religious feast days. The work was first published at Beijing between 1636 and 1642 and was reprinted several times, including in 1842 at Shanghai. Louis Pfister, SJ, *Notices biographiques et bibliographiques sur les Jésuites de l'ancienne mission de Chine, 1552 à 1773*, Variétés sinologiques 59 (Shanghai: Imprimerie de la Mission Catholique, 1932–1934), 109. One of Dias's sources in composing the *Shengjing zhi jie* was the first volume of Sebastianus Barradas, SJ, *Commentaria in concordiam et historiam evangelicam*, 4 vols. (1599). See Nicolas Standaert, ed., *Handbook of Christianity in China*, Vol. 1: *635–1800* (Leiden: Brill, 2001), 623.

96. Shen et al., *Zhaoran gonglun*, f. 4b (V, 2047).

97. Shen et al., *Zhaoran gonglun*, f. 7a (V, 2052).

98. Shen et al., *Zhaoran gonglun*, f. 3a (V, 2044).

99. *Catechism of Catholic Doctrine* (*Yaoli wenda*) (Hong Kong: Catholic Truth Society, 1967), 32.

100. Shen et al., *Zhaoran gonglun*, f. 3a–b (V, 2044–2045).

101. Shen et al., *Zhaoran gonglun*, f. 11a (V, 2060).

102. Shen et al., *Zhaoran gonglun*, f. 12a (V, 2062).

103. Shen et al., *Zhaoran gonglun*, f. 11b (V, 2061), 12b (V, 2063).

104. Letter of Antonio Caballero a Santa Maria to the Father Provincial Alonso de San Francisco, June 18, 1656, in *Sinica franciscana*, Vol. 2: *Relations et epistolas Fratrum Minorum saeculi 16 et 17*, ed. Anastasiius van den Wyngaert, OFM (Quaracchi-Florence: Collegium S. Bonaventurae, 1933), 446.

105. Jennes, *Four Centuries*, 45.

106. Servière, *Histoire*, 1:91.

107. Shen et al., *Zhaoran gonglun*, f. 9b (V, 2057).

108. Shen et al., *Zhaoran gonglun*, f. 9b (V, 2057). Monseigneur Alexandre de Govea was a secular priest made part of the third order of Franciscans. The king of Portugal nominated him as bishop of the diocese of Beijing, a position he assumed on January 18, 1784. Pfister, *Notices biographiques*, 942.

109. Shen et al., *Zhaoran gonglun*, f. 10a–b (V, 2058–2059).

110. Shen et al., *Zhaoran gonglun*, f. 12a (V, 2062).

111. Gotteland argued against women chanting the liturgy without men by referring to scripture, citing what appears to be Matthew 18:20: "For where two or three are gathered in my name, there am I in the midst of them" (Revised Standard Version). Gotteland claimed that since Jesus did not divide males and females, neither should the Chinese. But it is difficult to see how single-sex chanting would violate the Christian principle of equality of the sexes before God, particularly in the Catholic Church, which has made so many distinctions based on gender. Nan (Gotteland), *Wubang lun*, f. 12b–14b (V, 2102–2106).

112. Nan (Gotteland), *Wubang lun*, f. 13b (V, 2104).

113. Nan (Gotteland), *Wubang lun*, f. 14a (V, 2105).

114. Jennes, *Four Centuries*, 109–10.

115. Robert E. Entenmann, "Christian Virgins in Eighteenth-Century Sichuan," in *Christianity in China: From the Eighteenth Century to the Present*, ed. Daniel H. Bays (Stanford, CA: Stanford University Press, 1996), 184–86.

116. Menegon, *Ancestors*, 301–56.

117. Entenmann, "Christian Virgins," 180–81.

118. Servière, *Histoire*, 1:130.

119. Nan (Gotteland), *Wubang lun*, f. 12b (V, 2102).

120. Jennes, *Four Centuries*, 172–73.

121. Brandt, *Les Lazaristes*, 27; Fang, *Zhongguo Tianzhujiao*, 3:246–48.

122. Wei, *La politique missionnaire*, 471.

123. Wei, *La politique missionnaire*, 518.

124. Servière, *Histoire*, 1:95.

125. Servière, *Histoire*, 1:96.

126. Jeremy Clarke, SJ, *Catholic Shanghai: A Historical, Practical and Reflective Guide* (St. Louis, MO: Institute of Jesuit Sources, 2012), 77–87.

127. Charbonnier, *Guide to the Catholic Church in China*, 449–53.

CHAPTER 3

1. Jacques Leclercq, *Vie du Père Lebbe, le tonnerre qui chante au loin* (Tournai, Belgium: Casterman, 1955), 12.

2. Catholic University of America, *New Catholic Encyclopedia* (New York: McGraw Hill, 1967), 3:602. In 2000, when a list was prepared of 120 Catholics, martyred in China between 1648 and 1930, to be canonized by John Paul II, Perboyre's name was deleted, although it had been on a earlier form of this list.

3. Leclercq, *Vie*, 26, 45.

4. Leclercq, *Vie*, 30–31.

5. Leclercq, *Vie*, 35–36.

6. Leclercq, *Vie*, 47.

7. Leclercq, *Vie*, 64.

8. Ernest P. Young, *Ecclesiastical Colony: China's Catholic Church and the French Religious Protectorate* (New York: Oxford University Press, 2013), 134–37.

9. Young, *Ecclesiastical Colony*, 255.

10. Young, *Ecclesiastical Colony*, 28–33.

11. Young, *Ecclesiastical Colony*, 117–19.

12. Leclercq, *Vie*, 132, 167.

13. Leclercq, *Vie*, 127–29.

14. Leclercq, *Vie*, 133–34.

15. Leclercq, *Vie*, 146.

16. Leclercq, *Vie*, 159–62.

17. Leclercq, *Vie*, 182.

18. Leclercq, *Vie*, 218; Young, *Ecclesiastical Colony*, 218–19.

19. Leclercq, *Vie*, 219–23.

20. Leclercq, *Vie*, 227–32.

21. Nicolas Standaert, ed., *Handbook of Christianity in China*, Vol. 1: *635–1800* (Leiden: Brill, 2001), 468–69.

22. Leclercq, *Vie*, 234–39.

23. Young, *Ecclesiastical Colony*, 230–31.

24. Leclercq, *Vie*, 262–63.

25. Young, *Ecclesiastical Colony*, 232; Leclercq, *Vie*, 274.

26. Young, *Ecclesiastical Colony*, 243–44; Leclercq, *Vie*, 282–91.

27. Young, *Ecclesiastical Colony*, 244–46.

28. Zhang Ruogu, *Ma Xiangbo xiansheng nianpu* (A Chronology of the Life of Mr. Ma Xiangbo) (III-33), Appendix 1 (Shanghai: Shangwu yinshuguan, 1939), 234, cited in Ruth Hayhoe and Lu Yongling, eds., *Ma Xiangbo and the Mind of Modern China, 1840–1939* (Armonk, NY: M. E. Sharpe, 1996), 89.

29. See the list of Catholic degree holders compiled by Nicolas Standaert and Adrian Dudink in *Handbook of Christianity in China*, Vol. 1: *635–1800*, ed. Nicolas Standaert (Leiden: Brill, 2001), 399–403.

30. Ruth Hayhoe, "Introduction," in Hayhoe and Lu, *Ma Xiangbo*, 2.

31. Li Tiangang, "Christianity and Cultural Conflict in the Life of Ma Xiangbo," trans. Ruth Hayhoe, in Hayhoe and Lu, *Ma Xiangbo*, 92.

32. Li, "Christianity and Cultural Conflict," 98.

33. Li, "Christianity and Cultural Conflict," 101.

34. Michael Kropp, "Ma Xiangbo (1840–1939) und die Modernisierung des chinesischen Bildungswesens," *Monumenta Serica* 42 (1994): 401.

35. Angelo Zottoli, *Cursus litteraturae sinicae neo-missionariis accomodatus*, 5 vols. (Shanghai: Tou-sè-wè, 1878–1882).

36. Li, "Christianity and Cultural Conflict," 104.

37. Li, "Christianity and Cultural Conflict," 105–8.

38. Li, "Christianity and Cultural Conflict," 111–12.

39. Li, "Christianity and Cultural Conflict," 117.

40. Li, "Christianity and Cultural Conflict," 93.

41. Hayhoe and Lu, *Ma Xiangbo*, 4; Zhu Weizheng, "Statesman and Centarian: Ma Xiangbo as Witness of China's Early Modernity," trans. Wu Xiaoming, in Hayhoe and Lu, *Ma Xiangbo*, 20.

42. Li, "Christianity and Cultural Conflict," 120.

43. Kropp, "Ma Xiangbo," 405.

44. Kropp, "Ma Xiangbo," 400.

45. Fang Hao, "Ma Xiangbo xiansheng de shengping jiqi sixiang," cited in Hayhoe and Lu, *Ma Xiangbo*, 124.

46. Jesuit Xu Zongze related this incident to Fang Hao. See Fang Hao, "Ma Xiangbo xiansheng nianpu xinbian," *Tianzhujiao xueshu yanjiusuo xuebao* 6 (1974): S38–S39.

47. Li, "Christianity and Cultural Conflict," 94–97.

48. Li, "Christianity and Cultural Conflict," 105.

49. Li, "Christianity and Cultural Conflict," 110.

50. Li, "Christianity and Cultural Conflict," 125.

51. Ma's translation was published under the title *Jiushi fuyin* (World-Saving Gospels). See Jost Oliver Zetzsche, *The Bible in China* (Nettetal, Germany: Steyler Verlag, 1999), 420.

52. Li, "Christianity and Cultural Conflict," 137.

53. Kropp, "Ma Xiangbo," 415–17.

54. Lu Yongling, "Standing between Two Worlds: Ma Xiangbo's Educational Thought and Practice," in Hayhoe and Lu, *Ma Xiangbo*, 158–60.

55. Lu, "Standing between Two Worlds," 165–67.

56. Kropp, "Ma Xiangbo," 418.

57. Kropp, "Ma Xiangbo," 419–21.

58. Li, "Christianity and Cultural Conflict," 138–39.

59. Luisa M. Paternicò, "Two Powers without Cannons—the Late-Qing Government and the Holy See," *Sino-Western Cultural Relations Journal* 35 (2013): 16.

60. Li, "Christianity and Cultural Conflict," 140.

61. "Ying Hua," in *Biographical Dictionary of Republican China*, ed. Howard L. Boorman, 4 vols. (New York: Columbia University Press, 1971), 4:56–58.

62. Donald Paragon, "Ying Lien-chih (1866–1926) and the Rise of Fu Jen, the Catholic University of Peking," *Monumenta Serica* 20 (1961): 167–72.

63. Paragon, "Ying Lien-chih," 173–75.

64. Paragon, "Ying Lien-chih," 178–81.

65. R. G. Tiedemann, *Handbook of Christianity in China*, Vol. 2: *1800–Present* (Leiden: Brill, 2010), 517–18.

66. Paragon, "Ying Lien-chih," 193–97.

67. "Ma Liang T. Hsiang-po," in *Biographical Dictionary of Republican China*, 2:473.

68. Kropp, "Ma Xiangbo," 423–25.

69. Paragon, "Ying Lien-chih," 199–200.

70. See the map in Young-tsu Wong, *A Paradise Lost: The Imperial Garden Yuanming Yuan* (Honolulu: University of Hawaii Press, 2001), 2.

71. Paragon, "Ying Lien-chih," 167.

72. Kropp, "Ma Xiangbo," 426–27.

73. Lu, "Standing between Two Worlds," 198–200.

74. Paragon, "Ying Lien-chih," 204–7; Kropp, "Ma Xiangbo," 428.

75. Edward J. Malatesta, SJ, "Two Chinese Catholic Universities and a Major Chinese Catholic Thinker: Zhendan Daxue, Furen Daxue, and Ma Xiangbo," in *Historiography of the Chinese Catholic Church: Nineteenth and Twentieth Centuries*, ed. Jerome Heyndrickx, CICM (Leuven, Belgium: Ferdinand Verbiest Foundation–KU Leuven, 1994), 237–38.

76. Kropp, "Ma Xiangbo," 429–30.

77. Kropp, "Ma Xiangbo," 432.

78. Lu, "Standing between Two Worlds," 200; Malatesta, "Two Chinese Catholic Universities," 237; Miroslav Kollár, *Ein Leben im Konflikt: P. Franz Xaver Biallas SVD (1878–1936). Chinamissionar und Sinologe im Licht seiner Korrespondenz* (Sankt Augustin, Germany: Institut Monumenta Serica, 2011), 118.

79. "Ch'en Yuan," in *Biographical Dictionary of Republican China*, 1:261–62.

80. Malatesta, "Two Chinese Catholic Universities," 238.

81. See Karl Josef Rivinius, SVD, *Im Spannungsfeld von Mission und Politik: Johann Baptist Anzer (1851–1903), Bischof von Süd-Shandong* (Nettetal, Germany: Steyler Verlag, 2010).

82. Kollár, *Ein Leben im Konflikt*, 3. The trilingual title of the new journal conveyed its collaborative intentions. "Serica" derives from the Latin word for China, *Ser, Seres* (silk), and *Monumenta Serica* means "monuments of China." The Chinese title of was *Huayi xuezhi* (Scholarly Journal of China and Its Neighboring Peoples). The English subtitle was *Journal of Oriental Studies*.

83. The Western editors included the well-known Mongolist Antoine Mostaert, CICM (1881–1971), Baron Alexander von Staël-Holstein (1876–1937), Dr. Gustav Ecke (1896–1971), and Dr. Ernst Schierlitz (1902–1940). The Chinese editors were Chen Yuan, Shen Jianshi (1887–1947), Zhang Xinglang (1888–1951), and Ying Qianli (1901–1961). Shen wrote a "review of reviews" section, which surveyed Chinese, Japanese, and Western publications.

84. In 1963 Fu Ren University was reestablished on a seventy-five-acre campus in Hsinchuang, a suburb of Taipei, Taiwan. It grew rapidly to a university of fifteen thousand students and faculty and staff of eleven hundred.

85. Edward J. Malatesta, SJ, *The Society of Jesus and China: A Historical-Theological Essay*, Discovery: Jesuit International Ministries 7 (St. Louis, MO: Institute of Jesuit Sources, 1997), 19, 22.

86. Paul P. Mariani, *Church Militant: Bishop Kung and Catholic Resistance in Communist Shanghai* (Cambridge, MA: Harvard University Press, 2011), 17–20.

87. Mariani, *Church Militant*, 27.

88. Mariani, *Church Militant*, 29.

89. John Tong, "The Church from 1949 to 1990," in *The Catholic Church in Modern China: Perspectives*, ed. Edmond Tang and Jean-Paul Wiest (Maryknoll, NY: Orbis Books, 1993), 7–11.

90. Donald E. MacInnis, *Religious Policy and Practice in Communist China: A Documentary History* (New York: Macmillan, 1972), 132.

91. Document 52, "The Christian Manifesto," in MacInnis, *Religious Policy*, 158–60.

92. Peter Tze Ming Ng, *Chinese Christianity: An Interplay between Global and Local Perspectives* (Leiden: Brill, 2012), 68–71.

93. Ng, *Chinese Christianity*, 187–88.

94. Tong, "The Church," 10.

95. Mariani, *Church Militant*, 33.

96. Mariani, *Church Militant*, 45–54.

97. W. Aedan McGrath, *Perseverance through Faith: A Priest's Prison Story. The Memoirs of Father Aedan McGrath*, ed. Theresa Marie Moreau (n.p.: XLibris, 2008), 43.

98. Mariani, *Church Militant*, 58–62.

99. Mariani, *Church Militant*, 46–53.

100. McGrath, *Perseverance through Faith*, 32–33, 41.

101. Mariani, *Church Militant*, 22.

102. Mariani, *Church Militant*, 68–71.

103. Mariani, *Church Militant*, 87–89.

104. Jean-Claude Coulet, *Les actes de Béda Tsang* (Paris: 1954), 1. Copies of this biography of Zhang Boda are rare. The author's name, Jean-Claude Coulet, is apparently a pseudonym for a French Jesuit in Shanghai in 1951 and personally familiar with many of the events described in the book. The biography was first published at Paris in a French edition and later translated into a slightly condensed English version published in Hong Kong. However, a search of Hong Kong libraries in 2014 found only one copy of the book.

105. Coulet, *Les actes*, 3–4.

106. Malatesta, *The Society of Jesus and China*, 34–35; Leo F. McGreal, SJ, "In Retrospect," in American Jesuits of Gonzaga College, *Portraits of China* (Shanghai: Tou-sè-wè Press, 1937), 1–4.

107. Charles J. McCarthy, SJ, "Christ Forms the Martyr," *Woodstock Letters* 92 (1963): 395–402.

108. McCarthy, "Christ Forms the Martyr," 401–2.

109. Coulet, *Les actes*, 5.

110. Coulet, *Les actes*, 10–12.

111. Coulet, *Les actes*, 13. The Chinese text of this resolution is reproduced, followed by a French translation, in Coulet, *Les actes*, 27–29.

112. Coulet, *Les actes*, 15–17.

113. Coulet, *Les actes*, 16, 30n.

114. McGrath, *Perseverance through Faith*, 85.

115. "The Finale of the Imperialists' Running Dog and Counter-Revolutionary, Beda Chang," *Jiefang ribao*, November 17, 1951, translated in "A Martyr Dies," *China Missionary Bulletin* 1 (January 1952): 16–18.

116. Jin Luxian, *The Memoirs of Jin Luxian*, Vol. 1: *Learning and Relearning, 1916–1982*, trans. William Hanbury-Tenison (Hong Kong: Hong Kong University Press, 2012), 160.

117. Coulet, *Les actes*, 16–18.

118. Jean-Claude Coulet, *Father Beda Chang: Witness for Unity* (Hong Kong: Catholic Truth Society, 1953), 26.

119. Coulet, *Les actes*, 18. The phrase "¡Viva Cristo Rey!" was the battle cry of the Cristeros who led a counterrevolution (*La Cristiada*, or the Cristero War) from 1926 to 1929 in Mexico against the anticlericism of the Mexican government.

120. Coulet, *Les actes*, 4.

121. Coulet, *Les actes*, 19.

122. Coulet, *Les actes*, 20.

123. "A Martyr Dies," 17.

124. Mariani, *Church Militant*, 157–62.

125. Mariani, *Church Militant*, 148–67.

126. Mariani, *Church Militant*, 25.

127. Mariani, *Church Militant*, 190–96.

128. There were two main types of imprisonment in Communist China. *Laogai* (reform through labor) was a more legal proceeding involving a trial. *Laodong jiaoyang* (abbreviated as *laojiao*), meaning "reeducation through labor," was an

administrative punishment carried out by police and created in 1955 to suppress "counterrevolutionaries" in government. See Fu Hualing, "Re-education through Labour in Historical Perspective," *China Quarterly* 184 (2005): 811.

129. Fox Butterfield, *China, Alive in the Bitter Sea* (New York: Times Books, 1982), 367–68.

130. Jin, *Memoirs*, 15–18.

131. Mariani, *Church Militant*, 29.

132. Jin, *Memoirs*, 37–38, 47–48.

133. Jin, *Memoirs*, 98.

134. Jin, *Memoirs*, 157.

135. Obituary of Lazlo Ladany, *New York Times*, September 26, 1990.

136. L. Ladany, *China News Analysis* 145, August 24, 1965, 5. Also see Simon Leys (Pierre Ryckmans), "The Art of Interpreting Nonexistent Inscriptions Written in Invisible Ink on a Blank Page," *New York Review of Books*, October 11, 1990.

137. Chinese Catholic Patriotic Association, *Chinese Catholic Church* 11 (December 1984), translated and cited by L. Landany, *The Catholic Church in China* (New York: Freedom House, 1987), 73–74.

138. Mariani, *Church Militant*, 214, 221; Lazlo Ladany, SJ, *The Catholic Church in China* (New York: Freedom House, 1987), 74.

139. Jin, *Memoirs*, 161–62. See also Jin's criticism of Gong on 213.

140. Ladany, *Catholic Church*, 76–77.

141. Jin Luxian lecture given in Germany on April 18, 1886, cited in Ladany, *Catholic Church*, 77.

142. Ladany, *Catholic Church*, 74.

143. Mariani, *Church Militant*, 215.

CHAPTER 4

1. D. E. Mungello, *Drowning Girls in China: Female Infanticide since 1650* (Lanham, MD: Rowman & Littlefield, 2008), 9–10.

2. See Michelle T. King, *Between Birth and Death: Female Infanticide in Nineteenth-Century China* (Stanford, CA: Stanford University Press, 2014), 87–92.

3. Gabriel Palâtre, SJ, *L'infanticide et l'Oeuvre de la Sainte-Enfance en Chine* (Shanghai: Autographie de la Mission Catholique à l'Orphelinat de Tou-Sè-Wè, 1875). This source includes a seventy-four-page appendix containing sixty-six transcribed Chinese documents translated by Oliver Durandière, SJ, and six folded leaves of facsimile copies of Chinese broadsheet illustrations. See also Françoise Lauwaert, *Le meurtre en famille. Parricide et infanticide en Chine (XVIIIe–XIXe siècle)* (Paris: Éditions Odile Jacob, 1999), 260.

4. Palâtre, *L'infanticide*, 200.

5. Examples of these illustrations are republished in Mungello, *Drowning Girls in China*, 16–43.

6. Wolfram Eberhard, *A Dictionary of Chinese Symbols*, trans. G. L. Campbell (London: Routledge, 1986), 83.

7. C. A. S. Williams, *Chinese Symbolism and Art Motifs*, 3rd rev. ed. (Rutland, VT: Charles E. Tuttle Company, 1993), 319.

8. Weijing Lu, "'A Pearl in the Palm': A Forgotten Symbol of the Father-Daughter Bond," *Late Imperial China* 31 (2010): 62–97.

9. Shen Fu, *Six Records of a Floating Life* (*Fu sheng liu ji*), trans. Leonard Pratt and Chiang Su-hui (London: Penguin, 1983), 39.

10. King, *Between Birth and Death*, 150.

11. Mungello, *Drowning Girls in China*, 52–55.

12. Mungello, *Drowning Girls in China*, 47–52; King, *Between Birth and Death*, 69–73.

13. Bernice J. Lee, "Female Infanticide in China," in *Women in China: Current Directions in Historical Scholarship*, ed. W. L. Guisso (Youngstown, NY: Philo Press, 1981), 167–68; Ping-ti Ho, *Studies on the Population of China, 1368–1953* (Cambridge, MA: Harvard University Press, 1959), 58–62.

14. Alain Sauret, "China's Role in the Foundation and Development of the Pontifical Society of the Holy Childhood," in *Historiography of the Chinese Catholic Church: Nineteenth and Twentieth Centuries*, ed. Jeroom Heyndrickx, CICM (Leuven: Ferdinand Verbiest Foundation–KU Leuven, 1994), 247–72. Also see Henrietta Harrison, "'A Penny for the Little Chinese': The French Holy Childhood Association in China," *American Historical Review* 113 (2008): 72–92; Fanchón Royer, "Charles de Forbin-Janson, Missionary Bishop," *Americas* 10 (1953): 196; Jean Charbonnier, *Histoire des Chrétiens de Chine: "Mémoire chrétienne"* (Paris: Coédition Desclée/Bégédis, 1992), 231.

15. Mungello, *Drowning Girls in China*, 77–80.

16. Louis Wei Tsing-sing (Tian Genghua), *La politique missionnaire de la France en Chine, 1842–1856* (Paris: Les Nouvelle Éditions Latines, 1960), 255.

17. J. B. Piolet, *Les missions catholiques françaises au XIX° siècle*, Vol. 3: *Chine et Japon* (Paris: Armand Colin, n.d.), 177–78.

18. Palâtre, *L'infanticide*, 165–70.

19. Herbert Giles (organizer), "The Prevalence of Infanticide in China," *Journal of the North China Branch of the Royal Asiatic Society* 20 (1885): 34, 36, 41.

20. Shen Xizhi et al., *Zhaoran gonglun* (Hengtang, 1846), reprinted in *Xujiahui cangshulou: Ming-Qing Tianzhujiao wenxian* (Chinese Christian Texts from the Zikawei Library), ed. Nicolas Standaert (Zhong Mingdan) et al., 5 vols. (Taipei: Faculty of Theology, Fujen Catholic University, 1996), f. 13b (V, 2065).

21. Shen et al., *Zhaoran gonglun*, f. 41a (V, 2066).

22. Shen et al., *Zhaoran gonglun*, f. 141a–b (V, 2066–2067).

23. Nan (Gotteland), *Wubang lun*, reprinted in *Xujiahui cangshulou*, f. 16b (V, 2110).

24. Li Jiugong, *Shensi lu* (A Record of Careful Meditations), reprinted in *Yesuhui Luoma danganguan Ming-Qing Tianzhujiao wenxian* (Chinese Christian Texts from the Roman Archives of the Society of Jesus), ed. Nicolas Standaert and Adrian Dudink, 12 vols. (Taipei: Ricci Institute, 2002), f. 1b (IX, 178).

25. Giles, "The Prevalence of Infanticide," 25–50.

26. Mungello, *Drowning Girls in China*, 79.

27. Mungello, *Drowning Girls in China*, 63–70.

28. Julia Stone, *Chinese Basket Babies: A German Missionary Foundling Home and the Girls It Raised (1850s–1914)*, Opera Sinologica 26 (Wiesbaden: Harrassowitz Verlag, 2013), 214.

29. Stone, *Chinese Basket Babies*, xx, 195.

30. The contemporary scholarship on infanticide in Chinese history is sometimes inaccurate; for example, an article published in 1981 mistakenly refers to Protestant missionaries as the "first foreigners to register serious concern at female infanticide" and fails to note the existence of Fr. Palâtre's study. See Lee, "Female Infanticide," 168. One of the few studies of infanticide in China to make use of economic statistics argues that there were demographic correlations between high food prices and female infanticide. See James Lee, Cameron Campbell, and Guofu Tan, "Infanticide and Family Planning in Late Imperial China: The Price and Population History of Rural Liaoning, 1774–1873," in *Chinese History in Economic Perspective*, ed. Thomas G. Rawski and Lillian M. Li (Berkeley: University of California Press, 1992), 145–76.

31. Harrison, "A Penny for the Little Chinese," 76–78.

32. Lu, "A Pearl in the Palm," 63.

33. See Sue Bradshaw, OSF, "Religious Women in China: An Understanding of Indigenization," *Catholic Historical Review* 68 (1982): 28–45; Beatrice Leung and Patricia Wittenberg, "Catholic Religious Orders of Women in China: Adaptation and Power," *Journal for the Scientific Study of Religion* 43, no. 1 (2004): 67–82.

34. See Robert E. Entenmann, "Christian Virgins in Eighteenth-Century Sichuan," in *Christianity in China: From the Eighteenth Century to the Present*, ed. Daniel H. Bays (Stanford, CA: Stanford University Press, 1996), 180–93; Jos. Jennes [Yan Dingen], CICM, *Four Centuries of Catechetics in China. Zhongguo jiaoli jiangshou shi*, trans. Eng. Albert Van Lierde [Li Pengju], trans. Chinese T'ien Yung-cheng [Tian Yongzheng], CICM (Taipei: Tianzhujiao Huaming Shuju, 1976), 109–10.

35. R. G. Tiedemann, "Catholic Religious Communities of Chinese Women," in *Handbook of Christianity in China*, Vol. 2: *1800–Present*, ed. R. G. Tiedemann (Leiden: Brill, 2010), 587–88; Jennes, *Four Centuries*, 172–73.

36. Ida Sala, *History of Our Canossian Missions*, Vol. 2: *China, 1868–1952* (Hong Kong: Daughters of the Charity of Canossa, 2003), 357–58.

37. Kenneth Scott Latourette, *A History of Christian Missions in China* (London: Society for Promoting Christian Knowledge, 1929), 234.

38. Sala, *History*, 575–76.

39. "N. 4—Opera Pia Lavori Femminili a Beneficio della Santa Infanzia, Guluba 31.12.1918," report signed by P. Luigi Rossi, preserved in the Canossian Archive, Rome.

40. Sala, *History*, 359–60.

41. "Uno Sprazzo di Luce—Storia di 25 Anni di Apostolato Canossiano—1891–1916" (A Ray of Light: History of 25 Years of the Canossian Apostles—1891–1916), Shensi Mle Kulupa Cina, Archivo Canossiano, Roma; Sala, *History*, 360–61.

42. Sala, *History*, 361–62.

43. Sala, *History*, 362.

44. Sala, *History*, 363.

45. "Uno Sprazzo di Luce," 5.
46. Sala, *History*, 370.
47. "Uno Sprazzo di Luce," 9.
48. Sala, *History*, 367.
49. "Uno Sprazzo di Luce," 9.
50. Sala, *History*, 371.
51. Sala, *History*, 370.
52. Sala, *History*, 37.
53. Sala, *History*, 369.
54. Sala, *History*, 381.
55. "Uno Sprazzo di Luce," 8.
56. "Uno Sprazzo di Luce," 8, says five new sisters arrived in 1913, but Sala, *History*, 575, lists the names of only four.
57. Eric Teichman, *Travels of a Consular Officer in North West China* (Cambridge: Cambridge University Press, 1921), 36.
58. Teichman, *Travels*, 200.
59. Ida Pruitt, *Working Woman of Han* (Stanford, CA: Stanford University Press, 1945), 145–50.
60. Sergio Ticozzi, "China at the Beginning of the Twentieth Century," in *Lost China: The Photographs of Leone Nani* (Milan: Skira, 2003), 21.
61. Sala, *History*, 364.
62. Sala, *History*, 380.
63. Gianni Criveller, *The Martyrdom of Alberico Crescitelli: Its Context and Controversy*, ed. Betty Ann Maheu, MM (Hong Kong: Holy Spirit Study Centre, 2004), 12.
64. Sala, *History*, 381–82.
65. Sala, *History*, 384–85.
66. Sala, *History*, 386–88.
67. Sala, *History*, 403–4.
68. Johannes Schütte, SVD, *Die katholische Chinamission im Spiegel der rotchinesischen Presse* (Münster: Aschendorffsche Verlagsbuchhandlung, 1957), 115.
69. Cartoon by Zhang Wenyuan, July 1953.
70. Schütte, *Die katholische Chinamission*, 330.
71. Schütte, *Die katholische Chinamission*, 330–32.
72. *Wenhui ribao* (Hong Kong), June 7, 1951, cited in Schütte, *Die katholische Chinamission*, 332.
73. *Wenhui ribao*, December 2, 1951.
74. *China Missionary Bulletin* (Hong Kong) 4 (1952): 306.
75. Schütte, *Die katholische Chinamission*, 334–36.
76. *Xinwen ribao*, July 5, 1953, cited in Schütte, *Die katholische Chinamission*, 336.

CHAPTER 5

1. Gianni Criveller, *The Martyrdom of Alberico Crescitelli: Its Context and Controversy*, ed. Betty Ann Maheu, MM (Hong Kong: Holy Spirit Study Centre, 2004), 25.

2. For a discussion of the sexual seductions of Chinese women by Fr. Bernardino Bevilacqua, OFM, and Fr. Alessio Randanini, OFM, in western Shandong and southern Zhili provinces from 1736 to 1741, see D. E. Mungello, *The Spirit and the Flesh in Shandong, 1650–1785* (Lanham, MD: Rowman & Littlefield, 2001), 124–135.

3. Much of the material in this chapter is based on research originally done for an article. See D. E. Mungello, "Fact and Fantasy in the Sexual Seduction of Chinese Converts by Catholic Priests: The Case of the 120 Martyrs," *Sino-Western Cultural Relations Journal* 23 (2001): 8–21.

4. A complete list of the 120 martyrs of China canonized in 2000 is found in the appendix.

5. Alessandra Stanley, "Pope Canonizes 120 Killed in China and One American," *New York Times*, October 2, 2000.

6. French Vincentian Father Jean Gabriel Perboyre (1814–1856) was deleted from the 1967 list of 119 martyrs, while Bishop Luigi Versiglia, SDB (1873–1930), and Fr. Callisto Caravario (1903–1930) were added to the 2000 list, making 120 martyrs. Catholic University of America, *New Catholic Encyclopedia*, 3:602–3.

7. See R. Molinari, "Canonization of Saints (History and Procedure)," in *New Catholic Encyclopedia*, 3:55–59.

8. "Zhongguo Tianzhujiao Aiguohui Zhongguo Tianzhujiao Zhujiaotuan fabiao shengming" (The Chinese Catholic Patriotic Association Issues a Statement on the Chinese Regional Bishops' Conference), *Renmin ribao*, September 27, 2000; Erik Eckholm, "China Protests Planned Canonization of 120," *New York Times*, September 27, 2000.

9. Ren Yanli, "Saints, Imperialists, and the Catholic Church's Discrimination against China," trans. Yao Ximing, *Heartland—Eurasian Review of Geopolitics* 1 (2001): 123–24. See also "Time to Forgive the Sinners of China," *Economist*, April 21–27, 2001, 34.

10. Chinese Regional Bishops' Conference, ed., *Les 120 nouveaux saints martyrs de Chine* (Taipei, 2000); Chinese Regional Bishops' Conference, ed., *Zhongguo xundao shengren chuan* (Taipei: Yongwang wenhua shiye youxiangongsi, 2000).

11. See "Zhongguo Tianzhujiao Aiguohui."

12. Shi Yan, "Jiekai sowei 'shengren' de mianmu,'" *Renmin ribao*, October 3, 2000.

13. Eugenio Menegon, *Ancestors, Virgins, and Friars: Christianity as a Local Religion in Late Imperial China* (Cambridge, MA: Harvard University Asia Center, 2009), 98.

14. Menegon, *Ancestors*, 316–24.

15. Anthony E. Clark, *China's Saints: Catholic Martyrdom during the Qing (1644–1911)* (Bethlehem, PA: Lehigh University Press, 2011), 61–65; Menegon, *Ancestors*, 98–99.

16. Fr. Chapdelaine was also known under the Chinese names Siding and Ma Aosiduo.

17. Zhen Shi, "Ma Lai yu Di'er Yapian Zhanzheng" (Auguste Chapdelaine and the Second Opium War), *Renmin ribao*, September 29, 2000.

18. *Zhongguo xundao shengren chuan* (Biographies of Martyred Saints in China), ed. Chinese Regional Bishops' Conference (Taipei: Yongwang wenhua shiye youxiangongsi, 2000), 142.

150

Notes to Pages 99–103

19. Jean Charbonnier, "Les 120 martyrs de Chine canonisés le 1er octobre 2000," in *Études et documents* (Paris: Archives des Missions Étrangères, 2000), 12:75; Herm. Wegener, SVD, *Heroes of the Mission Field*, trans. E. McCall (Techny, IL: Mission Press SVD, 1916), 51.

20. Charbonnier, "Les 120 martyrs de Chine," 76; [Pater] Roeser, SVD, *Zhonghua guangrong* (Die chinesischen Martyrer) (Yanzhou, Shandong: Yangzhou Catholic Church, 1925), 14.

21. "Lettre de M. Guillemin [i.e., Guillemain], préfet apostolique des missions du Quang-tong et du Quang-xi à MM. les directeurs de l'Œuvre de la Propagation de la Foi, Canton 8 juillet 1856," in *Annales de la propagation de la foi* (Lyon: M. P. Rusard, 1856), 28:462.

22. Ralph R. Covell, *The Liberating Gospel in China: The Christian Faith among China's Minority Peoples* (Grand Rapids, MI: Baker, 1995), 83–86.

23. Chinese Regional Bishops Conference, ed., *Zhonghua xundao shengren chuan*, 140. Cf. Zhen, "Ma Lai yu Di'er Yapian Zhancheng."

24. Roeser, *Zhonghua guangrong*, 16.

25. Charbonnier, "Les 120 martyrs de Chine," 80.

26. Chinese Regional Bishops Conference, ed., *Zhonghua xundao shengren chuan*, 141; "Lettre de M. Guillemin," 471–72.

27. The entry on Agnes Cao Guiying in *Les 120 nouveaux saints martyrs*, 18, gives the year of her move from Guizhou to Guangxi as 1852—an obvious error, since Fr. Chapdelaine did not arrive in Guizhou until February 1854 and would have been unable to issue the invitation to her in 1852.

28. Charbonnier, "Les 120 martyrs de Chine," 80.

29. "Lettre de M. Chapdelaine, missionnaire apostolique, à M. Albrand, supérieur du Séminaire des missions-étrangères, Kouang-tsao-pa, province du Kouei-tcheou [Guizhou], 10 julliet 1855," in *Annales de la propagation de la foi* (Lyon: M. P. Rusard, 1856), 28:459.

30. Charles O. Hucker, *A Dictionary of Official Titles in Imperial China* (Stanford, CA: Stanford University Press, 1985), 294–95.

31. "Lettre de M. Guillemin," 464; Chinese Regional Bishops Conference, ed., *Zhonghua xundao shengren chuan*, 141.

32. "Lettre de M. Guillemin," 465–66.

33. "Lettre de M. Guillemin," 468.

34. "Lettre de M. Guillemin," 469.

35. On the dynamics of martyrdom in Shandong, see Mungello, *Spirit*, 3, 28, 74, 110. On wondrous signs, see in the same work, 5–6.

36. E-tu Zen Sun, trans. and ed., *Ch'ing Administrative Terms: A Translation of the Terminology of the Six Boards with Explanatory Notes* (Cambridge, MA: Harvard University Press, 1961), 275–76.

37. Sun, *Ch'ing Administrative Terms*, 290.

38. "Lettre de M. Guillemin," 473.

39. "Lettre de M. Guillemin," 474.

40. Wegener, *Heroes*, 67–68. A remarkable photograph of prisoners in these cages appears in Jonathan D. Spence and Annping Chin, *The Chinese Century:*

A Photographic History of the Last Hundred Years (New York: Random House, 1996), 24–25.

41. "Lettre de M. Guillemin," 474–75.

42. Sun, *Ch'ing Administrative Terms*, 270.

43. "Lettre de M. Guillemin," 376.

44. Roeser, *Zhonghua guangrong*, 18.

45. "Lettre de M. Guillemin," 476–77.

46. Wegener, *Heroes*, 68.

47. "Lettre de M. Guillemin," 478.

48. Sun, *Ch'ing Administrative Terms*, 275.

49. Sun, *Ch'ing Administrative Terms*, 278.

50. "Lettre de M. Guillemin," 478–79.

51. "Lettre de M. Guillemin," 479–80.

52. See Robert des Rotours, "Quelques notes sur l'anthropophagie en Chine," *T'oung Pao* 50 (1963): 386–427; Robert des Rotours, "Encore quelques notes sur l'anthropophagie en Chine," *T'oung Pao* 54 (1968): 1–49.

53. S. Wells Williams, *The Middle Kingdom: A Survey of the Geography, Government, Literature, Social Life, Arts, and History of the Chinese Empire and Its Inhabitants*, 2 vols. (New York: Charles Scribner's Sons, 1898), 1:514.

54. See Zheng Yi, *Scarlet Memorial: Tales of Cannibalism in Modern China*, trans. and ed. T. P. Sym (Boulder, CO: Westview Press, 1996).

55. Adrien Launay, *Histoire générale de la Société des missions-étrangères*, 3 vols. (Paris: Téqui, 1894), 3:331–35, cited in Henri Cordier, *L'expédition de Chine de 1857–58. Histoire diplomatique* (Paris: Félix Alcan, 1905), 22.

56. Jean Charbonnier, *Histoire des Chrétiens de Chine: "Mémoire chrétienne"* (Paris: Coédition Desclée/Bégédis, 1992), 229.

57. Kenneth Scott Latourette, *A History of Christian Missions in China* (London: Society for Promoting Christian Knowledge, 1929), 273.

58. Criveller, *The Martyrdom*, 15–16.

59. Criveller, *The Martyrdom*, 17–18.

60. Boxer activity in Shanxi province is treated in Anthony E. Clark, *Heaven in Conflict: Franciscans and the Boxer Uprising in Shanxi* (Seattle: University of Washington Press, 2015).

61. "Uno Sprazzo di Luce—Storia di 25 Anni di Apostolato Canossiano—1891–1916" (A Ray of Light: History of 25 Years of the Canossian Apostles—1891–1916), Shensi Mle Kulupa Cina, Archivo Canossiano, Roma, 7; Ida Sala, *History of Our Canossian Missions*, Vol. 2: *China, 1868–1952* (Hong Kong: Daughters of the Charity of Canossa, 2003), 168.

62. *Les 120 nouveaux saints martyrs*, 84.

63. Criveller, *The Martyrdom*, 29.

64. Criveller, *The Martyrdom*, 20.

65. Criveller, *The Martyrdom*, 30–31, identifies Teng Shangxian with the "Ten Cun-ie" (Teng Cunye, or Village Elder Teng) mentioned in PIME sources.

66. Criveller, *The Martyrdom*, 32–33.

67. Criveller, *The Martyrdom*, 36–38.

68. Criveller, *The Martyrdom*, 40–42.
69. Zhang Li and Liu Jiantang, eds., *Zhongguo jiao'an shi* (Chengdu: Sichuan sheng shehui kexue yuan chubanshe, 1987), cited in Criveller, *The Martyrdom*, 33–35.

CHAPTER 6

1. Document 19 (March 1982), "The Basic Viewpoint and Policy on the Religious Question in China during the Period of Socialism," in John Tong, "The Church from 1949 to 1990," in *The Catholic Church in Modern China: Perspectives*, ed. Edmond Tang and Jean-Paul Wiest (Maryknoll, NY: Orbis Books, 1993), 19–20.
2. [David Macdonald Paton], "First Thoughts on the Débâcle of Christian Missions in China," *International Review of Mission* (Geneva) 40, no. 160 (October 1951): 411.
3. Hong Kong *Mission Bulletin* statistics, as cited in Lazlo Ladany, SJ, *The Catholic Church in China* (New York: Freedom House, 1987), 20. According to the *Annuaire de l'Église catholique en Chine 1949*, cited in Beatrice Kit Fun Leung, "The Missionaries," in *Handbook of Christianity in China*, Vol. 2: *1800–Present*, ed. R. G. Tiedemann (Leiden: Brill, 2010), 793–94, the 1948 records give the number of Catholic missionaries in China at 5,112 sisters, 2,676 priests, and 632 brothers. The power of the Jesuits in 1951 is indicated by their 1951 membership in China of 888 priests and lay brothers, several of whom were Chinese.
4. Paul P. Mariani, *Church Militant: Bishop Kung and Catholic Resistance in Communist Shanghai* (Cambridge, MA: Harvard University Press, 2011), 210.
5. David Macdonald Paton, *Christian Missions and the Judgment of God* (London: SCM Press, 1953).
6. The Zhejiang provincial campaign to remove crosses and demolish churches that are not part of the Chinese Catholic Patriotic Association and the Protestant Three-Self Patriotic Movement is a recent manifestation of the blending of Catholic and Protestant churches by Chinese Communist officials. The government has published a list of sixty-four targeted Christian churches (including both Catholic and Protestant churches). See www.asianews.it/news-en/Zhejiang:-list-and-pictures-of-64 (May 21, 2014).
7. Paton, *Christian Missions and the Judgment of God*, 2nd ed. (Grand Rapids, MI: William B. Eerdmans, 1996), 84.
8. Joseph R. Levenson, *Confucian China and Its Modern Fate: A Trilogy*, Vol. 1: *The Problem of Intellectual Continuity* (Berkeley: University of California Press, 1958), 121.
9. Levenson, *Confucian China*, 120.
10. Levenson, *Confucian China*, 123.
11. Jacques Gernet, *Chine et Christianisme: Action et réaction* (Paris: Gallimard, 1982). This widely read book was published in German, Italian, English, and Chinese editions. See Jacques Gernet, *Christus kam bis nach China: Eine erste Begegnung und ihr Scheitern*, trans. Christine Mäder-Virágh (Zürich: Artemis, 1984); Jacques Gernet, *Die Begegnung Chinas mit dem Christentum*, trans. Roman Malek (Sankt Augustin,

Germany: Institut Monumenta Serica, 2012); Jacques Gernet, *Cina e cristianesimo: Azione e reazione*, trans. Adriano Prosperi (Casale Monferrato, Italy: Marietti, 1984); Jacques Gernet, *China and the Christian Impact: A Conflict of Cultures*, trans. Janet Lloyd (New York: Cambridge University Press, 1985); Jacques Gernet, *Zhongguo he Jidu jiao: Zhongguo he Ouzhou wen hua zhi bi jiao*, trans. Geng Sheng, rev. sup. ed. (Shanghai: Shanghai Guji Chuban she, 2003).

12. In contrast to Levenson, with his pessimism about the survival of Confucianism in modern China, Wm. Theodore de Bary held a far more optimistic view. See Arthur Waldron's review of de Bary's *Confucian Tradition and Global Education: The Tang Chun-I Lectures for 2005* in *Sino-Western Cultural Relations Journal* 31 (2009): 70–74.

13. Gernet's *Chine et Christianisme: Action et réaction* was reprinted in an edited, revised, and corrected version with a different subtitle as *Chine et Christianisme: La première confrontation* (Paris: Gallimard, 1991).

14. One of the leading scholars who devoted his early career to studying the entry of Buddhism into China, Erik Zürcher, though initially agreeing with Gernet, would eventually come to a conclusion about Christianity's historical adaptation to China that contradicted Gernet's argument. Zürcher's views evolved and diverged from Gernet's on one crucial point. As he moved more deeply into the seventeenth-century interaction of the Jesuit Giulio Aleni with the literati in Fujian province, Zürcher developed new insights. By 1990, he wrote that the reception of Jesuit accommodation in Fujian province "contradicts the thesis (brilliantly presented by Jacques Gernet) that the Chinese, due to their ingrained cultural preoccupations, virtually were unable to assimilate the basic ideas of Christianity—the *Diary* [*Kouduo richao*] shows us striking examples of the opposite." Erik Zürcher, "The Jesuit Mission in Fujian in Late Ming Times: Levels of Response," in *Development and Decline of Fukien Province in the 17th and 18th Centuries*, ed. Eduard B. Vermeer (Leiden: Brill, 1990), 456.

15. Kwang-ching Liu, ed., *American Missionaries in China: Papers from Harvard Seminars* (Cambridge, MA: East Asian Research Center, Harvard University, 1966).

16. Paul A. Cohen, *China and Christianity: The Missionary Movement and the Growth of Chinese Antiforeignism, 1860–1870* (Cambridge, MA: Harvard University Press, 1963), 3–60.

17. Lu Tongliu, "Goutong Zhong-Xi wenhua de xianquzhe—Li Madou," *Renmin ribao*, November 4, 1979.

18. Bob Whyte, *Unfinished Encounter: China and Christianity* (London: Collins, 1988), 204–5.

19. Daniel H. Bays, ed., *A New History of Christianity in China* (Malden, MA: Wiley-Blackwell, 2012), 136.

20. David Aikman, *Jesus in Beijing* (Washington, DC: Regnery, 2003), 48.

21. Kim-Kwong Chan and Alan Hunter, trans., *Prayers and Thoughts of Chinese Christians* (Boston: Cowley, 1991), 22–23.

22. Alan Hunter and Chan Kim-kwong, "Growth of the Chinese Church since 1949," in Tiedemann, *Handbook*, 2:812.

23. Tong, "The Church," 18.

24. *Zhongguo zongjiao bangao 2013*, ed. Jin Shi and Qiu Yonghui (Beijing: Shehui Keshui wenxian chubanshe, 2013).

25. Richard P. Madsen, "Beyond Orthodoxy: Catholicism as Chinese Folk Religion," in *China and Christianity: Burdened Past, Hopeful Future*, ed. Stephen Uhalley Jr. and Xiaoxin Wu (Armonk, NY: M. E. Sharpe, 2001), 233–49.

26. See the list of Catholic degree holders compiled by Nicolas Standaert and Adrian Dudink in *Handbook of Christianity in China*, Vol. 1: *635–1800*, ed. Nicolas Standaert (Leiden: Brill, 2001), 399–403.

27. D. E. Mungello, *The Spirit and the Flesh in Shandong, 1650–1785* (Lanham, MD: Rowman & Littlefield, 2001), 111–18.

28. Bays, *New History*, 164.

29. Bays, *New History*, 174.

30. Hunter and Chan, "Growth of the Chinese Church," 2:816–17.

31. Tong, "The Church," 22–23.

Bibliography

"A Martyr Dies." *China Missionary Bulletin* 1 (January 1952): 16–18.

Aikman, David. *Jesus in Beijing.* Washington, DC: Regnery, 2003.

American Jesuits of Gonzaga College. *Portraits of China.* Shanghai: Tou-sè-wè Press, 1937.

Arlington, L. C., and William Lewisohn. *In Search of Old Peking.* Beijing: Henri Vetch, 1935.

Bangert, William V., SJ. *A History of the Society of Jesus.* 2nd ed. St. Louis, MO: Institute of Jesuit Sources, 1986.

Barmé, Geremie R. "The Gardens of Perfect Brightness, a Life in Ruins." *East Asian History* 11 (1996): 111–58.

Bays, Daniel H., ed. *A New History of Christianity in China.* Malden, MA: Wiley-Blackwell, 2012.

———. *Christianity in China: From the Eighteenth Century to the Present.* Stanford, CA: Stanford University Press, 1996.

Biallas, P. Franz Xaver, SVD. *Konfuzius und sein Kult: Ein Beitrag zur Kulturge-schichte Chinas und ein* Führer *zur Heimatstadt des Konfuzius.* Peking-Leipzig: Pekinger Verlag, 1928.

Boorman, Howard L., ed. *Biographical Dictionary of Republican China.* 5 vols. New York: Columbia University Press, 1967–1971.

Bradshaw, Sue, OSF. "Religious Women in China: An Understanding of Indigeniza-tion." *Catholic Historical Review* 68 (1982): 28–45.

Brady, Anne-Marie. *Friend of China: The Myth of Renwi Alley.* London: Routledge, 2002.

Brandt, Joseph van den. *Les Lazaristes en Chine, 1697–1935. Notices biographiques.* Beiping: Imprimerie des Lazaristes, 1936.

Bryan, William Jennings. *Letter to a Chinese Official, Being a Western View of East-ern Civilization.* New York: McClure, Phillips, 1906.

Bulfoni, Clara, and Anna Pozzi, eds. *Lost China: The Photographs of Leone Nani.* Milan: Skira Editore SpA, 2003.

Butterfield, Fox. *China, Alive in the Bitter Sea.* New York: Times Books, 1982.

Catholic University of America. *New Catholic Encyclopedia.* New York: McGraw Hill, 1967.

Chan, Kim-kwong, and Alan Hunter, trans. *Prayers and Thoughts of Chinese Christians.* Boston: Cowley, 1991.

Chapdelaine, Auguste. "Lettre de M. Chapdelaine, missionnaire apostolique, à M. Albrand, supérieur du Séminaire des missions-étrangères, Kouang-tsao-pa, province du Kouei-tcheou [Guizhou], 10 julliet 1855." In *Annales de la propagation de la foi*, 28: 459. Lyon: M. P. Rusard, 1856.

Charbonnier, Jean. "Les 120 martyrs de Chine canonisés le 1er octobre 2000." In *Études et documents* (Paris: Archives des Missions Étrangères, 2000).

———. *Guide to the Catholic Church in China.* Singapore: China Catholic Communication, 2000.

———. *Histoire des Chrétiens de Chine: "Mémoire chrétienne."* Paris: Coédition Desclée/Bégédis, 1992.

Chinese Regional Bishops' Conference, ed. *Les 120 nouveaux saints martyrs de Chine.* Taipei, 2000.

———, ed. *Zhongguo xundao shengren chuan.* Taipei: Yongwang wenhua shiye youxiangongsi, 2000.

Clark, Anthony E. *China's Saints: Catholic Martyrdom during the Qing (1644–1911).* Bethlehem, PA: Lehigh University Press, 2011.

———. *Heaven in Conflict: Franciscans and the Boxer Uprising in Shanxi.* Seattle: University of Washington Press, 2015.

Clarke, Jeremy, SJ. *Catholic Shanghai: A Historical, Practical and Reflective Guide.* St. Louis, MO: Institute of Jesuit Sources, 2012.

Cohen, Paul A. *China and Christianity: The Missionary Movement and the Growth of Chinese Antiforeignism, 1860–1870.* Cambridge, MA: Harvard University Press, 1963.

Cole, H. M. "Origins of the French Protectorate over Catholic Missions in China." *American Society of International Law* 34 (1940): 473–91.

Colombel, Fr. "Ch. VI. Le Kiang-nan." In *Les missions catholiques françaises au XIX° siècle*, edited by Jean-Baptiste Piolet, SJ, 173–74. Paris: Librairie Armand Colin, 1902.

Cordier, Henri. "Nécrologiè. Aloys Pfister." *T'oung Pao* 2 (1891): 460–64.

———. *L'expédition de Chine de 1857–58. Histoire diplomatique.* Paris: Félix Alcan, 1905.

Coulet, Jean-Claude [Claude Larre, SJ]. *Les actes de Béda Tsang.* Paris: 1954.

———. *Father Beda Chang: Witness for Unity.* Hong Kong: Catholic Truth Society, 1953.

Couling, Samuel. *The Encyclopedia Sinica.* Shanghai: Kelly & Walsh, 1917.

Criveller, Gianni. *The Martyrdom of Alberico Crescitelli: Its Context and Controversy*, edited by Betty Ann Maheu, MM. Hong Kong: Holy Spirit Study Centre, 2004.

Cummins, J. S. *A Question of Rites: Friar Domingo Navarrete and the Jesuits in China.* Aldershot, UK: Scholar Press, 1993.

Dawson, Raymond. *The Chinese Chameleon: An Analysis of European Conceptions of Chinese Civilization*. London: Oxford, 1967.

Dehergne, Joseph, SJ. *Répertoire des Jésuites de Chine de 1552 à 1800*. Rome: Institutum Historicum Societatis Iesu, 1973.

Dickinson, Goldsworthy Lowes. *The Autobiography of G. Lowes Dickinson and Other Unpublished Writings*, edited by Dennis Proctor. London: Gerald Duckworth, 1973.

————. *Letters from a Chinese Official, Being an Eastern View of Western Civilization*. New York: McClure, Phillips, 1904.

Dudink, Adrian. "The Chinese Christian Books of the Former Beitang Library." *Sino-Western Cultural Relations Journal* 26 (2004): 46–59.

————. "The Chinese Texts in the Zikawei Collection in Shanghai: A Preliminary and Partial List." *Sino-Western Cultural Relations Journal* 33 (2011): 1–41.

Eben von Racknitz, Ines. *Die Plünderung des Yuanming yuan. Imperiale Beutenahme im britisch-französischen Chinafeldzug von 1860*. Stuttgart: Franz Steiner Verlag, 2012.

Eberhard, Wolfram. *A Dictionary of Chinese Symbols*. Trans. G. L. Campbell. London: Routledge, 1986.

Entenmann, Robert E. "Christian Virgins in Eighteenth-Century Sichuan." In *Christianity in China: From the Eighteenth Century to the Present*, edited by Daniel H. Bays, 180–93. Stanford, CA: Stanford University Press, 1996.

Fang Hao. "Ma Xiangbo xiansheng nianpu xinbian." *Tianzhujiao xueshu yanjiusuo xuebao* 6 (1974): 1–59; 7 (1975): 1–114.

————. *Zhongguo Tianzhujiao shi renwu chuan*. 3 vols. Hong Kong: Xianggang Gongjiao Zhenlixue Hui, 1973.

Fu Hualing. "Re-education through Labour in Historical Perspective." *China Quarterly* 184 (2005): 811–30.

Gernet, Jacques. *Chine et Christianisme: Action et reaction*. Paris: Gallimard, 1982.

Giles, Herbert (organizer). "The Prevalence of Infanticide in China." *Journal of the North China Branch of the Royal Asiatic Society* 20 (1885): 25–50.

Golvers, Noël. "The Provenances of the Western Books in the Former (and Current) Xujiahui (Zikawei) Library, Shanghai." *Sino-Western Cultural Relations Journal* 36 (2014): 24–42.

Gotteland, Claude (Nan Gelu). *Wubang lun*. Reprinted in *Xujiahui cangshulou: Ming-Qing Tianzhujiao wenxian*. Chinese Christian Texts from the Zikawei Library, edited by Nicolas Standaert, Adrian Dudink, Yi-long Huang, Ping-yi Chu, et al., f.1a–21a (V, 2079–2119). 5 vols. Taipei: Faculty of Theology, Fujen Catholic University, 1996.

Guillemain. "Lettre de M. Guillemin [i.e., Guillemain], préfet apostolique des missions du Quang-tong et du Quang-xi à MM. les directeurs de l'Œuvre de la Propagation de la Foi, Canton 8 juillet 1856." In *Annales de la propagation de la foi*, 28: 462. Lyon: M. P. Rusard, 1856.

Han Yu-shan. *Elements of Chinese Historiography*. Hollywood, CA: W. M. Hawley, 1953.

Harrison, Henrietta. "'A Penny for the Little Chinese': The French Holy Childhood Association in China." *American Historical Review* 113 (2008): 72–92.
———. *The Missionary's Curse and Other Tales from a Chinese Catholic Village.* Berkeley: University of California, 2013.
Hayhoe, Ruth, and Lu Yonglong, eds. *Ma Xiangbo and the Mind of Modern China, 1840–1939.* Armonk, NY: M. E. Sharpe, 1996.
Hevia, James L. *Cherishing Men from Afar: Qing Guest Ritual and the Macartney Embassy of 1793.* Durham, NC: Duke University Press, 1995.
———. "Loot's Fate: The Economy of Plunder and the Moral Life of Objects 'From the Summer Palace of the Emperor of China.'" *History and Anthropology* 6 (1994): 319–45.
Heyndrickx, Jerome, CICM, ed. *Historiography of the Chinese Catholic Church: Nineteenth and Twentieth Centuries*, edited by Jerome Heyndrickx, CICM. Leuven, Belgium: Ferdinand Verbiest Foundation–KU Leuven, 1994.
Ho, Ping-ti. *Studies on the Population of China, 1368–1953.* Cambridge, MA: Harvard University Press, 1959.
Huang Xiaojuan. "Christian Communities and Alternative Devotions in China, 1780–1860." PhD diss., Princeton University, 2006.
Huang Zhiwei. "Xujiahui cangshulou" (The Xujiahui [Zi-ka-wei] Library). Trans. Norman Walling, SJ. *Tripod* (July–August 1992), 22–35.
Hummel, Arthur, ed. *Eminent Chinese of the Ch'ing Period.* Washington, DC: Government Printing Office, 1943.
Jennes, Jos., CICM. *Four Centuries of Catechetics in China.* Eng. trans. Albert Van Lierde; Chinese trans. T'ien Yung-cheng, CICM. Taipei: Tianzhujiao Huaming Shuju, 1976.
Jin Luxian. *The Memoirs of Jin Luxian.* Vol. 1: *Learning and Relearning, 1916–1982.* Trans. William Hanbury-Tenison. Hong Kong: Hong Kong University Press, 2012.
King, Michelle Tien. *Between Birth and Death: Female Infanticide in Nineteenth-Century China.* Stanford, CA: Stanford University Press, 2014.
Kollár, Miroslav. *Ein Leben im Konflikt: P. Franz Xaver Biallas SVD (1878–1936). Chinamissionar und Sinologe im Licht seiner Korrespondenz.* Sankt Augustin, Germany: Institut Monumenta Serica, 2011.
Kropp, Michael. "Ma Xiangbo (1840–1939) und die Modernisierung des chinesischen Bildungswesens." *Monumenta Serica* 42 (1994): 397–443.
Ku Hung-ming. *The Spirit of the Chinese People: With an Essay on "The War and the Way Out."* Beijing: Peking Daily News, 1915. Translated as *Der Geist des chinesischen Volkes und der Ausweg aus dem Krieg.* Jena: Eugen Diederichs, 1917.
Ladany, Lazlo, SJ. *The Catholic Church in China.* New York: Freedom House, 1987.
Latourette, Kenneth. *History of Christian Missions in China.* London: Society for Promoting Christian Knowledge, 1929.
Launay, Adrien. *Histoire générale de la Société des missions-étrangères.* 3 vols. Paris: Téqui, 1894.
Laurence, Patricia. *Lily Briscoe's Chinese Eyes: Bloomsbury, Modernism, and China.* Columbia: University of South Carolina Press, 2003.
Lauwaert, Françoise. *Le meurtre en famille. Parricide et infanticide en Chine (XVIIIe–XIXe siècle).* Paris: Éditions Odile Jacob, 1999.

Lazzarotto, Angelo S., and Gianni Criveller. *Alberico Crescitelli 1863–1900. Martire in China*. Bologna: Editrice Missionaria Italiana, 2005.

Leclercq, Jacques. *Vie du Père Lebbe, le tonnerre qui chante au loin*. Tournai, Belgium: Casterman, 1955. Translated by George Lamb as *Thunder in the Distance: The Life of Père Lebbe*. New York: Sheed & Ward, 1958.

Lee, Bernice J. "Female Infanticide in China." In *Women in China: Current Directions in Historical Scholarship*, edited by W. L. Guisso, 163–77. Youngstown, NY: Philo Press, 1981.

Lee, James, Cameron Campbell, and Guofu Tan. "Infanticide and Family Planning in Late Imperial China: The Price and Population History of Rural Liaoning, 1774–1873." In *Chinese History in Economic Perspective*, edited by Thomas G. Rawski and Lillian M. Li, 145–76. Berkeley: University of California Press, 1992.

Leung, Beatrice, and Patricia Wittenberg. "Catholic Religious Orders of Women in China: Adaptation and Power." *Journal for the Scientific Study of Religion* 43, no. 1 (2004): 67–82.

Levenson, Joseph R. *Confucian China and Its Modern Fate: A Trilogy*. Berkeley: University of California Press, 1958–1965.

Leys, Simon (Pierre Ryckmans). "The Art of Interpreting Nonexistant Inscriptions Written in Invisible Ink on a Blank Page." *New York Review of Books*, October 11, 1990.

Li Jiugong. *Shensi lu* (A Record of Careful Meditations). Reprinted in *Yesuhui Luoma danganguan Ming-Qing Tianzhujiao wenxian (Chinese Christian Texts from the Roman Archives of the Society of Jesus)*, edited by Nicolas Standaert and Adrian Dudink, 9:119–238. 12 vols. Taipei: Ricci Institute, 2002.

Liu, Kwang-ching, ed. *American Missionaries in China: Papers from Harvard Seminars*. Cambridge, MA: East Asian Research Center, Harvard University, 1966.

Loewe, Michael. *Early Chinese Texts: A Bibliographical Guide*. Berkeley, CA: Society for the Study of Early China, 1993.

Lu Weijing. "'A Pearl in the Palm': A Forgotten Symbol of the Father Daughter Bond." *Late Imperial China* 31 (2010): 62–97.

Lu Xun. *Selected Works of Lu Xun*. Trans. Yang Hsien-I and Gladys Yang. 4 vols. Beijing: Foreign Languages Press, 1956–1960.

MacInnis, Donald E. *Religious Policy and Practice in Communist China: A Documentary History*. New York: Macmillan, 1972.

Malatesta, Edward J., SJ. *The Society of Jesus and China: A Historical-Theological Essay*. Discovery: Jesuit International Ministries No. 7. St. Louis, MO: Institute of Jesuit Sources, 1997.

Mariani, Paul P. *Church Militant: Bishop Kung and Catholic Resistance in Communist Shanghai*. Cambridge, MA: Harvard University Press, 2011.

Marx, Karl. *Marx on China: Articles from the New York Daily Tribune, 1853–1860*. London: Lawrence & Wishart, 1951.

Maughm, W. Somerset. *On a Chinese Screen*. Reprint, New York: Paragon House, 1990.

Maxwell-Stuart, P. G. *Chronicle of the Popes*. London: Thames & Hudson, 1997.

McBrien, Richard P. *Lives of the Popes: The Pontiffs from St. Peter to John Paul II*. New York: HarperCollins, 1997.

McCarthy, Charles J., SJ. "Christ Forms the Martyr." *Woodstock Letters* 92 (1963): 395–402.

McGrath, W. Aedan. *Perseverance through Faith: A Priest's Prison Story. The Memoirs of Father Aedan McGrath*, edited by Theresa Marie Moreau. N.p.: XLibris, 2008.

Menegon, Eugenio. *Ancestors, Virgins, and Friars: Christianity as a Local Religion in Late Imperial China.* Cambridge, MA: Harvard University Press, 2009.

Minamiki, George, SJ. *The Rites Controversy: From Its Beginnings to Modern Times.* Chicago: Loyola University Press, 1985.

Moidrey, Joseph de, SJ. *La hiérarchie catholique en Chine, en Corée et au Japan (1307–1914).* Shanghai: Zikawei, 1914.

Mungello, D. E. *Curious Land: Jesuit Accommodation and the Origins of Sinology.* Stuttgart: Franz Steiner Verlag, 1985.

————. *Drowning Girls in China: Female Infanticide since 1650.* Lanham, MD: Rowman & Littlefield, 2008.

————. "Fact and Fantasy in the Sexual Seduction of Chinese Converts by Catholic Priests: The Case of the 120 Martyrs." *Sino-Western Cultural Relations Journal* 23 (2001): 8–21.

————. *The Great Encounter of China and the West, 1500–1800.* 4th ed. Lanham, MD: Rowman & Littlefield, 2013.

————. "Reinterpreting the History of Christianity in China: Historiographical Review." *Historical Journal* 55, no. 2 (2012): 533–52.

————. "The Return of the Jesuits to China in 1841 and the Chinese Christian Backlash." *Sino-Western Cultural Relations Journal* 27 (2005): 9–46.

————, ed. *The Rites Controversy: Its History and Meaning.* Nettetal, Germany: Steyler Verlag, 1994.

————. *The Spirit and the Flesh in Shandong, 1650–1785.* Lanham, MD: Rowman & Littlefield, 2001.

————. *Western Queers in China: Flight to the Land of Oz.* Lanham, MD: Rowman & Littlefield, 2012.

————. "The Xujiahui (Zikawei) Library of Shanghai in 1986." *China Mission Studies (1550–1800) Bulletin* 8 (1986): 41–56.

Ng, Peter Tze Ming. *Chinese Christianity: An Interplay between Global and Local Perspectives.* Leiden: Brill, 2012.

Palâtre, Gabriel, SJ. *L'infanticide et l'Oeuvre de la Sainte-Enfance en Chine.* Shanghai: Autographie de la Mission Catholique à l'Orphelinat de Tou-sè-wè, 1875.

Paragon, Donald. "Ying Lien-chih (1866–1926) and the Rise of Fu Jen, the Catholic University of Peking." *Monumenta Serica* 20 (1961): 165–226.

Paton, David Macdonald. *Christian Missions and the Judgment of God.* London: SCM Press, 1953.

[————]. "First Thoughts on the Débâcle of Christian Missions in China." *International Review of Mission* (Geneva) 40, no. 160 (October 1951): 411–20.

Pfister, Louis, SJ. *Notices biographiques et bibliographiques sur les Jésuites de l'ancienne mission de Chine, 1552 à 1773.* Variétés sinologiques 59. Shanghai: Imprimerie de la Mission Catholique, 1932–1934.

Piolet, J. B. *Les missions catholiques françaises au XIX° siècle.* Vol. 3: *Chine et Japon.* Paris: Armand Colin, n.d.

Pirès-Pereira to Raphael Umpierres, letter dated January 15, 1835, at Beijing, Scritture riferite in Congresso, Cina e Regni adiacenti (Prop. S.R.), *Archives of the Sacred Congregation of the Propaganda* (Rome) 8: 314–15.

Porter, Andrew. "'Cultural Imperialism' and Protestant Missionary Enterprise, 1780–1914." *Journal of Imperial and Commonwealth History* 25, no. 3 (September 1997): 367–91.

Pruitt, Ida. *Working Woman of Han.* Stanford, CA: Stanford University Press, 1945.

Reinders, Eric. *Borrowed Gods and Foreign Bodies.* Berkeley: University of California, 2004.

Ren Yanli. "Saints, Imperialists, and the Catholic Church's Discrimination against China." Trans. Yao Ximing. *Heartland—Eurasian Review of Geopolitics* 1 (2001): 123–24.

Rivinius, Karl Josef, SVD. *Im Spannungsfeld von Mission und Politik: Johann Baptist Anzer (1851–1903), Bischof von Süd-Shandong.* Nettetal, Germany: Steyler Verlag, 2010.

Roeser, [Pater], SVD. *Zhonghua guangrong* (Die chinesischen Martyrer). Yanzhou, Shandong: Yangzhou Catholic Church, 1925.

Rossi, Luigi. "N. 4—Opera Pia Lavori Femminili a Beneficio della Santa Infanzia, Guluba 31.12.1918." Report, preserved in the Canossian Archive, Rome.

Rotours, Robert des. "Encore quelques notes sur l'anthropophagie en Chine." *T'oung Pao* 54 (1968): 1–49.

———. "Quelques notes sur l'anthropophagie en Chine." *T'oung Pao* 50 (1963): 386–427.

Royer, Fanchón. "Charles de Forbin-Janson, Missionary Bishop." *Americas* 10 (1953): 196.

Sala, Ida. *History of Our Canossian Missions.* Vol. 2: *China, 1868–1952.* Hong Kong: Daughters of the Charity of Canossa, 2003.

Sauret, Alain. "China's Role in the Foundation and Development of the Pontifical Society of the Holy Childhood." In *Historiography of the Chinese Catholic Church: Nineteenth and Twentieth Centuries,* edited by Jeroom Heyndrickx, CICM, 247–72. Leuven, Belgium: Ferdinand Verbiest Foundation–KU Leuven, 1994.

Schütte, Johannes, SVD. *Die katholische Chinamission im Spiegel der rotchinesischen Presse.* Münster: Aschendorffsche Verlagsbuchhandlung, 1957.

Servière, Joseph de la, SJ. *Histoire de la mission du Kiang-nan.* 2 vols. Shanghai: T'ou-sè-wè Orphanage, 1914.

Shen Fu. *Six Records of a Floating Life* (*Fu sheng liu ji*). Trans. Leonard Pratt and Chiang Su-hui. London: Penguin, 1983.

Shen Xizhi et al. *Zhaoran gonglun* (Hengtang, 1846), reprinted in *Xujiahui cangshulou: Ming-Qing Tianzhuyao wenxian* (Chinese Christian Texts from the Zikawei Library), edited by Nicolas Standaert (Zhong Mingdan) et al. 5 vols. Taipei: Faculty of Theology, Fujen Catholic University, 1996.

Shi Yan. "Jiekai sowei 'shengren' de mianmu" (Revealing the True Colors of the So-Called Saints). *Renmin ribao,* October 3, 2000.

162 Bibliography

Sommervogel, Carlos, SJ. *Bibliothèque de la compagnie de Iésu.* 12 vols. Brussels and Paris, 1890–1932.
Spence, Jonathan D., and Annping Chin. *The Chinese Century: A Photographic History of the Last Hundred Years.* New York: Random House, 1996.
———. *The Gate of Heavenly Peace: The Chinese and Their Revolution, 1895–1980.* Hammondsworth, UK: Penguin, 1982.
———. *God's Chinese Son: The Taiping Heavenly Kingdom of Hong Xiuquan.* New York: Norton, 1996.
Ssu-ma Ch'ien. *Selections from Records of the Historian.* Trans. Yang Hsien-I. Beijing: Foreign Languages Press, 1979.
Standaert, Nicolas, ed. *Handbook of Christianity in China.* Vol. 1: *635–1800.* Leiden: Brill, 2001.
Stone, Julia. *Chinese Basket Babies: A German Missionary Foundling Home and the Girls It Raised (1850s–1914).* Opera Sinologica 26. Wiesbaden: Harrassowitz Verlag, 2013.
Sun, E-tu Zen, trans. and ed. *Ch'ing Administrative Terms: A Translation of the Terminology of the Six Boards with Explanatory Notes.* Cambridge, MA: Harvard University Press, 1961.
Sweeten, Alan Richard. *Christianity in Rural China: Conflict and Accommodation in Jiangxi Province, 1860–1900.* Ann Arbor, MI: Center for Chinese Studies, 2001.
Tang, Edmond, and Jean-Paul Wiest, eds. *The Catholic Church in Modern China: Perspectives.* Maryknoll, NY: Orbis Books, 1993.
Teichman, Eric. *Travels of a Consular Officer in North West China.* Cambridge: Cambridge University Press, 1921.
Tiedemann, R. G., ed. *Handbook of Christianity in China.* Vol. 2: *1800–Present.* Leiden: Brill, 2010.
——— [Dideman]. *Huabei de baoli he gonghuang: Yiheduan yundong de qianxi jidujiao chuanbo he shehui chongtu* (Violence and Fear in North China: Christian Mission and Social Conflict on the Eve of the Boxer Uprising). Trans. Cui Huajiao. Nanjing: Jiangsu People's Publishing Co., 2011.
Tong, John. "The Church from 1949 to 1990." In *The Catholic Church in Modern China: Perspectives,* edited by Edmond Tang and Jean-Paul Wiest, 7–27. Maryknoll, NY: Orbis Books, 1993.
Uhalley, Stephen, Jr., and Xiaoxin Wu, eds. *China and Christianity: Burdened Past, Hopeful Future.* Armonk, NY: M. E. Sharpe, 2001.
"Uno Sprazzo di Luce—Storia di 25 Anni di Apostolato Canossiano—1891–1916" (A Ray of Light: History of 25 Years of the Canossian Apostles—1891–1916). Shensi Mle Kulupa Cina, Archivo Canossiano, Roma.
Van Damme, Daniel, OFM. *Necrologium Fratrum Minorum in Sinis.* 3rd ed. Hong Kong: Tang King Po School, Kowloon, 1978. 1st ed. compiled by Joannes Ricci, OFM (1934); 2nd ed. compiled by Kilian Menz, OFM (1944).
van den Wyngaert, Anastasiius, OFM, ed. *Sinica franciscana.* Vol. 2: *Relations et epistolas Fratrum Minorum saeculi 16 et 17.* Quaracchi-Florence: Collegium S. Bonaventurae, 1933.

Verhaeren, H., CM *Catalogue de la Bibliothèque du Pé-t'ang.* Beijing: Imprimerie des Lazaristes, 1949.

Waldron, Arthur. "Review of Wm. Theodore de Bary's *Confucian Tradition and Global Education. The Tang Chun-I Lectures for 2005.*" *Sino-Western Cultural Relations Journal* 31 (2009): 70–74.

Wegener, Herm., SVD. *Heroes of the Mission Field.* Trans. E. McCall. Techny, IL: Mission Press SVD, 1916.

Wei Tsing-sing, Louis. *La politique missionnaire de la France en Chine, 1842–1856.* Paris: Les Nouvelle Éditions Latines, 1960.

Wenzel-Teuber, Katharina. "Stastisches Update 2013 zu Religionen und Kirchen in der Volksrepublik China." *China heute* 33, no. 1 (181) (2014): 20–31.

Whyte, Bob. *Unfinished Encounter: China and Christianity.* London: Collins, 1988.

Wiest, Jean-Paul. "Bringing Christ to the Nations: Shifting Models of Mission among the Jesuits in China." *Catholic Historical Review* 83 (1997): 654–90.

Wilkerson, Endymion. *Chinese History: A Manual.* Cambridge, MA: Harvard University Asia Center, 1998.

Williams, C. A. S. *Chinese Symbolism and Art Motifs.* 3rd rev. ed. Rutland, VT: Charles E. Tuttle, 1993.

Williams, S. Wells. *The Middle Kingdom: A Survey of the Geography, Government, Literature, Social Life, Arts, and History of the Chinese Empire and Its Inhabitants.* 2 vols. Rev. ed. New York: Charles Scribner's Sons, 1898.

Wong, Young-tsu. *A Paradise Lost: The Imperial Garden Yuanming Yuan.* Honolulu: University of Hawaii, 2001.

Wu Jingzi. *The Scholars* (*Rulin waishi*). Trans. Yang Hsien-I and Gladys Yang. Beijing: Foreign Languages Press, 1957.

Yates, M. T. *Records of the General Conference of the Protestant Missionaries of China Held at Shanghai, May 10–24, 1877.* Shanghai: Presbyterian Mission Press, 1878.

Young, Ernest P. *Ecclesiastical Colony: China's Catholic Church and the French Religious Protectorate.* New York: Oxford University Press, 2013.

Young, John D. *Confucianism and Christianity: The First Encounter.* Hong Kong: Hong Kong University Press, 1983.

Zetzsche, Jost Oliver. *The Bible in China.* Nettetal, Germany: Steyler Verlag, 1999.

Zhang Li and Liu Jiantang, eds. *Zhongguo jiao'an shi* (History of Religious Incidents in China). Chengdu: Sichuan sheng shehui kexue yuan chubanshe, 1987.

Zhang Ruogu. *Ma Xiangbo xiansheng nianpu* (A Chronology of the Life of Mr. Ma Xiangbo) (III-33), Appendix 1. Shanghai: Shangwu yinshuguan, 1939.

Zhang Xianqing. *Guan fu, zongzu yu Tianzhujiao: 17–19 shiji Fuan xiangcun jiaohui de lishi xushi* (State, Lineage and Catholicism: A Narrative of the History of the Church in Seventeenth- to Nineteenth-Century Rural Fuan). Beijing: Zhonghua shuju, 2009.

Zhen Shi. "Ma Lai yu Di'er Yapian Zhanzheng" (Auguste Chapdelaine and the Second Opium War). *Renmin ribao*, September 29, 2000.

Zheng Yi. *Scarlet Memorial: Tales of Cannibalism in Modern China.* Trans. and ed. T. P. Sym. Boulder, CO: Westview Press, 1996.

"Zhongguo Tianzhujiao Aiguohui Zhongguo Tianzhujiao Zhujiaotuan fabiao sheng-ming" (The Chinese Catholic Patriotic Association Makes a Statement on the Chinese Catholic Bishops' Conference). *Renmin ribao*, September 27, 2000.

Zhongguo zongjiao bangao 2013 (Annual Report on Religions in China 2013). Edited by Jin Ze and Qiu Yonghui. Beijing: Shehui Keshui wenxian chubanshe, 2013.

Zottoli, Angelo. *Cursus litteraturae sinicae neo-missionariis accomodatus*. 5 vols. Shanghai: Tou-sè-wè, 1878–1882.

Zürcher, Erik. "The Jesuit Mission in Fujian in Late Ming Times: Levels of Response." In *Development and Decline of Fukien Province in the 17th and 18th Centuries*, edited by Eduard B. Vermeer, 417–57. Leiden: Brill, 1990.

———, trans. *Kouduo richao, Li Jiubiao's Diary of Oral Admonitions: A Late Ming Christian Journal. Translated, with Introduction and Notes by Erik Zürcher.* 2 vols. Monumenta Serica Monograph Series LVI/1–2. Nettetal, Germany: Steyler Verlag, 2007.

Index

abandoned children. *See* female
  infanticide; orphanages
abortion: debate, 75; sex-selective,
  73, 76
accommodation, 116; Jesuit, 15, 39,
  45, 51
accusations of US-Vatican
  collaboration, 87–90, *91*
Adinolfi, Francesco, SJ, 46
Ad sinarum gentes, 64
Alcock, Rutherford, 21
America. *See* United States
American Board of Commissioners for
  Foreign Missions, 56–57
American exceptionalism, 10, 12
American Jesuits, 60. *See also* Jesuits
Anderson, Rufus, 56
Anglo-French forces, 2–5, 98
Annales de la Sainte-Enfance, 74
Annam, 98
anti-accommodationism, 50
anti-Americanism, 57, 61, *62*, 87–90, *91*
anti-Catholicism, 1, 55–69, 87–92
anti-Japanese, 49, 52, 61
Anti-Rightest Campaign, 115
Antonucci, Gregorio, OFM, 77–78,
  80, 86
Anzer, Johann Baptist, SVD, 55
apostasy, 64

Archinti, Teresa, 79, 86
arrogance, European, 31
Arrow War. *See* Second Opium War
Assyrian Church (Nestorianism), 78
astronomical observatory: Sheshan, 37;
  Zikawei, 24
atheism, 110, 114
Aurora Academy (Zhendan
  Xueyuan), 49
Aurora University. *See* Zhendan Daxue

baby towers, 72
Baijiazhai, 100
Bai San (Pe-san), 100
Bai Xiaoman, Laurence, 99, 101, 102
baptism of moribund infants, 74, 76,
  90–92
Basset, Jean, MEP, 138n77
Battaglini, Marina, 138n84
Battaiola, Serfina, 84
beatas, 35, 97
beatification, 94
Beijing court, 15
Beijing-Vatican relations. *See* Vatican-
  Beijing relations
Beitang Library, 24
Benedict XIV, 19
Benedict XV, 43, 44, 54
Benedictines, 54–55

About the Author

D. E. Mungello, the grandson of Italian and German immigrants, was raised in a small town in southwestern Pennsylvania. After obtaining his doctorate at the University of California at Berkeley, he focused on Sino-Western history. His research in Europe and China led to the production of *Curious Land: Jesuit Accommodation and the Origins of Sinology* (1985) and *The Great Encounter of China and the West, 1500–1800* (four editions, 1999–2013). In 1979 in Germany he founded the *Sino-Western Cultural Relations Journal.* His recent books have examined the more neglected and sensitive areas of Sino-Western history, including *Drowning Girls in China: Female Infanticide since 1650* (2008) and *Western Queers in China: The Flight to the Land of Oz* (2012). He has also published articles in *VIA* (*Voices in Italian Americana*) and the *Gay and Lesbian Review.* His first teaching position was at Lingnan College in Hong Kong, and he is currently professor of history at Baylor University in Waco, Texas.

Printed in the USA
CPSIA information can be obtained
at www.ICGtesting.com
LVHW041610100124
768674LV00005B/75